CHAT
REFERENCE

DATE DUE

DEC 18 2003	
12/3/03	
NOV - 1 2009	
Nov 22	
NOV 15 2009	
MAY - 9 2016	
NOV 14 2016	

CHAT REFERENCE

A Guide to Live Virtual Reference Services

Jana Smith Ronan

LIBRARIES

UNLIMITED

A Member of the Greenwood Publishing Group

Westport, Connecticut • London

Library of Congress Cataloging-in-Publication Data

Ronan, Jana
    Chat reference : a guide to live virtual reference services / by Jana Smith Ronan
        p.   cm.
    Includes bibliographical references and index.
    ISBN 1–59158–000–5 (alk. paper)
    1. Electronic reference services (Libraries). 2. Electronic reference services
    (Libraries)—Computer programs. 3. Electronic reference services (Libraries)—
    United States—Case studies. I. Title.
    Z711.45.R66 2003
    025.5′24—dc21   2003051639

British Library Cataloguing in Publication data is available.

Library of Congress Catalog Card Number: 2003051639
ISBN: 1–59158–000–5

First published in 2003

Libraries Unlimited, Inc., 88 Post Road West,Westport, CT 06881
A Member of the Greenwood Publishing Group, Inc.
www.lu.com

Printed in the United States of America

The paper used in this book complies with the
Permanent Paper Standard issued by the National
Information Standards Organization (Z39.48–1984).

10 9 8 7 6 5 4 3 2 1

CONTENTS

CONTENTS

PREFACE

In order to survive, the library must develop a symbiotic relationship with its parent community. Successful libraries serve their community and are rewarded for their service. The community benefits from the information and services provided by the library; the library benefits from receiving a strong political, economic, and cultural status. Both community and library grow and evolve together. A community that neglects its library will need to develop other means for satisfying its informational needs—or go without. If a library fails to provide useful information and services, the community will turn elsewhere for those functions. In each of these cases, the library will wither and die—and the community will also suffer.

David Tyckoson, 2001

Several years ago, I visited a language arts classroom where students were learning in a virtual environment, something I had never experienced before. The system was the University of Florida Networked Writing Environment (NWE), and students were using an early virtual reality software program called MOO (Multi-User Dungeon Object Oriented). The instructor was leading a class discussion of a literary work by chatting in this virtual environment, prompting both students sitting at computers in the classroom and others logged on from home to respond with interpretations of key passages. The instructor would ask a question, aloud or in MOO via text-based chat, and the students would type responses. He would post a URL, and the students would cut it from the text of the chat, paste it into a separate web browser and look at the web page. The students were multitasking, using a word-processing program to take notes, surfing the Web, and messaging the rest of the class. Some students were also composing e-mails in yet another computer application. The room was filled with the sound of keys clicking as the class responded to the instructor's and their fellow students' electronic postings, punctuated only by the occasional sound of laughter at a comment. Silent words rolling across the screen were the only feedback from the students attending class online. Every person in the classroom was engrossed in the online conversation, seemingly unaware that they were learning how to write. As I watched, I wondered not only how the library could support this type of scholarly activity, but also how librarians could work with students online. There had to be some way to integrate the power of computer-based real-time communication into our services to serve students, faculty, and staff more effectively. I signed up for an account with the NWE and have never looked back.

When we developed our real-time reference service, RefeXpress, at the University of Florida, we spent long hours investigating software and trying to determine how reference communication in real time could benefit online and remote users. We visited chat rooms and online communities and consulted with local university experts and programmers as we struggled to learn the basics of instant messaging, MOO, and Internet Relay Chat (IRC). If there had been other libraries to look to as examples or literature to read on the subject, our task would have been much easier. Outside of some isolated tests of chat and instant messaging in libraries, there weren't any real models in the library world to follow. For the most part, these trials were situated in academic libraries enjoying the rich technological and online networking support that affiliation with a university system brings. There was the experimental IRC channel that Bill Drew set up to serve library users, before implementing instant messaging in the SUNY Morrisville Library. The Internet Public Library and Joe Janes ran a MOO-based reference service from 1995–2000. Temple University's online messaging system, TalkBack, developed by Sam Stormont, was another early system. At the University of Florida, we, too, experimented. We set up a reference MOO and then later moved to more sophisticated call center software.

Setting up a reference service using one of these real-time systems was challenging for all but the most motivated libraries and librarians. It's true that there was an abundance of documentation in print and on the Web for setting up these early systems, and the software was inexpensive if not free. Setting up a system offering text-based chat required a level of technical expertise that placed implementation out of the range of most librarians. This was especially true at small institutions lacking a supportive information technology department, good networking, or computer savvy librarians with time to tinker. With the busy workload most reference librarians carry, learning how to set up a computer server and then installing the messaging software and programming the interface was just too much to ask. Most libraries concentrated on serving online user needs by developing e-mail reference services and web sites, as well as purchasing information resources online.

Yet at the University of Florida, we felt an impetus to investigate real-time communication to be responsive to our online community's needs. When we started our real-time reference project in 1999, it was apparent that the reference services we offered at the time were not meeting the needs of certain faculty, students, and staff, most notably, those who preferred to conduct research online. With the exception of our popular e-mail-based "Ask a Reference Question" service, reference services were provided from traditional style desks, situated by entrances where users could see us smiling at them as they entered the building. Like many libraries of the last decade, our reference operation remained solidly "bricks and mortar." The emphasis on the physical illustrated a disconnect between our reference operations and the rapid migration of information sources and services, such as course reserves, to a digital model of distribution. E-mail reference services did not meet many users' requests for immediate help in solving a connection problem or interpreting database results while online. This realization fueled our determination to explore ways to provide better reference service online.

The trend of using library resources outside the physical confines of the library is not likely to end. As libraries continue to purchase more databases and other information resources online, it becomes easier for users to access all kinds of full-text materials outside the confines of the library walls. The continually expanding amount of information provided via proprietary online databases or freely available on the Internet is terribly seductive. As one undergraduate recently noted in a library focus group, "I was a lot more dependent on librarians and stuff, where now I feel like because of computers and technology, I don't have to worry about whether someone is going to be there. I can just come and do everything on my own by myself" (Young and Seggern 2001, 162). It's common knowledge that many people prefer to wade through thousands of hits yielded by a sloppy Google search, the vagaries of AskJeeves, or even a bad search in a library database to making a trip to the library. Up to now, have librarians given users who prefer to communicate and research online a viable alternative? Is it reasonable to require that this growing group of the user population continue to approach us on our own terms for our services, either by hanging up their modem connection to call us on the phone or by traveling to the library? Is this being responsive to our community's needs? No, it is not. We must strive to develop a more symbiotic relationship with our online clientele.

The current interest in adding real-time technology to reference services is heartening. It represents a positive step toward positioning the institution of the library where it needs to be—in the heart of the online community. It is a necessary change in our service model if we are to provide high-quality reference services to people at the point of need. At the start of the millennium, the phenomenon of electronic communication has reached a critical mass, heretofore not experienced in our culture. Computers have never been more affordable, and most people can obtain an inexpensive Internet account through their local discount store or telephone company. Instant messaging programs vie for market share, bundling their program with computer operating systems or purchase of an Internet account. Many libraries are holding workshops on providing online services to users with handheld computers such as Palms or Visors, which can transmit e-mail and search Web-based library databases. Cell phones proliferate, some with built-in messaging features that allow users to send e-mails or chat in real time with friends. The number of users that can be reached with real-time reference services is growing rapidly, as are the number of real-time software programs and hosted services that libraries can and should use to communicate with their clientele.

This book is intended as a blueprint to lead the reader through the many decisions and considerations involved in setting up a real-time reference service. Chapters 1 and 2 delve into the historical development of computer-based chat, introducing the major types of chat systems. Discussions cover IRC, instant messaging, MOO, and simple chat programs with a Web interface, as well as more sophisticated software packages such as courseware and call center software from vendors including Live Assistance, WebCT, LSSI, Docutek, divine, QuestionPoint, and Digi-Net. For the readers struggling to decide if their library users are ready for a chat service, Chapter 3 suggests measures for assessing a community's receptivity and computer access to online assistance. Chapter 4 brings consideration of software functionality and user needs to a conclusion, offering a framework to apply in selecting the best real-time software for your unique environment.

The remainder of the book focuses on human and organizational issues, starting with staffing and training in Chapters 5 and 6, moving on to administration issues for public, academic, and special libraries in Chapter 7. Many examples of policies and guidelines from practicing services are given in Chapter 8, followed by Chapter Nine's consideration of techniques for effectively chatting with a remote user. Because real-time reference is so new, it can be challenging to publicize; Chapter 10 presents some strategies for promoting virtual reference services.

Chapters 11 through 15 are case studies written by contributors selected from five very different, yet equally successful, real-time reference services. Leading off is an examination of *Talk to a Librarian LIVE* at the SUNY Morrisville College Library, by Bill Drew. Talk to a Librarian Live is a fine example of a library taking advantage of a widely used and freely available software, AOL Instant Messenger, to reach users. The case study by DeAnne Luck, of *Ask A Librarian* at the library of Austin Peay State University, demonstrates that incorporating chat into duties at the reference desk is one strategy for launching a new service when staffing is scarce. Shelle Witten, of the library of the Paradise Valley Community College, details how ten autonomous community college libraries formed *Librarians Online*, a chat reference cooperative, powered by LSSI's *Virtual Reference Toolkit*. Carol Ann Borchert shares how her institution uses library school graduate students to staff the *Virtual Library Reference Chat* at the University of South Florida. She also describes the challenges of working with users in IRC. In the final case study, Mimi Pappas and Colleen Seale of the University of Florida, part of the *RefeXpress* planning team, write about the challenges of setting up a real-time reference service from scratch. These case studies bring a broader understanding of the strategies that can be employed in providing synchronous-based reference. Think of them as "snapshots in time" of some real pioneers in real-time reference. Some have continued to improve their online assistance by adjusting staffing and service hours, whereas others have even adopted new software. My heart-felt thanks to these knowledgeable chat librarians for writing about their experiences, and contributing so largely to this work.

I also owe a debt of gratitude to John F. Ronan, Mimi Pappas, Pam Cenzer, and Martin Dillon for their invaluable assistance in editing this work. To Marilyn Ochoa, Colleen Seale, Gary Cornwell, Carol Turner, Ann Lindell, LeiLani Freund, Peter Malanchuk, Sherman Butler, Carol Drum, Bill Covey, and other staff at the University of Florida Libraries, thank you for your insights and for shouldering some of my duties this past year, giving me much-needed time to research and write.

REFERENCES

Rheingold, Howard. 2002. *Smart Mobs: The Next Social Revolution*. Cambridge, MA: Perseus.

Tyckoson, David. 2001. "What Is the Best Model of Reference Service?" *Library Trends* 50 (fall): 183–96.

Young, Nancy J., and Marilyn Von Seggern. 2001. "General Information Seeking in Changing Times: A Focus Group Study." *Reference & User Services Quarterly* 41: 159–69.

1 INTRODUCTION TO CHAT AND BASIC REAL-TIME SOFTWARE

Probably the most bewildering and time-consuming aspect of planning a real-time reference service is sorting through the wide variety of software that supports on-line conferencing in real time. Until about a year ago, little had been written about the application of chat-based software in libraries, but the surge in interest has led to more and more articles and reviews of software packages. When studying the literature, librarians can find an abundance of case studies and analyses in the literature of the business world, where chat has been used on web sites for years to improve customer relations and sales. What it boils down to is that libraries (and businesses) have a wide variety of choices.

The spectrum of chat software ranges from free or inexpensive software, such as instant messaging or Internet Relay Chat (IRC) that supports text-based conferencing between two or more users, to sophisticated and often expensive software used in call centers that combines text-based chat with sound, video, white-boarding, voice over Internet protocol (VOIP) and the ability to send users web pages and files. But with such a broad range of software to choose from, where does one start? The goal of this chapter is to introduce the reader to the basic characteristics and features of the major categories of software that enable one to carry on a conversation in real time with another user via the Internet.

It would be easier to choose a system if some standards for chat reference existed, but at this point, academic, public, and special libraries are still experimenting with real-time reference software. There are, however, two major sets of guidelines being drafted that will likely influence librarians' selection of software in the future. There are the *Guidelines for Implementing and Maintaining Virtual Reference Services* being drafted by an ad hoc committee within the Machine Assisted Reference Section (MARS) of the Reference and User Services Association

(RUSA), part of the American Library Association. Then there is the *Question/ Answer Transaction Protocol* that is being drafted by the National Information Standards Organization (NISO). However, librarians can learn from the pioneers who have already established online reference systems.

Libraries such as Miami University Library and Morris Library at Southern Illinois University at Carbondale took advantage of local talent to program their own chat software from scratch. Miami runs its "Ask A Question" service with locally developed software called *Rakim;* Morris Library's software is called *Morris Messenger* (Fagan and Calloway 2001). Many libraries, such as the Morrisville College Library (SUNY), have adopted open source software or inexpensive shareware such as *AOL Instant Messenger (AIM)*, to set up chat reference services. Others are purchasing relatively inexpensive software such as *ConferenceRoom* or *ChatSpace* to add a chat component to their reference services. The most popular option at the time of writing, however, seems to be to contract with services such as the *Virtual Reference Toolkit* or *VRT* (Library Systems & Services LLC or LSSI), *24/7 Reference,* or *LivePerson* to host services on a remote server, as the University of Tennessee Libraries at Knoxville and the Denver Public Library have done. The major issues that seem to be determining the approach institutions take include budget, local computing cultures, availability of technical expertise, and last, but perhaps most important, software features.

In this chapter, we look at simple real-time systems that offer text-based chat functionality, in the order of their historical development. These systems include instant messaging, IRC, and MOO. Also covered is Web-based software that overlays or incorporates the previously mentioned types of software, such as *ConferenceRoom* and *ChatSpace*. The chapter introduces more sophisticated software with advanced features such as push page and white-boarding. These include LSSI's *VRT, LiveAssistance, QuestionPoint,* and divine's *Virtual Reference Desk.*

INTERNET RELAY CHAT—IRC

Internet Relay Chat, or IRC, is a popular and flexible way of conferencing in real time. Developed in 1988 by Jarkko Oikarinen in Finland, IRC is a public domain technology that is supported by many operating systems, making it a versatile and accessible option for offering real-time reference. Before the development of IRC, Internet users chatted using a variety of programs such as "talk" on UNIX based systems, but there wasn't an established protocol to support text-based messaging across platforms. As McConnell (2002) noted, "IRC created a standard mechanism for creating multi-party conversations, and for networking chat servers. This enabled very large numbers of people to converse online through a large network of publicly operated IRC servers." Efnet, Dalnet, Undernet, and IRCnet are the major IRC networks operating today, but there are many smaller networks as well. Because IRC technology is in the public domain, it is easy to find client programs that allow users to connect and chat. The Finnish University and Research Network archives a variety of clients.

IRC from the User's Perspective

To get connected to the IRC network, you need some type of IRC client program. Some IRC networks, such as Dalnet, offer web pages with embedded Java clients. Many users chat by connecting to a server-based client such as *ircii* (Unix or Linux) via their dial-up account's shell. Other people install freeware or shareware IRC clients, such as *mIRC*, on their computers. Using the client software, you establish a connection to an IRC server, which connects you to the network of IRC servers across the Internet, and join a channel. A channel is a virtual space or room where users can congregate and chat with each other. Thousands of discussion channels are available on any subject and can even be built spontaneously if desired. These virtual discussion spaces can be public, private (one-on-one), and moderated.

What is it like to use IRC? Internet Relay Chat is a fast-paced chat environment, especially when several users are logged on and talking in the same channel. IRC users behave much like people at cocktail parties or large social gatherings, where people join one group and talk for a while, then move on to another group of people as their interest waxes and wanes. When on IRC, you will see people joining channels, lurking or talking, and leaving for other channels. Some of this activity is pictured in a session using the mIRC client as pictured in Figure 1.1.

Communication is primarily text based, and it is public unless you use special commands to address your remarks to specific users. Some types of IRC-based software can be configured to offer cues or features that would be useful in real-time reference. These include creating triggers that make the computer beep at appropriate moments (such as when a user posts a question) and the ability to send files to users. Some software supports clickable URLs (Uniform Resource Locators) in the text of the chat. For example, some IRC systems automatically convert any text string beginning with "http://" or "https://" or "file://" into a hyperlink on which the user can click to launch a web site or download a file. In other IRC-based software, it is possible to encase a web address in a pair of tags similar to HTML (HyperText Markup Language). For example, if I was working with a user in this system and wanted to direct her to the Google web site, I could type the following message: "Nell, try searching [url] http://www.google.com [/url]."

IRC and the Librarian

What does the librarian or user need to know to use IRC successfully? Chatting in IRC can be as simple as typing what you want to say in the input box and submitting it to the rest of the channel by hitting the enter key. More complex functions include using numerous special commands to send private messages; transmitting sound, graphic, or other files; silencing or kicking off a troublesome user; or even emoting. Seasoned IRC users are familiar with a range of these commands, but librarians will want to set up a supporting web site with clear instructions to teach

Figure 1.1. Internet Relay Chat session using mIRC.

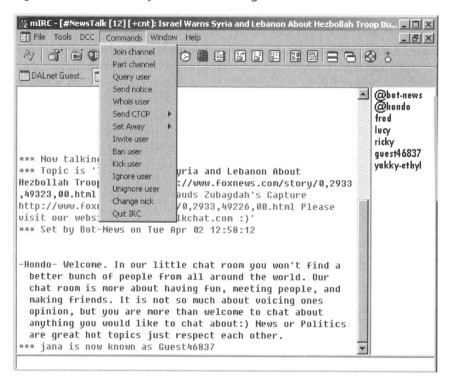

new users. A good web site to consult for more information about how IRC works is *A Short IRC Primer* (Pioch et al. 1997).

Setting Up IRC

Setting up an IRC server to host a chat reference service requires some computer expertise, but the software is free, and web-based documentation is abundant. Assuming that you already have a computer server on which to install an IRC program, the first step is to choose the most appropriate IRC server software or daemon for your operating system. Daemons are available for most operating systems. Download and install the daemon and configure it to connect to an IRC network or to operate separately. An IRC can be set up to be connected to other IRC networks so people can find it through other networks, or it can be set up to allow access only through the address on your server. Setting it up to operate independently reduces the possibility of nonlibrary users joining your reference channel and disrupting conversation. Once you have the IRC server configured and running, you'll need to let users know how to reach the chat reference service. One way to do this is to create an accompanying web site, with the address and port number of your IRC server, hyperlinks to web sites to download client software, and a simple guide to chatting in your service, all prominently featured on the page. You could even embed a Java-based client such as *Objirc Chat* on your reference web site to generate a chat window automatically using a plug-in, rather than requiring users to download and configure an IRC client. This would make connecting to your reference service as easy as possible for your less technologically inclined library users.

Hosted IRC

There is an alternative to running an entire IRC server to host your real-time service if setting up a server sounds too difficult or time-consuming. Consider setting up a library channel on an existing IRC server operated on your campus or by another local computer group. To set up a reference assistance channel on an existing IRC system, first connect to the system, then issue the command to create a new channel (/join #name). For example, you could issue the command "/join #library help," and a new channel named "library help" would appear. It is very easy. The downside of creating a channel on a hosted IRC server is that when you exit, you lose ownership to anyone who happens to be online in the channel at that given time. The new owner or channel operator inherits complete control and can change settings or even delete the entire channel. There are two approaches to solving this problem, both of which involve creating what is called a "robot" or "bot." A bot is an automatically running software program that can be programmed to act as the owner and keep the channel open. It is possible to do this without assistance from the hosted IRC's system operator (sysop), but it involves keeping your computer online and connected to the IRC at all times. A more permanent option is to contact the sysop, register the channel, and request that the sysop create the bot for you, eliminating the need to stay connected to the IRC at all times. This is admittedly a very truncated treatment of hosted IRCs and channels. To learn more about channels, bots, and IRC programming, consult *A Short IRC Primer* (Pioch et al. 1997) and *Learn Internet Relay Chat* (Toyer 1997).

If setting up an IRC server or establishing a library reference channel on an established IRC server seems daunting, a commercial web-based chat package based on the IRC protocol is one alternative. These software packages are easier to install and relatively economical; see "Web-Based Chat Software" later in this chapter for more information.

IRC AT A GLANCE

Advantages:
- Software free or inexpensive
- Java clients available so that users can reach librarians by web browser alone
- Requires lower bandwidth

Disadvantages:
- Old technology, text-based
- May require user to install software to reach librarians
- Typically lacks features such as push page, escorting, and databases of conversational phrases repeatedly used by librarians
- Users may need to learn commands to use IRC effectively, to join a channel, to send a private message to the librarian, or even to log off

IRC Software Archives
Finnish University and Research Network
ftp://ftp.funet.fi/pub/unix/

IRC daemons (Book of IRC)
http://www.bookofirc.com/software/servers/

IRCDHELP
http://www.ircdhelp.org/ircdvers.html

Clients
irc.org (includes links to Objirc, ircii, and mIRC)
http://www.irc.org/links.html

MOO (MULTI-USER DOMAIN OBJECT-ORIENTED)

Another type of real-time program that is popular for recreational and educational use is the virtual reality software called MOO (Multi-User Domain Object-Oriented). Simply defined, MOOs are "text-based virtual environments hosted on a computer which allows users to log in and participate in the world" (Taylor 2000). These virtual environments are much richer in functionality and detail than an IRC channel. For example, most MOOs offer a series of spaces or rooms to traverse and interactive objects that respond to commands (words used in text messaging) or the user's presence. Davies, Shield, and Weininger (1998) define this software as "a database of information responding in real time to commands entered by a user (or player) accessing the server on which the MOO resides." Probably the most widely known application of this communication technology in libraries was the MOO that the Internet Public Library (IPL) operated from 1995 to 2000, staffed with volunteer librarians and operating two hours daily (Shaw 1996). The entry point for the IPL MOO is pictured in Figure 1.2.

A more current example of a library MOO can be found at the University of New Brunswick (UNB). UNB Libraries uses the technology to teach library skills to groups of distance-learning students in real time, using the web-based *enCore* MOO software. The Library lobby of the UNB MOO is pictured in Figure 1.3.

Like IRC, MOO incorporates a text-based chat component, but unlike IRC a MOO "is a living, ever-changing textual environment" (Holmevik and Haynes 2000b). There are hundreds of online MOO worlds patterned after actual or

Figure 1.2. Entrance to the Internet Public Library MOO.

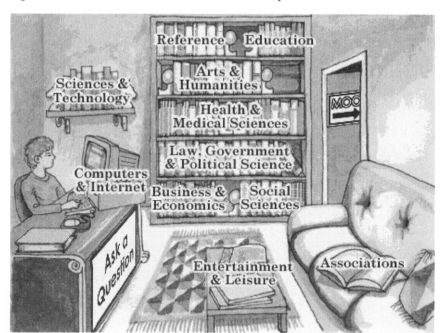

imagined universities, buildings, forests, and other environments. In the University of Florida Libraries' now-defunct reference MOO, librarians greeted users in a virtual library foyer but also had two private discussion spaces called the "Reference Desk" and the "Office." There was also a space called the "Classroom," designated for group instruction.

In a MOO, a type of MUD (multi-user domain), users are not limited to simply chatting but can wander through a maze of richly descriptive spaces, build virtual rooms, and create or react to a wide variety of objects such as robots, containers, message boards, or slides. MUDs first appeared on the Internet around 1979 as simple text-based environments where gaming enthusiasts could congregate online to play Dungeons and Dragons and other games. Incidentally, MUD is also correctly defined as multiple user dimension, multiple user dungeon (from an early Internet role-playing game), or multiple user dialogue (*The MUD Faq* 2002). MOOs were developed more than a decade later, in the early 1990s, as programmers extended the functionality of MUD software to allow anyone with an account to create rooms and alter the environment. For an idea of what a purely text-based environment looks like, there is a screen snapshot of the popular *Lambda MOO* in Figure 1.4. Note the rich description of "The Living Room." The "Welcome poster," "fireplace," "couch," and "Cockatoo" are a few of the objects with which users can interact.

Figure 1.3. Library lobby of the University of New Brunswick MOO.

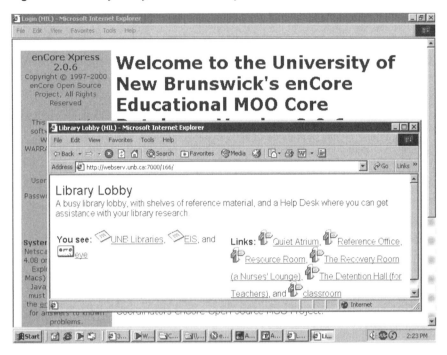

Figure 1.4. In the "Living Room" of the Lambda MOO.

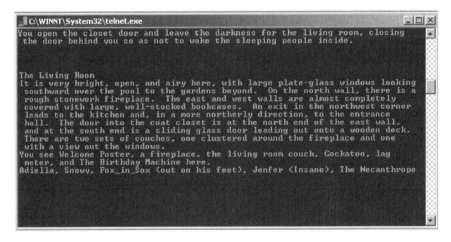

Using a MOO to Chat

Like IRC, conversation in a MOO can be extremely fast paced, depending on the number of people participating and the drift of the conversation. Most MOOs support connections from guests or registered users via clients on the users' computers or through web-based Java telnet applets. Once connected, you can use basic commands to see who is online, to chat, to describe your character or change your username, or to explore various rooms. "As users begin to MOO, many notice that 'chatting' seems to be the only available activity" (Davies, Shield, and Weininger 1998). For some, MOO evokes a vision of gaming enthusiasts hammering commands on their keyboard to propel themselves through an imaginary cyberworld of medieval castles to slay dragons or battle evil wizards. MOO is, however, much more than a gaming environment and is a popular tool for teachers of writing and composition. While it is true that "many do exist simply for socializing and playing games, educational MOOs, such as *schMOOze University*, offer a variety of learning activities and projects that move well beyond this. For example, *schMOOze University* comprises a virtual campus, complete with classrooms and self-study tutorials, dormitories, libraries, a graffiti wall, a games room, and much more" (Davies, Shield, and Weininger 1998). Exploring a MOO such as *Connections* or *LambdaMOO* can be like reading a work of fiction, as you read descriptions of rooms and the objects you find in them and as you see the messages that are generated as you leave one virtual room for another. Users who log on as guests may wander through the MOO, enjoying these features. Registered users have more privileges. They can map out the location of virtual rooms and build them, as well as create virtual objects that react and even chat with users. The interactive, creative, text-intensive nature of the MOO makes it an excellent tool to teach writing, currently the main application of this interactive medium in college and university settings.

Using a MOO can be more challenging than using IRC. Because MOO is more than just a space to chat, users need to know some basic commands. For example, a user may have to issue a command such as "connect guest" at the welcome page (as seen in Figure 1.6) to get connected or preface comments with the command "say" to talk with other participants. In strictly text-based MOOs lacking a graphical user interface such as JHCore, users have to master additional commands if they wish to travel from virtual room to virtual room or interact with some of the more advanced objects such as bots or slides. Happily, there is software that presents many of the commands in a point-and-click interface for users and librarians. *enCore* is one variety of MOO that includes a Web interface for users. Even with a graphical interface, however, the rich descriptive and interactive environment inherent in MOOing may present substantial barriers for first-time users uncomfortable with experimentation. The learning curve is even steeper for librarians who will work with a host of more advanced commands to create the virtual environment including rooms, robots, and so on.

Setting Up a MOO

Using a MOO can be a fun way to create a reference service. The University of Texas at Dallas maintains an online learning environment called LinguaMoo, where faculty can gather virtually to converse or teach classes. MOO software enables librarians to design an imaginary world much like (or very different from) your physical library while supporting multimedia. This sets it apart from some other real-time programs, which rely on conversation alone. Software such as *JHCore*, *eDUcore*, and *enCore* are powerful open-source programs that require no client download for a user to connect. Most people already have a telnet client loaded on their computer that works with their web browser, so downloading is not necessary. Free Java applets such as *Cup-O MUD* are available to create a web page with a chat window–type interface for the telnet-based *JHCore*, and *enCore* comes with a built-in server-side client called *Xpress* that creates a web interface. "Through the *Xpress* interface, people can browse your MOO as a non-interactive hypertext, or use the integrated *Xpress* MOO client to communicate with others online" (Holmevik and Haynes 2000a). In other words, the user can travel through the MOO by pointing and clicking, yet can chat with the librarian or other users. "The web interface allows you to connect web pages, images, sound files, Real Audio and video streams, Shockwave animations, Java applets and more to objects in your MOO" (Holmevik and Haynes 2000a).

MOO programs such as *JHCore*, *eDUcore*, and *enCore* give librarians the ability to control the number of users that can log on and feature robust databases that can be programmed to generate automated help features and canned responses for librarians and to create interactive robots that will respond to users. Librarians can program a rich and descriptive virtual environment featuring "rooms" that include customized features with which users may interact. For example, librarians could create virtual handouts to hand to online users that answer common questions such as, "What are the library hours?" In a purely text-based MOO, you can ask a user to pick up an object and "look" at it, which is a command to display the object's description, or instruct the user to click on the handout if using the web-based interface.

Setting up a MOO does require at least some basic knowledge of MOO programming concepts. I recommend two books in this area, the first, *MOOniversity*, written by English composition instructor Cynthia Haynes and MOO programmer Jan Run Holmevik (2000a). The second is a collection of essays titled, *High Wired: On the Design, Use, and Theory of Educational MOOs*, edited by Holmevik and Haynes (2001). Both are excellent guides to installing and programming a MOO, as well as the educational applications of the software. In addition, the articles by Shaw (1996) and Eustace and McAfee (1995) provide tips on customizing a MOO for reference use.

Hosted MOO Services

If running a MOO locally at your library is not a viable option but you are interested in the medium, you might wish to investigate a hosted service. There are

Figure 1.5. Log-on page for the RefeXpress MOO.

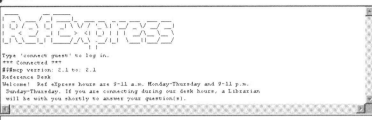

Ref eXpress is a library reference discussion space where you can ask librarians at the University of Florida for help with your research.

Above this text you should see a window with a connection to *Ref eXpress*. (The JAVA applet works best with Netscape Navigator, so use that if you can.)

- Type **connect guest** in the bottom box to begin.
- Type **say** followed by some text to type in a question and converse with librarian.
- Type **@quit** to logoff Ref eXpress.

Please do not use the forward, back or home button on your browser during a *Ref eXpress* session, as you may be disconnected.

Ref eXpress is a pilot program offered from March 13 through May 4, 2000. Please complete the web survey to let us know if you like this new service.

Hours | Help | Rules | FAQ | New Browser Window | Survey | Email a Reference Question

RefeXpress Development Team:
Bradley Dilger, Ann Lindell, Mimi Pappas, Alice Primack, Jana Ronan, John F. Ronan, Colleen Seale.
Copyright (c) 2000 University of Florida George A. Smathers Libraries. All Rights Reserved.
P. O. Box 117001 Gainesville, FL 32611-7001
Acceptable Use, Copyright, and Disclaimer Statement
Send comments and/or questions about this site to
ronan@mail.uflib.ufl.edu.
Last Updated March 7, 2000

many MOOs and MOO wizards (administrators) that offer hosting on their servers. The local MOO administrator at the University of Florida (MOOville) helped me pilot the first stage of our real-time reference service on one of its servers, as pictured in Figure 1.5. If you don't have a local MOO at your institution, you may wish to investigate setting up a room on an existing MOO on an educational system such as *Connections* or contract with *Diversity University* for services (rates are posted on the organization's web site; Diversity University 1997).

MOO AT A GLANCE

Advantages:
- Extend reference services to students in MOO writing programs
- If used for distance education or for local classes, users will be familiar with it
- Inexpensive or free

- Some MOO software supports web pages, images, sound, video, animation
- Possible to program alert features and frequently used sayings for librarians
- Possible to program "clickable" URLs
- Can work with many users at one time for bibliographic instruction or be restricted to one user at a time

Disadvantages:
- Primarily text based
- Command driven, unless programmed for graphical interface
- Not intuitive for first time users, although IRC and instant messaging users will grasp it quickly
- Lacks features such as web escorting
- Learning curve exists for commands
- Some programming knowledge necessary to install and operate

MOOs Mentioned in Text
Connections
http://web.nwe.ufl.edu/~tari/connections/

Diversity University
http://moo.dumain.du.org:8000/

LambdaMOO
http://www.gotham-city.net/lambda.html

LinguaMOO
http://lingua.utdallas.edu:7000/

MOOville
http://web.nwe.ufl.edu/writing/help/moo/

SchMOOze University
http://schmooze.hunter.cuny.edu:8888/

University of New Brunswick Libraries
http://www.unb.ca:7000/166/

Selected MOO Software
eDUcore (Diversity University) http://www.du.org/educore/
enCore http://lingua.utdallas.edu/encore/
JHCore http://sourceforge.net/projects/jhcore/
LambdaCore ftp://ftp.lambda.moo.mud.org/pub/MOO/

INSTANT MESSAGING (IM)

In a brief article concerning the security of instant messaging that was published recently in *The Independent* (London), 7 January 2002, technology editor Charles Arthur touched on the development of the medium. "Instant messaging is a phenomenon, though rather like text messaging on mobiles, it isn't new. It appeared in 1984, before the Net, when sites were islands that you dialed into separately. Some bulletin boards implemented a protocol that allowed real-time person-to-person communication—you typed some text, which got sent over your modem and phone line to another user logged onto the same system" (Arthur 2002). In 1986, a company named Mirablis invented a new type of Internet-based instant messaging that also incorporated presence awareness, a feature that enables users to determine if someone is online and willing to accept a chat session. This early software was called *ICQ*, a phonetic spelling of the phrase "I seek you."

ICQ and other instant messaging programs work differently from IRC; messages are not routed through the server (with IRC, a live connection is maintained with the IRC server at all times). In IM, a user opens a client program and logs on. The IM client notifies the IM server at the other end that the user is online, sending the server user IP and port numbers. Then the server notifies the IM client if any of the people on a contact or "buddy" list are online, so that the user can instant message them directly, based on their IP and port numbers. Arthur (2002) notes that "Buddy Lists are like interactive address books: the names come alight when someone is online and available to chat." This means that when users open an instant messaging session with their buddies, they create a direct connection to the person with whom they are chatting, bypassing the server.

Instant messaging programs allow users to chat privately one-on-one, leave messages for others, send files, play games, and talk, depending on the IM program. Third-party add-ons, such as *AIM Speech*, read messages out loud to users, making instant messaging even more flexible. Because the business world in particular finds instant messaging useful, IM programs are in constant competition, and features are continually being upgraded and added.

At Columbia University, the Augustus C. Long Health Sciences Library uses AIM to conference online with their patrons seeking assistance. Users can initiate an IM session with a librarian at the web page pictured in Figure 1.6. The page also includes a link to an archive where users can download a copy of AIM. In the simulated session in Figure 1.7, a librarian assists "Nell" in searching a database by talking her through the process in the IM window.

Choosing the Right IM for Your Users

When selecting an instant messaging program, care should be taken for several reasons. Despite the best efforts of the Internet Engineering Task Force (IETF), at this time there is no established protocol for instant messaging. *AIM*, the dominant player in this area of communication, uses a proprietary protocol, and at the time of writing seems unwilling to share it with the rest of the IM industry. This means that if you select *Yahoo! Messenger* as the software for your virtual reference service, you may or may not be able to chat with people using other IM software. There are IM clients that support multiple programs, however; *Trillian*, *Imici Messenger*, and *Odigo* also support *AIM*, *Yahoo! Messenger*, *ICQ*, and MSN *Messenger*. This means that if you use *Trillian*, you can combine the buddy lists of your friends using *AOL*, *Yahoo! Messenger*, and other programs.

Figure 1.6. Log-on page for the Augustus C. Long Health Sciences Library's Ref Chat (AIM).

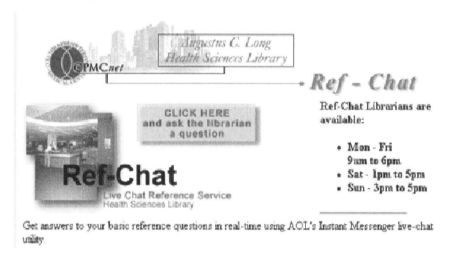

Figure 1.7. Simulation of librarian using AIM to assist a person using a database.

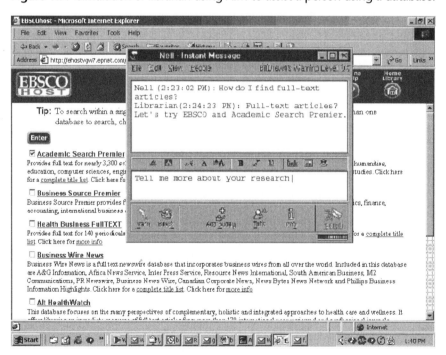

Security

Security is another issue to consider when using IM. "The ability to maintain an 'always-on' connection means that you are opening up a 'channel' to your computer's desktop, thereby raising the vulnerability of client systems to viruses, security breaches, spam messages, junk mail, and abuse by other users" (NPTalk 2000). Another potential problem for services running off a hosted instant messaging service such as *Yahoo! Messenger* or *MSN Messenger* is that, as ZDNet computer applications columnist Vaughnan-Nichols (2001) noted, there is no guarantee that messages aren't read at the servers or in transit over the Internet by someone using a network scanner. He recommends running virus programs on the gateway or router computer as well as virus protection programs on librarians' computers. For optimal security, he recommends running the IM service on a local server behind a firewall and disabling any voice messaging or file transfer features. Although most libraries using this technology are operating from hosted services such as *MSN Messenger* or *AIM*, you can purchase IM server software and run your service locally to enhance security. Such programs include *Jabber Server, Bantu, Odigo Open Instant Messaging Server (OIMS),* or *Imici SMB Server.*

Device-Based Versus Network-Based IM

Another consideration is whether to choose a device-based or a network-based IM system. Device-based IM means that a user's configuration information, such as lists of contacts, are stored on the same computer as the client software and are not accessible if the user logs on at another location. Network-based instant messaging programs, such as *ActiveIM*, store user configurations on the server, enabling the user to access settings regardless of the computer, cell phone, PDA (personal digital assistant), or other device that is used to connect and chat. For example, *AIM* allows users to export their buddy list for installation on another computer (which can be unwieldy) or access their list and send messages through a web browser using *AIM Express*. Network-based IM may be the best option for a reference operation because it frees librarians to connect at the computer of their choice in the most convenient location.

Other Features

Other issues to consider when choosing an IM are cross-platform accessibility, audio capabilities, and other special features. One desirable feature is cross-platform accessibility to allow Macintosh, Windows, Unix, and other users access to your real-time reference services. This means that the IM server software should have client software for each of these operating systems. Other worthwhile features include video, user control of his or her visibility online, the ability to chat with more than one user at a time, active URLs, programmed emoticons, and file sharing. Another feature, VOIP, allows chatters to hear each other and users to telephone the librarian through the instant messenger's audio capabilities. The clarity of VOIP is only as good as the network connectivity, however; in less than optimal conditions, it may transmit in only one direction. Finally, the amount of memory that the IM program requires on computers is an important consideration, as is the speed of transfer. You may wish to skip some of the aforementioned features if implementing them means that users will experience lag time while chatting or if they will have to install a large software program on their computers to connect. For more on IM, see "How Instant Messaging Works" by Jeff Tyson (2002) and Joseph Yue's (2000) presentation on implementing ICQ in a library setting.

INSTANT MESSAGING AT A GLANCE

Advantages:
- Software is free or inexpensive
- One-on-one communication
- Many users are familiar with the technology
- Some programs incorporate voice technology

Disadvantages:
- Security issues
- May require user to install software to reach librarians
- May include advertising or other distracting features such as stock quotes, pop-up ads, and animation
- Easy access to other recreational chat spaces may confuse users
- Typically lacks features such as push page, escorting, and databases of conversational phrases repeatedly used by librarians
- Primarily text based

Selected IM Software

ActiveIM
http://www.cs.berkeley.edu/~mikechen/im/

AIM (AOL Instant Messenger)
http://www.aim.com/index.adp

Bantu
http://corp.bantu.com/

ICQ
http://www.icq.com/download/

Imici
http://www.imici.com/

Jabber Server
http://www.jabber.org/

MSN Messenger
http://messenger.msn.com/

Odigo
http://www.odigo.com/

Trillian
http://www.trillian.cc/

Yahoo! Messenger
http://messenger.yahoo.com/

WEB-BASED CHAT SOFTWARE

Having established some grounding in earlier, but still widely used, types of real-time communication software, I now consider a popular and adaptable type of program for real-time reference: web-based chat software. For our purposes, let's define this software as any program that creates a chat window on a web page, allowing users to exchange messages with a librarian without having to install a special piece of software on their computers. Web-based chat falls into two broad categories that I call "hybrid" and "prepackaged."

Web-Based IRC and MOO

One way to improve dramatically the functionality of a traditional IRC- or MOO-based operation is to create a web-based interface. Adding a web interface eliminates the need for people to find, install, and master software to access your real-time service. Java applets such as *jIRC*, *Cup-O MUD*, or *MOOtcan* are readily available in various archives on the Internet. Two of the larger archives are the Sun Microsystems Java archive and Internet.com's Java Boutique. You can also use a search engine such as Google or AltaVista to locate other archives. Figure 1.5 displays what this type of connection looks like in the now-defunct *RefeXpress* library MOO.

In this building-block approach, library staff members either maintain an IRC or MOO server at their facility or establish a channel or room with a hosted service, in addition to creating and maintaining a web site for the user interface. If you are leaning toward using IRC or MOO, this configuration removes barriers such as software installation for the user but adds an extra level of complexity for the library when installing and maintaining the service. This type of interface tends to be user friendly, with many of the basic communication and navigation commands programmed into buttons or pull-downs, depending on the Java applet you adopt.

How does it work? Library staff members design an entry page for their chat reference service that contains an embedded Java applet (many tutorials on this subject exist on web sites such as *WebMonkey*, the *Java Boutique*, or at *Focus on Java*). When the user initiates a chat, the web server sends the user's computer the Java applet, which quickly loads and creates a chat window. Applets vary in complexity, so a worthwhile feature is a simple interface that removes the need for a new user to master anything but how to type messages in the send box and

Figure 1.8. Composite of the University of North Texas Libraries' log-on page, overlaid with a chat session.

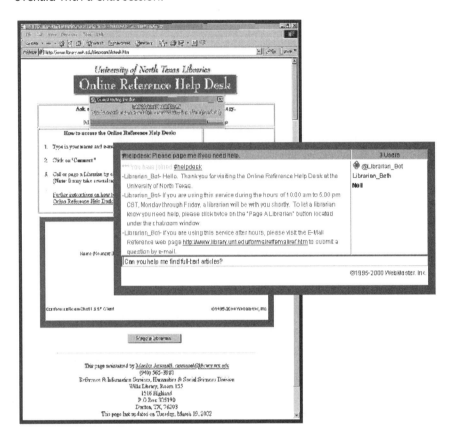

then hit an enter key to transmit it to the librarian on duty. Librarians will need access to advanced commands to create a new channel or to remove a disruptive user. Most applets also support advanced commands for the librarians who staff the service and other experienced users to send private messages and perform other functions. Some applets even support push, sound, video, and white-boarding. This approach is probably the most viable for libraries seeking to reach established online communities using IRC or MOO. It is also possible to program a complete web-based chat program, or just an interface for IRC or MOO, using Perl, CGI, ASP, VBScript, and XML with Java. If this option appeals to you, read Tom Corcotoi's (n.d.) tutorial in *Programmer's Resource* for a good introduction. Another place to consult is *The CGI Resource Index*, a web site that lists many free and inexpensive scripts. Keep in mind that an easier alternative might be to find shareware or commercial software that incorporates all of this programming for you (see Figure 1.8).

Prepackaged Options

There are numerous prepackaged software programs available for purchase or free downloading to create a web-based chat service. Although many of these programs incorporate IRC, Java, and HTML in the programming to create an easy-to-use interface, others employ relational databases or other strategies to create the chat feature. As you evaluate these packages, remember that free or inexpensive versions of web-based communication software tend to lack advanced features that enhance provision of reference service such as push page or databases of preprogrammed responses. They are designed mainly to facilitate text-based chat, although some do support the transfer of files.

There are many commercial web-based software packages available, such as *ChatSpace, ParaChat, VolanoChat,* and *RealChat.* One typical example of a web-based package based on IRC is *ConferenceRoom,* used to create the "Online Reference Help Desk" at the University of North Texas Libraries. *WebMaster* bundles IRC server software and a web-based user interface in *ConferenceRoom,* which runs on operating systems ranging from Windows and Linux to Apple OSX and Solaris. The program comes in a zipped file that you can purchase and download from the *WebMaster* site, and it self-installs. Another IRC-based software package that is rated highly in reviews at Internet.com is *ChatSpace 2.1,* used by the libraries of the Boeing Company and the Fitchburg State College Library. *ChatSpace* runs on Windows servers, allows up to 100 people to be connected at a time and is advertised as free for online communities that number under 10,000 users. Like the hybrid approach, these IRC-based programs allow users to initiate a chat session through their web browser while supporting advanced IRC commands such as private messaging or creating channels. When evaluating this type of software, it is usually easy to test the software in action. Often the companies either offer limited trials of the software or maintain a demonstration chat room using the software on their web site (see Figure 1.9).

Other Options for Web-Based Chat

Finding a program that works with IRC or MOO is not the only option you have to create a web-based chat service. It is possible to purchase web-based chat software powered with Java servlets or Perl, CGI, ASP, or VBScript in combination with relational databases or to program your own. Needless to say, the latter approach requires a certain level of programming knowledge. There are tutorials on the Web and in popular computing magazines to help guide a programmer in creating a home-grown chat program. Another option is to use an open-ware program such as *jzChat,* that may be downloaded from the Web. Business and computer trade magazines carry numerous reviews of these types of software, as do online magazines and web sites focusing on the computer industry and the Internet (*C|NET, Internet.com,* and *ZDNet* are a few web sites that provide reviews). In addition, *JUMBO!* lists several types of chat programs for download or purchase. It is surprising that more libraries are not taking

Figure 1.9. User's view of a chat session using *Rakim* at the Miami University Libraries.

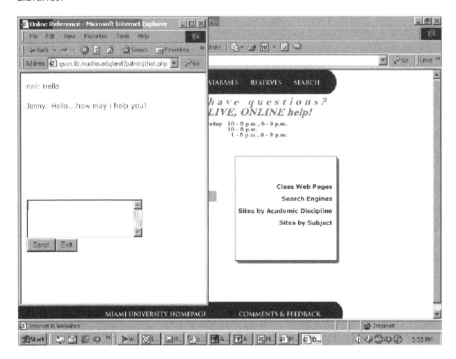

this approach. One notable exception would be Miami University Libraries' chat service, developed completely in-house, named *Rakim*.

WEB-BASED CHAT SOFTWARE AT A GLANCE

Advantages:
- Java applets allow users to connect without installing client software on their computers
- Software is inexpensive or even free if hosted on chat company's servers
- "Clickable" URLs
- Many include push page (where the librarian can send the user a web page)
- One-on-one communication
- Some programs incorporate voice technology

Disadvantages:
- Some packages offer only one software interface for both users and librarians
- May include advertising or other distracting features such as stock quotes, pop-ups, and animation
- Easy access to other recreational chat spaces may confuse users
- Having to handle interruptions in public rooms (if using free, hosted service)

- Typically lacks features such as escorting and databases of conversational phrases repeatedly used by librarians
- Primarily text based

Selected Web-Based Software

ChatSpace
http://www.chatspace.com/

ConferenceRoom
http://www.conferenceroom.com

Echat
http://www.e-scripts.com/echat/

ParaChat
http://www.parachat.com

Rakim
http://styro.lib.muohio.edu/rakim/

RealChat
http://www.rcsoft.net/

VolanoChat
http://www.volano.com/

The goal of this chapter has been to provide the reader with an overview of basic types of software, such as instant messaging, IRC, and MOO, that can create text-based chat and communication online in real time. This understanding will allow readers to select more effectively the best software for their particular situation. Remember that advances are continual in communication software, so consult current reviews of software of the business world to complete your evaluation. New chat and instant messaging software constantly debuts in the marketplace. Even if you decide not to implement any of the software discussed in this section, you will have a better understanding of the more advanced software, discussed in Chapter 2, that often incorporates instant messaging or IRC in a suite of interconnected software.

REFERENCES

Arthur, Charles. 2002. "Network: Let Your Fingers Do the Talking; Instant Messaging Is a Phenomenon. But It Isn't New, and Fierce Debates Continue about the Use and Abuse of It." *The Independent* (London), (7 January), 9. Available online at http://www.independent.co.uk or in LexisNexis (accessed 7 March 2002).

Corcotoi, Tom. n.d. "How to Build Your Own Web Based ASP Chat System." *Programmers Resource.com.* Available online at http://www.programmers resource.com/articles/buildachat.asp (accessed 7 March 2002).

Davies, Lawrence B., Lesley Shield, and Markus J. Weininger. 1998. "Godzilla Can MOO, Can You? MOOs for Construction, Collaboration & Community and Research." *The Language Teacher* 22. Available online at http://www.jalt-publications.org/tlt/files/98/feb/davies.html (accessed 27 February 2002).

Diversity University. 1997. *Establishing an Online Virtual World for Education.* Available online at http://www.du.org/educore/MOOsetup_main.html (accessed 27 February 2002).

Eustace, Ken, and Malcolm McAfee. 1995. *Beyond the WEB and the MOO in Education.* Paper presented at the ACEC'95 Conference, 9–13 July, Perth, Australia. Available at http://www.csu.edu.au/research/sda/Papers/webmoo2.html (accessed 31 August 2002).

Fagan, Jody Condit, and Michele Calloway. 2001. "Creating an Instant Messaging Reference System." *Information Technology and Libraries* (December 20). Available online at http://www.lita.org/ital/2004_fagan.html (accessed 31 August 2002).

Holmevik, Jan Rune, and Haynes, Cynthia. 2000a. *enCore Educational MOO Core Database: Administrators Guide.* Available online at http://lingua.utdallas.edu/encore/readme.html (accessed 13 March 2002).

Holmevik, Jan Rune, and Cynthia Haynes. 2001. *High Wired: On the Design, Use, and Theory of Educational MOOs,* second edition. Ann Arbor: University of Michigan Press.

Holmevik, Jan Rune, and Cynthia Haynes. 2000b. *MOOniversity: A Student's Guide to Online Learning Environments.* Boston: Allyn and Bacon.

McConnell, Brian. 2002. "Web-Enabling Your Call Center." *HelloDirect.com* (January 31). Available online at http://telecom.hellodirect.com/docs/Tutorials/WebEnableCallCenter.1.033099-P.asp (accessed 14 May 2003).

"The Mud Faq." 2002. "1.1 What is a MUD?" *The Mud Connector.* Available online at http://www.mudconnect.com/mudfaq/ (accessed 31 August 2002).

"NPTalk: Instant Messaging." 2000. *NPT: Nonprofits' Policy and Technology Project.* Available online at http://www.ombwatch.org/npt/nptalk/may2000/im.html (accessed 28 January 2002).

Pioch, Nicolas, Owe Rasmussen, Michelle A. Hoyle, and Joseph Lo. 1997. *A Short IRC Primer.* Edition 1.2 (January 1). Available online at http://www.irchelp.org/irchelp/ircprimer.html#Behave (accessed 21 January 2002).

Shaw, Elizabeth. 1996. *Real-Time Reference in a MOO: Promise and Problems* (April). Available online at http://www.google.com/search?q=cache:sQCD_F7QeTsC:www~personal.si.umich.edu/~ejshaw/research2.html (accessed 19 March 2002).

Taylor, Tina Lynn. 2000. "Living Digitally: Embodiment in Virtual Environments." Ph.D. diss., Brandeis University.

Toyer, Katherine. 1997. *Learn Internet Relay Chat.* Plano, TX: Wordwise.

Tyson, Jeff. 2002. "How Instant Messaging Works." *How Stuff Works, Inc.* http://www.howstuffworks.com/instant-messaging1.htm (accessed 29 January 2002).

Vaughan-Nichols, Steven. 2001. "Instant Messaging—Better Safe Than Sorry" (October 25). *ZDNet Tech Update.* Available online at http://techupdate.zdnet.

com/techupdate/stories/main/0,14179,2815785,00.html (accessed 22 January 2002).

Yue, Joseph. 2000. "The Use of ICQ in Providing Real Time Reference Services." Paper presented at *Facets of Digital Reference*. The Virtual Reference Desk 2nd Annual Digital Reference Conference, 16–17 October, Seattle, WA. Available online at http://www.vrd.org/conferences/VRD2000/proceedings/Yue11–20.shtml (accessed 27 March 2002).

WEB SITES CITED

AltaVista
    http://www.altavista.com

The CGI Resource Index
    http://cgi.resourceindex.com/Programs_and_Scripts/Perl/Chat

C/NET
    http://www.cnet.com

Cup-O MUD
    http://www.du.org/java/CupOmud/

Focus on Java
    http://java.about.com/library/weekly/mpreviss.htm

Google
    http://www.google.com

Internet.com
    http://www.internet.com

Internet.com Java Boutique
    http://javaboutique.internet.com/network/chat.html

jIRC
    http://www.jpilot.com/java/irc/support.html

JUMBO!
    http://www.jumbo.com/chat/

jzChat
    http://www.javazoom.net/jzservlets/jzchat10/jzchat.html

MOOtcan
    http://cmc.uib.no/~sindre/mootcan/

Sun Microsystems Java Archive
    http://java.sun.com/applets/

WebMonkey
    http://hotwired.lycos.com/webmonkey/index.html

ZDNet
    http://www.zdnet.com/

2 ADVANCED REAL-TIME SOFTWARE

There are many types of more advanced software programs than IRC, MOO, or instant messaging (IM) that hold promise for real-time reference services for online library users. In addition to simple text-based chat, they offer sophisticated features such as escorting, pushing or sending web pages to users, white-boarding and powerful knowledge bases. This chapter seeks to explore the advantages and disadvantages of the major types of software in this category, from courseware packages used to conduct classes online to suites of powerful software used in e-commerce to run web-based call centers. The pros and cons of implementing a hosted real-time reference service will also be examined here, because most hosted systems such as LSSI's *Virtual Reference Toolkit (VRT)* and the Metropolitan Cooperative Library System's *24/7 Reference* service use call center software. Other software and hosted services discussed in this chapter include *WebCT*, HorizonLive's *ReferenceDesk Live*, *eCollege*, Docutek's *VRLplus*, Digi-Net's *eLibrarian*, *LiveAssistance*, divine's *Virtual Reference Desk* (VRD), Convey's *OnDemand*, eGain's *Live Web Suite*, and the *QuestionPoint Collaborative Reference Service* (a joint project of the Library of Congress and OCLC, the Online Computer Library Center.)

COURSEWARE

One unique type of software that the libraries at Bryn Mawr and the University of Philadelphia are using to provide real-time reference services is courseware, suites of software normally used to manage distance-learning classes. Many colleges and universities, nonprofit organizations, and private businesses use programs such as *WebCT*, *Blackboard*, *Prometheus*, *ERes*, or *eCollege* to facilitate delivery of course content online. Programs such as *WebCT* and *Prometheus* include text-based chat, audio

Figure 2.1. Chat session from the user's perspective at Michigan State University Libraries (*VRLplus*).

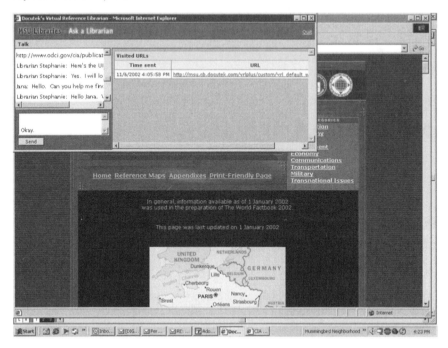

chat, file sharing, white-boarding, and the ability to push users slides or files—all features that could easily be adapted to reference work. The functionality of this category of software varies by vendor. Some vendors bundle a full array of multimedia and Internet features in a basic package, and others parcel out features such as audio chat in additional modules that must be purchased separately. For example, Docutek has a special library component called *VRLplus* that can be purchased to extend the capabilities of the *ERes* electronic reserve program to e-mail, escorting, transcripts, and creating an expert system. Figure 2.1 illustrates a VRLplus session, from a user's perspective. In this online reference encounter, the user is looking for a map.

Another reason to consider courseware is that online learners should be able to migrate easily to a library chat service based on software they have mastered for courses or training, as well as for the visibility that product placement within online courses would afford reference services. For a comparison of features across some of the leading brands of courseware, please consult Table 2.1.

Accessibility and Courseware

Authentication or Accounts? Librarians need to be aware that accessibility can be an issue in programs such as *WebCT* or *e-College*. To start with, most courseware packages require users to log on with an institutional account that may be

Table 2.1 Comparison of courseware features.

	Blackboard	eCollege	HorizonLive 3.0	*VRLplus*	WebCT
Communication					
Chat	yes	yes	yes	yes	yes
Moderated chat	yes	yes	yes		yes
Rooms	yes	yes		yes	yes
Transfer users	no		no	yes	no
E-mail (built-in)	yes	yes	yes	yes	yes
Private messenging	yes	yes	yes	no	yes
VOIP	no	yes	2-way	no	no
Streaming video	no	yes	yes	no	no
Special features					
Push URL	yes	unclear	yes	yes	no
Whiteboard	yes	no	yes	yes	yes
Slides	yes	yes	yes	yes	yes
Application sharing	yes	yes	yes	yes	yes
File exchange	yes	yes	yes	yes	some
Form sharing	no	no	yes	yes	no
Transcripts	yes		yes	yes	yes
Knowledgebase	no		polling feature	yes	no
FAQs	URLs	URLs	yes	URLs, responses	URLs
Statistics	no	yes	yes	yes	no
User Interface					
Account needed	yes	yes	account or guest	log on required	account or guest
System	Mac, Windows	Mac, Windows	Windows, UNIX, Mac32 MB RAM, RealPlayer or QuickTime, Sound card and speakers	Mac, Windows, UNIX	Mac, Windows
Browser	IE, Netscape	IE, Netscape	IE, Netscape	IE, Netscape	IE, Netscape
Java required	yes	yes	yes	no	yes
508 compliant (for disabilities)	yes	yes	yes		yes
Customize	yes	yes		yes	yes
Librarian Interface					
Special client	Web based	Web based	Web based	Web based	Web based
Built-in browser	yes	yes	yes	yes	yes
System					
Installation assistance	yes	yes	Included	Included	yes
Standalone or hosted	both	hosted	both	both	standalone
Server requirements	2 CPU Ultrasparc II 450 MHz 2 CPU Pentium III, 800 MHz, 2 GB RAM Webserver: Apache or IIS	N/A	customized by HorizonLive for library	Windows 2000 Web Server, Pentium III. 667 MHz+, 256 MB memory, 9.1 GB hard drive	Linux/UNIX- 512 MB 1 GB MS OS 10 MB Disk space
HTTP tunnelling (through firewalls)				yes	problems
Pricing	per user		seats, concurrent users	seats	varies by product

authenticated or to create an account "on-the-fly" before they are able to connect and ask a question. Passwording a real-time reference service might deter some people who prefer anonymity, who are in a hurry, or who find the mechanics of establishing an account problematic because they lack technical proficiency. The log-on process may discourage people most in need of assistance from a librarian online.

Computer Literacy Another accessibility factor to consider is that courseware does require a certain level of computer literacy to navigate. Many instructors using courseware to teach arrange for their students to have a hands-on orientation to the software at the beginning of the course, indicating that at least general assistance in learning the software is necessary. Even if the text-based chat function is easy to use, more advanced features such as white-boarding or file sharing may be complicated for users and librarians. For example, *ReferenceDesk Live* as implemented at the Lippincott Library at the University of Pennsylvania's Wharton School of Business offers two-way live audio for communication but is a confusing interface if one's computer isn't properly configured to connect immediately. The user can see the librarian online trying to communicate using streaming audio, but it's difficult to find the alternative communication channels to send a return message. Even for libraries in the enviable position of serving users in a homogenous computing environment, such as a large corporation or a middle school that has a contract with Apple, one cannot assume user proficiency with the technology. As Laurie Harrison (2001) puts it so aptly, "technical accessibility does not ensure usability." As the education coordinator at the Resource Centre for Academic Technology at the University of Toronto, Harrison conducted a survey of selected courseware's features and foibles, concluding that the user's level of experience is a "key factor in success."

Critical Mass When evaluating the potential that courseware might hold for your library services, keep in mind that courseware is primarily designed for students to use over several weeks or months, during which time they learn to navigate and become comfortable with the interface. If your target audience already uses the software for classes, business meetings, or other online conferencing, they will probably find a real-time reference service offered in the same medium accessible. Unfortunately, courseware may not be the best means to provide help to users on a one-time-only or occasional basis, as is often the case in reference work.

Selection and Installation

Most courseware packages are available as plug-and-play systems to be installed and administered on a local library server (*WebCT, Eres*) or through remote hosting (*Blackboard, HorizonLive*). Because of the high cost of these integrated systems and limited usability, I recommend considering courseware as a medium for real-time reference only if you can join an established system. If your parent institution uses courseware, economics alone may be a compelling reason to use in reference, if only temporarily, to learn more about virtual reference. It may be possible to form a partnership with another department or piggyback on the institutional license at little or no additional cost. If considering an independent purchase, be aware that this powerful software often starts at the $10,000 to $15,000 range (hosted or locally operated), not including such hidden costs as hardware and ancillary software. Pricing also may depend on the number of courses and people enrolled at an institution or business.

Courseware at a Glance

Advantages:
- Features include text-based chat, audio chat, file sharing, white-boarding, and push page, integrated into a single interface
- One-on-one or group communication, often moderated
- Instructor console makes configuration of the service and administration easier
- May be able to partner with another department or program (e.g., distance-learning unit)
- May be able to connect reference points within online courses

Disadvantages:
- Requires large amount of bandwidth
- Complex interface to master
- Logging on requires account
- Lacks features such as escorting, databases of conversational phrases
- Expensive
- If hosted, may include distracting advertising
- If hosted, may not be able to set hours of access

Selected Courseware Software:

Blackboard
http://www.blackboard.com

eCollege
http://www.ecollege.com/index.html

Prometheus (Blackboard)
http://company.blackboard.com/prometheus/

ReferenceDesk Live (RDL) from HorizonLive
http://www.horizonlive.com/

Virtual Reference Librarian (*VRLplus*) from Docutek
http://www.docutek.com

WebCT
http://www.webct.com

CALL CENTER SOFTWARE

Currently the most sophisticated chat-based software is the type of software that call centers use to reach consumers, as implemented on the web sites of large corporations such as Lands' End, America Online, Walgreens, or Monster.com. A call or web center is an online help desk where customer service representatives handle consumer questions and problems. It sounds a lot like a reference desk, doesn't it? Call centers use expensive suites of software to enable representatives to process large numbers of chats (and phone calls), to triage these queries and forward them to the appropriate representative or department, to log transactions, and to collect information about customers.

Definition and Features

Call center software typically incorporates text-based chat, web browsing, Voice over Internet Protocol (VoIP), streaming video, e-mail, white-boarding, and application sharing, as well as special features such as preprogrammed phrases to aid representatives in answering customers quickly. The prime objective of this powerful type of software is to provide an extremely user-friendly interface for on-line consumers, while offering as few barriers to accessing help or sales assistance as possible. Therefore, call center software typically does not require downloading or installation of software components on the user's side, outside of clicking an "okay" button to accept a Java applet.

Some call center software packages, such as divine *Virtual Reference Desk (VRD)*, (powered by *NetAgent*) and Digi-Net eLibrarian (also called *Groopz*), even enable companies to define "web zones" or groups of web pages for the purposes of monitoring user activity. If a consumer travels into the "web zone," the software will automatically generate a chat session with the user, send a floating "bubble" across the user's screen inviting him or her to chat, or alert the customer service representative to the user's presence in the zone. It is debatable whether this feature is appropriate for a library given privacy and courtesy concerns, but it is an interesting capability nevertheless.

Probably the most useful and coveted characteristic of this type of software is the escorting or co-browsing feature, which allows a customer service representative to lead a consumer through a series of web pages step-by-step. Some programs offer bi-directional escorting, in which the librarian sets the program to follow the user. This enables the librarian to diagnose a problem by "watching" the user's actions as she or he navigates through a database or the library web site. A few examples of call center software that are currently being used in public, college, private, and school libraries are divine *VRD*, eGain *Live Web*, Convey *OnDemand*, LSSI *VRT*, *QuestionPoint*, *RightNowLive*, and *LiveAssistance*. Table 2.2 compares features such as escorting, VOIP across several software packages.

Users and Call Center Software

Users find it easy to access chat reference services supported by call center software because the user interface is totally web-based. Users fill out a form on a web page, submitting information such as their name, e-mail address, and question. Some libraries collect only a minimum of information about a user before they log on, whereas others, such as the Keystone Library Network's *Virtual Information Desk (VID)*, use the form to get a jump on the reference interview. The *VID* collects the user's name, e-mail address, affiliation, level of education, sources consulted, and the reference question. At the other end of the spectrum is the

Table 2.2a Comparison of call center software features by vendor.

	LivePerson	LiveAssistance	LiveHelper	Virtual Reference Desk (divine)	24/7 Reference from MCLS (eGain software)
Communication					
Chat	yes	yes	yes	yes	yes
Initiate a chat	yes	yes	no	add-on component	no
e-mail (built in)	no	no	no	yes	no
Automatically e-mail chat transcripts	yes (but not automatic)	yes (but not automatic)	yes	yes	yes
Private messaging	Corporate version	no	yes	yes	yes
Remote control of user's computer	no	no	Corporate version	no	no
See user typing	no	no	no	yes	no
Streaming video	no	May be future enhancement	no	no	no
System stallers	Corporate version	no		yes	yes
VOIP	in development (Hear)Me	no	Corporate version	yes	no
Special Features					
Push (send) pages to user	Y	yes	Pro & Corporate versions	yes	yes
Escorting/co-browsing	no	no	no	yes	yes
Bi-directional escorting (follow the user)	no	no	no	yes	yes
Application sharing	no				no
FAQs, canned messages	URLs, responses	URLs, responses	Pro & Corporate versions	URLs, responses	yes
File exchange	via URL in chat			yes	yes
Form sharing (fill in form together)	yes	no		yes	yes
Knowledgebase	yes			no	
Alert features	yes	yes	yes	sound, popups	yes
Librarian can terminate session	yes	yes		yes	yes
Queues/routing	yes	yes	yes	yes	yes
Search transcripts/get user history	yes	yes	yes	yes	yes
Transfer calls to another librarian	Corporate version	yes	yes	yes	yes
Categorize questions	Corporate version	yes		yes	
reports/statistics	yes	yes	yes	yes	yes
Survey/evaluation tool built-in	yes	yes	no	add-on component	yes
Spellchecker	Corporate version	no		yes	yes
Redirection or display message when closed	yes	yes	yes	yes	yes
Detect user browser, OS	Corporate version	no		yes	yes
Traffic monitoring (see incoming calls)	yes	no	yes	yes	yes

FAQs=frequently asked questions; HTTP, hypertext transfer protocol;
URL=uniform resource locator.

University of Florida, where all that is actually needed to log on is a name or pseudonym (although the form also asks for an e-mail address and question). Once the server receives the form from the user, it generates the actual chat session by transferring a Java applet or ActiveX control to the user's computer. All the user need do is click on a button to accept or reject the applet or control.

Once the user is connected, he or she sees some combination of a web page and a chat window, enabling the user to converse with the librarian on duty while he or she looks at the web page(s).

Table 2.2b Comparison of call center software features by vendor.

	Virtual Reference ToolKit (LSSI - eGain software)	QuestionPoint (enhanced communications)	eLibrarian (Groopz software from Digi-Net)	RightNow Live
Communication				
Chat	yes	yes	yes	yes
Initiate a chat	no	yes	yes	no
e-mail (built in)	add-on component	no		optional
Automatically e-mail chat transcripts	yes	yes	yes	yes, and moving mouse
Private messaging	yes	coming		yes
Remote control of user's computer	yes	yes	no	no
See user typing	no	see cursor	yes	yes, and moving mouse
Streaming video	no	yes		no
System stallers	yes		yes	no
VOIP	no	yes		no
Special Features				
Push (send) pages to user	yes	yes	yes	yes
Escorting/co-browsing	yes	yes	no	yes
Bi-directional escorting (follow the user)	yes	yes	no	no
Application sharing	add-on	yes		yes
FAQs, canned messages	yes	URLs, responses	URLs, responses	URLs
File exchange	yes	yes	text, music, images, video, applications, files, web pages	no
Form sharing (fill in form together)	yes	yes		yes
Knowledgebase	add-on	yes		yes
Alert features	yes	yes	yes	yes
Librarian can terminate session	yes	yes	yes	yes
Queues/routing	yes	yes	yes	yes
Search transcripts/get user history	yes	yes	yes	yes
Transfer calls to another librarian	yes	coming	yes	yes
Categorize questions		no		yes
reports/statistics	yes	yes		yes
Survey/evaluation tool built in	yes	no	no	yes
Spellchecker	yes	no	no	yes
Redirection or display message when closed	yes	yes	yes	yes
Detect user browser, OS	yes	yes		no
Traffic monitoring (see incoming calls)	yes	yes	yes	yes

VOIP=voice over Internet protocol; FAQ=frequently asked questions; OS=operating system.

The applets or controls that are used to create a seamless connection normally remain resident—although invisible—on the user's computer. One program, *On-Demand* (which is used to power the chat component of *QuestionPoint*), can be configured to install a permanent button advertising the library chat service on the user's web browser.

Comparison Shopping

When comparing call center software programs, one major difference to look for is the way in which the software presents the chat session. Some use frames to

Table 2.2c Comparison of call center software features by vendor.

	LivePerson	LiveAssistance	LiveHelper	Virtual Reference Desk (divine)	24/7 Reference from MCLS (eGain software)
Users Interface					
Platform	Mac, Windows, Linux	Windows, Mac, AOL	PC		Mac, Windows
Browser	yes (less support for Netscape/Macs)	All	IE best	IE, Netscape (works with Opera)	yes
Java enabled	yes	yes	yes	Java, Active X	yes
Cookies enabled	no	yes	yes		yes
Window	Floating window	Floating window	Floating window	frames	frames
Customize log-in form, chat skin	yes	yes (extra)	Pro & Corporate versions	yes	login
Proxy compatible	open certain ports	yes	With user ID and password	yes	yes
(Disabilities)	no	no		no	no
Librarian's Interface					
Special client	Web			Client or Web	n/a
Built-in browser	no	no	no	yes	yes
Identifies patrons by IP address (re tracking & history)	yes	yes		yes	yes
System					
Standalone or hosted	hosted	hosted	hosted	either	remote server
Pricing	seats	seats	seats	seats	seats
Maintenance package available	yes		yes	yes	yes
Connect multiple servers running the call center software	no			yes	yes
HTTP tunneling (chat behind firewall)	•				no
Training and Assistance					
Documentation	yes	yes	yes	yes	yes
Vendor training included	yes	yes	no	yes	yes
Timesharing, sharing reference desk with other libraries or institutions	no	yes	no	yes	yes

VOIP=voice over Internet protocol; FAQ=frequently asked questions; OS=operating system.

divide the screen into half web browser and half chat window, and others gener-ate the chat session in an independent window that floats over the web page. If you look at Figure 2.2, you can see that VRD presents a built-in web browser in the top frame, and the chat session in the lower frame. Nell, the user, is looking for a map of Uzbekistan, which displays in the top half of the window, in the up-per frame. With eGain's product (Figure 2.3), the presentation is more vertical, with the browser being presented in a frame on the left, and the chat session in a smaller frame on the right. The map of France appears to the left. Using the frames approach, any pages that the librarian pushes or sends to the user displays in the section of the screen devoted to the web browser, although pages can be programmed to open in an independent window as needed.

LiveAssistance, RightNow Live, and *OnDemand* use a different approach, one where an independent chat window floats above the web browser on the user's screen. In Figure 2.4, a librarian at Austin Peay State University is using Live Assistance chat to show a user how to find videos. As you can see, the chat win-dow is small, leaving most of the screen free for display of content. *RightNow Live,* the chat software used at the University of South Florida libraries, operates in

Table 2.2d Comparison of call center software features by vendor.

	Virtual Reference ToolKit (LSSI - eGain software)	QuestionPoint (enhanced communications)	eLibrarian (Groopz software from Digi-Net)	RightNow Live
Users Interface				
Platform	Mac, Windows	Windows, Mac, Unix		
Browser	IE, Netscape	IE, Netscape		IE, Netscape
Java enabled	yes	VIP plug-in	yes	Java, Active X
Cookies enabled		no		yes
Window	frames	yes	floating window	floating window
Customize log-in form, chat skin	login	yes	login, chat skin	yes
Proxy compatible	open certain ports	independent	yes	yes
(Disabilities)	no	n/a		yes
Librarian's Interface				
Special client	n/a	yes	Web	web
Built-in browser	yes	no	no	no
Identifies patrons by IP address (retracking & history)	yes	no	yes	yes
System				
Standalone or hosted	either	hosted	either	both
Pricing	seats	by profile	seats	
Maintenance package available	yes	yes	yes	yes
Connect multiple servers running the call center software	yes	n/a	yes	yes
HTTP tunneling (chat behind firewall)	yes	yes	yes	yes
Training and Assistance				
Documentation	yes	yes	yes	yes
Vendor training included	yes	yes	yes	yes
Timesharing, sharing reference desk with other libraries or institutions	yes	yes	no	no

IP=internet provider; HTTP=hypertext transfer protocol

much the same way, as pictured in Figure 2.5. When the librarian on duty sends a map to the user, the map opens in a new window. Figure 2.6 pictures the software *OnDemand* (Convey) in action, as the librarian on duty at the University of Wisconsin, Madison, helps a user once again find a map of France. (Incidentally, the *OnDemand* software is now licensed to libraries exclusively through the *QuestionPoint* project; *QuestionPoint* participants can opt to purchase the *OnDemand* live reference component or use the simple text-based chat that comes free of charge with a subscription.) Figure 2.7 is a snapshot of a user session in *eLibrarian* (Digi-Net), the software system adopted by OhioLink, early in Fall 2002 when the system was still in development.

Both approaches to the user interface have their advantages. With the frames approach, the librarian has more control over the screen that the user will see, but there is less space to display content. With the other approach, web pages pushed by the librarian display behind the chat window, which means that there is a danger of content being by the chat window. It's difficult to control the location of the chat window because the users' local configuration may affect the size of the window and where it pops open, and because the user can reposition the window by dragging it to a new place on the screen.

Figure 2.2. Chat session from the user's perspective RefeXpress, University of Florida Libraries (divine *VRD*).

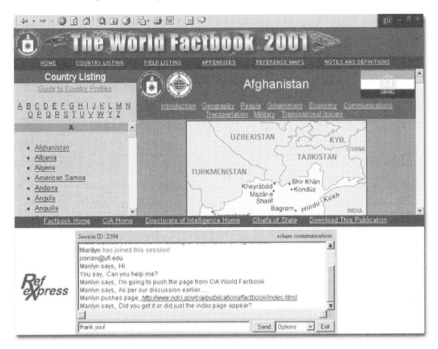

At the end of the session, with frames-based software, the software can be configured to leave the user at the last web page viewed during the session with the librarian, at the page the user accessed to start the chat session, or at other, predetermined web pages. With the floating chat window approach, the user simply clicks on the exit or logoff button, and the floating window disappears.

The Librarian's Interface

By now you should have a feel for how the call center software works from a user's perspective. But what is it like for the librarian? Call center software may require that a special client program be installed on computers where librarians will be working to create the librarian's console or that may be delivered from the server via a web page and Java applet. Some software packages include a client and web-based access (divine *VRD*), which is good for times when the librarian can't get to a computer with the client program. The client provides a powerful interface that can be complex, as shown in the following figures. Figure 2.8 is a screen snapshot of a UF librarian's computer screen, as the librarian works with a patron. Figure 2.9 is a snapshot of the LSSI *VRT* client for librarians. Although there are some differences in how the call center software implements this from package to package, the librarian's interface typically is composed of a built-in

Figure 2.3. Composite of the user log on screen overlaid with an actual reference session at the KNOWITNOW 24X7, CLEVNET Library (LSSI *VRT*).

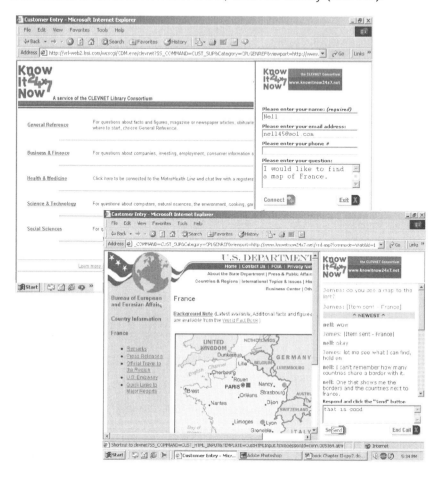

web browser, alert devices, a chat window, and features for rapidly delivering answers such as lists of preprogrammed phrases (or canned responses), web pages, and PowerPoint tutorials.

Value-Added Features

Preprogrammed phrases are probably the most useful feature to compare when choosing a software package. For example, when users log on, the librarian can greet them by choosing a greeting from a wide array of preprogrammed phrases that display on the librarian's side, or by keying in a favorite greeting into the chat box. In the University of Florida's real-time reference service, these preprogrammed phrases include responses such as, "Hello, my name is . . . ," "What is your e-mail

Figure 2.4. Chat session from the user's perspective at the Austin Peay State University Libraries (*LiveAssistance*).

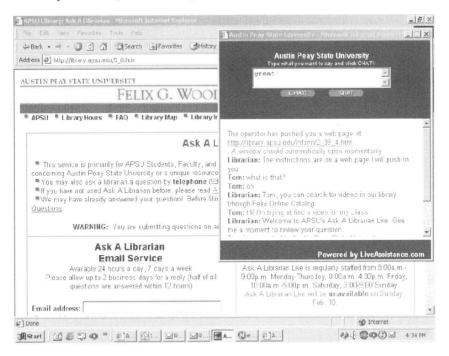

address," "It may take me a few minutes to find the answer," "Did I answer your question?" and many other comments and questions that *RefeXpress* librarians find themselves repeating over and over during a reference interview. Any systems seriously under consideration should provide the facility for adding such comments to a list that is available to the librarian as well as the systems administrator. Some software programs such as Digi-Net *eLibrarian* offer a limited number of canned responses, while others such eGain *LiveWeb* and LSSI *VRT* offer a much more expansive collection, as well as the ability to organize phrases in folders by category for easy retrieval. Some systems even incorporate built-in e-mail modules to allow librarians to follow-up sessions via e-mail, or even to merge chat and e-mail reference operations into one system, streamlining the library's virtual reference system.

Private messaging between librarians is another helpful function. Web-based call center software often includes a separate instant messaging utility to allow librarians to communicate privately outside of the main chat. As librarians may transfer calls to another librarian in this software, private messaging helps the first librarian provide some context for the librarian taking over the query or fielding the referral.

Most call center programs archive transcripts of sessions with users in built-in or separately operating relational databases, with access built in through the librarian's

Figure 2.5. Chat session from the user's perspective at the University of South Florida Libraries (*RightNowLive*).

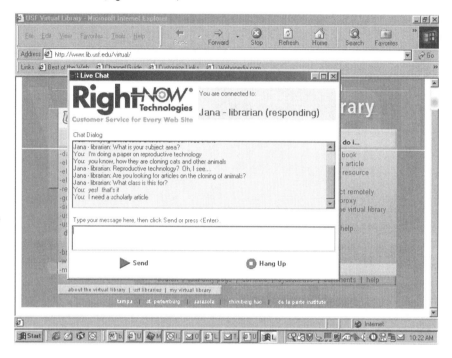

interface. Systematic storage of these transcripts enables librarians to have easy access to records of sessions to assist in answering a question, to study reference queries online, to compile and publish statistics, and even to generate knowledge bases of commonly asked questions and answers for users to browse. Some programs allow librarians to activate a feature that retrieves past transcripts for review. This is useful as a source of additional context with repeat users. Access to this data varies, with some systems allowing easy access to all staff and others having the ability to set levels of authority so that staff can see only records of their own sessions with users, supervisors can follow the work of their employees, and so forth.

Call center software also has alert and automated response features that make it easier to multitask and work with multiple users. It is important to give users feedback when they try to log on to a chat reference system, even if the librarian is busy. Programs such as eGain *Interact* or *HumanClick* feature programmable automated responses that notify the user that the librarian is busy. The user might see a message in the chat box such as, "Thank you for your question. The librarian will be with you shortly." One handy automated response is something I call "the babysitter." It is a hold script in divine *VRD* that can be programmed to deliver messages to a user at regularly timed intervals while you leaf through books in the reference stacks or search a database.

Figure 2.6. Chat session from the user's perspective at the University of Wisconsin, Madison Libraries (Convey *OnDemand*).

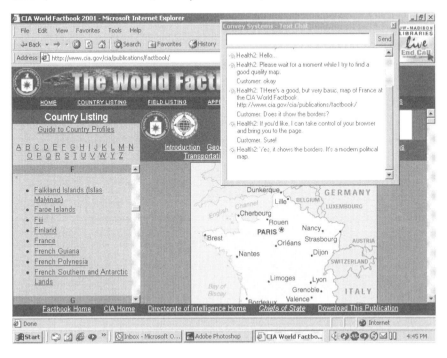

Closely related to programmable automated responses are alert features. Unlike primitive text-based chat programs, most call center software has elaborate systems to alert representatives with sound or visual cues that a user has logged on or of user activity. These cues are usually beeps or tones accompanied by popup windows that spin to the foreground of the computer screen. Alerts help the librarian keep in touch with the user when multitasking or searching other programs for answers. They also relieve staff from the stress of staring at a computer screen while waiting for users to log on. Instead, librarians can be productive and check their e-mail, search databases, write reports, or even catch up on professional reading.

User Management

One fascinating aspect of call center software is the way that the software manages log-ons through queues and assignment of sessions to representatives. Software such as eGain's *Live* and *Interact*, divine *VRD*, Digi-Net *eLibrarian*, and others create internal subdivisions called queues, much like the channels in IRC-based systems. As users log on, the software puts them in a queue, where users wait for the next available librarian to take their question. This is, of course,

Figure 2.7. Chat session from the user's perspective at the Ohio Library and Information Network, OhioLINK (*eLibrarian*).

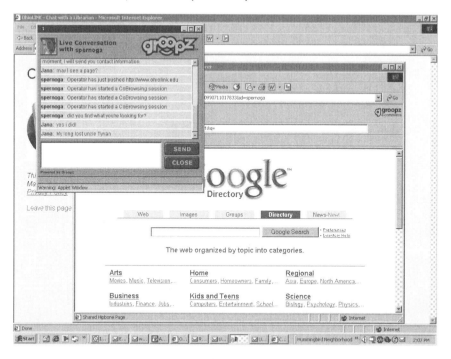

invisible to the user, who sees only a message such as, "Next in queue, please wait for the next available librarian." Although most virtual reference services program the software to feed questions automatically to the librarian or librarians online in the order they were received, you can also program the software to let the librarians pull users from the queue.

Most call center software packages support multiple queues; you can create several queues thereby enabling libraries to run several independent "help lines" on one server, maximizing costs, performance, and maintenance. The software can be programmed to send users to a certain queue or service line based on the web page the chat link was on or, conversely, let the user select a queue from a listing on the web page. This is how large hosted services and consortia operate, using a network of internal queues. There are systems that use algorithms to balance the number of questions among librarians. Others employ "skills-based routing" to route questions "based on the subject matter, language, academic level or other criteria" (Coffman, Henshall, and Fiander 2003, Appendix 1, p. 29).

An example might be *AskUsQuestions.com,* an Ohio cooperative providing real-time reference services to more than twenty libraries. If I choose "Ashtabula County Public Library" from the pull-down as I log on, the divine *VRD* software (also called *NetAgent*) drops me in the queue with the Ashtabula librarians, not

Figure 2.8. divine *VRD* Librarian Client.

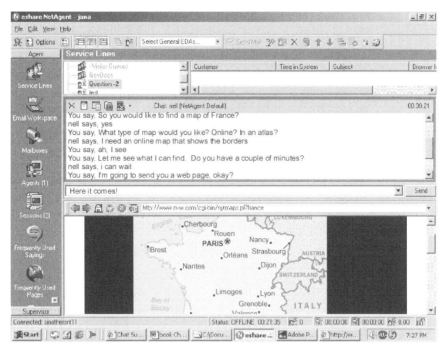

the librarians from the McKinley Memorial Library (unless they are minding the Ashtabula queue for some reason). Another example is the *RefeXpress* and *Gov-Xpress* services at the University of Florida. These sites function off the same divine *VRD* server but operate as completely independent services with separate service hours. Web pages with programmed variables are used to deposit *RefeXpress* patrons into the *RefeXpress* queue and people seeking government documents assistance into the *GovXpress* queue. Librarians staffing the two services can see users log on for *RefeXpress* and *GovXpress*, but their accounts are programmed to accept only sessions with users accessing the appropriate service. Large real-time reference applications service providers (ASPs) such as *24/7 Reference* or LSSI *VRT* use a complex network of service queues to connect users rapidly to the appropriate library.

Call center software is an excellent fit for libraries that would like to share software and hardware costs while maintaining independently operated real-time reference services.

Pricing and System Requirements

Software such as eGain's *Live Web* suite, divine *VRD*, and *LiveAssistance* are typically priced by seats, or the number of representatives (agents) that may be

Figure 2.9. LSSI *VRT* Librarian Client.

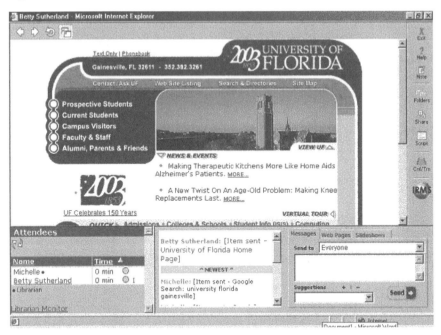

online simultaneously to take questions. Prices often start at $2,000 or more a seat. This is in combination with the cost of the software for the computer server (if you plan to run your real-time reference operation locally) or the maintenance and service fees if using ASPs such as LSSI's *VRT*, the Metropolitan Cooperative Library System's *24/7 Reference*, *LiveAssistance*, or *RightNow*. The CLEVnet Consortium estimated the cost for a year's service (five seats) via *VRT* is approximately $44,400 (Carterette and Feldman 2003).

Because of the complexity and power of such software, running the system locally requires a robust computer server and a solid network infrastructure, including a compatible SQL database, a web server, and an e-mail server. With some systems such as divine's *VRD* or eGain's *Live Web*, features may be purchased in modules. You can start with the baseline chat component, then add e-mail management, VoIP, or videoconferencing components later if desired. Other programs come bundled into one package—take it or leave it. If the software requires that librarians load clients onto their computers, take into consideration the memory and speed requirements that the system requires of your computers. At the University of Florida, we increase the amount of random access memory (RAM) on computers to at least 128 K to support the librarian client software. Another factor to examine when choosing the system is whether it is possible to set the number of questions that each agent or librarian can field at one time. For example, *VRD* can be configured so that staff can work with anywhere from one to six users, although I personally do not recommend setting it higher than two at a time.

Installation and Training

Training and installation are a crucial part of the vendor's overall software package. Some companies such as divine require that the computer staff and librarians administrating the software attend special training sessions, and then send a team of software engineers to perform the initial installation on site and hold more training sessions for staff. Other companies such as LSSI train the librarians at the institution but also offer continuing education opportunities via online workshops. Be sure to evaluate the software's administrative module that the chat service administrator will use to set up librarian accounts, configure and customize the user and librarian interface, build preprogrammed phrases, and compile statistical reports. Do follow the evaluation checklist given in Figure 4.4 of Chapter 4 closely to avoid unwelcome surprises after signing the contract. Pay particular attention to the usability of the librarian's console or interface and the administrative module, because you will want peak functionality in this part of the software. Don't find out after it's too late that the operating systems clash or that the new call center software doesn't work with a crucial in-house component, such as the relational database. Table 2.2 presents features across several popular software packages used in real-time reference as of February 2003.

For more information on web-based call center software, I recommend "Assessing Web Enabled Call Center Technologies," by Bernett and Jarmillo (2001) and *A Virtual Reference Primer* (Coffman, Henshall, and Fiander 2002). If you are interested in using call center software, but your resources make installing software and maintaining a networked complex of computer servers impractical, the following section on hosted real-time services may provide other alternatives. A hosted service such as LSSI *VRD* or *24/7 Reference* offers most of the benefits of call center software without the maintenance issues.

Call Center Software at a Glance

Advantages:
- Extremely friendly and intuitive user interface
- One-on-one communication
- Accessible via web browser for users
- Powerful features to aid in answering questions (push page, escorting, databases of conversational phrases)
- Alert features, transcripts, ability to transfer sessions to another librarian
- Some programs incorporate voice and video technology
- Often enables private conferencing outside the chat feature
- Often available for purchase in modules
- Vendors provide training

Disadvantages:
- Expensive whether hosted or installed locally
- Steep learning curve to use features efficiently
- Librarian's interface may be complex
- Librarians may need to install special client software to reach answering features
- Some programs require high bandwidth (especially if using VOIP, audio, or white-boarding)

Selected Call Center Vendors:

eGain Live Web
http://www.egain.com/

HumanClick
http://www.humanclick.com/

Live Person
http://www.liveperson.com/

LiveAssistance
http://www.liveassistance.com/

Livehelper
http://www.livehelper.com/

NetAgent (see Virtual Reference Desk, divine)

OnDemand Convey Systems (now integrated into QuestionPoint enhanced communications)
http://www.conveysystems.com/implementation.asp

QuestionPoint Collaborative Reference Service
http://www.questionpoint.org

RightNow Live
http://www.rightnow.com/

24/7 Reference
http://www.247ref.org/

Virtual Reference Desk (VRD), divine
http://www.divine.com/vrd

Virtual Reference Toolkit, LSSI (eGain)
http://www.vrtoolkit.net

HOSTED REAL-TIME SERVICES

By this point in your reading, it is hoped that you have a better understanding of the types of software or systems that support synchronous communication for a reference service in your library. There is a wide variety of programs to select from, including instant messaging, IRC, MOO, courseware, web-based chat, and call center software. You may have decided to try a particular type of software but are wondering whether it would be wise to operate the software locally on computers at your library or to go with an ASP to host your service.

Hosting or Using an ASP

Subscribing to a hosted chat service is an attractive option for a variety of reasons, and ASPs are abundant. If you are leaning toward the hosted option, do be aware that the more expensive the ASP or host, the more assistance and services you will receive in setting up and running a real-time reference operation.

Some ASPs operating IM, IRC, MOO, or even web-based chat may offer little more than space on a remote computer for your service, along with initial assistance with set-up. It really depends on the organization offering the service. There are many places to set up a free real-time reference service such as *Connections, Yahoo! Chat,* or on an existing IRCnet server, but the drawback is that these services often operate on a shoestring. Many rely on volunteer help. This makes them a less stable choice; you may wish to investigate how long they have been in operation and what their rate of downtime has been in the past. Clearly some expertise is required to participate. If your library has staff that enjoys dabbling in computer programming and building web pages, a free host may be a good option.

Advantages of the Hosted Approach

There are many reasons that contracting for synchronous services with an ASP is attractive. The main advantages are provision of computer space and expertise, ease of setup and training, options for outsourcing reference queries, and increased opportunities for collaboration with other libraries.

Computer Support Although many libraries, both big and small, already have a network infrastructure to tap into when planning a real-time reference service (either in-house or through an affiliation with a university, corporation, school district, or other entity), there are many that do not but would like to establish online reference assistance. Contracting with companies such as *ChatSpace* or LSSI *VRT* relieves your library from the daunting task of buying and setting up expensive new hardware, installing and configuring chat and networking software, tending to maintenance issues, troubleshooting, and keeping up with software upgrades. Hosting enables your library to use sophisticated software with minimal fuss.

I do not recommend pursuing a freely hosted service if your library requires extensive assistance in developing your service. An ASP such as *ConferenceRoom* or *ChatSpace* offers inexpensive hosting. *ChatSpace* charges a low of $50 a month for one hundred or fewer concurrent users. Commercial operations such as *Blackboard, ElementK,* or a call center vendor such as *LiveAssistance, LivePerson,* LSSI *VRT, 24/7 Reference,* or divine *VRD* may be better in this situation because they provide more consistent support and service. Many of these services have been running real-time services for some time and offer stable systems with little computer downtime. Be sure to evaluate the robustness and speed of communication by logging onto the vendor's site a couple of times and chatting. Don't stop there; find an operational site, such as a library that has purchased the service or even a business, and test it during times of the day when Internet traffic is at a peak.

It's also a good idea to check on an ASP's track record in business literature. Call or web centers are hot topics now, as are instant messaging and chat; you will find plenty of reviews in related publications. Online library discussion groups devoted to virtual reference issues, such as DIG_REF and Livereference, are another source. Be sure to search the archives of these online groups for past discussions of software.

When deciding on a service, one important thing to keep in mind is that although a few ASPs specialize in serving libraries, most support e-commerce. Library-oriented ASPs offer a considerable advantage in that they understand the reference environment and may be able to help you anticipate problems that typically arise in creating a new real-time reference service.

Training Staff training is an important part of setting up an effective chat reference service. Many of the more sophisticated hosted services feature "jump-start" training for librarians to get a service up and running, as well as continuing support online. Library vendors are the stars here. Although most call center ASPs offer onsite training, it is usually targeted to the business sector. These trainers do not understand how their product will be implemented in an educational or library setting.

If you are in the market for call center software, contracting with a library ASP may be better for settings where librarians and staff are unfamiliar with synchronous communication. In my experience, librarians who have never chatted before find e-commerce jargon and examples confusing or even threatening. Vendors focused on the library market, such as LSSI, *24/7 Reference,* or *QuestionPoint,* employ librarians as trainers and use examples and vocabulary designed to put library staff at ease. This is not to say that the training issues are insurmountable if a nonlibrary vendor's package is superior in other respects. Many libraries augment the initial training with other outside trainers or local workshops. In addition to the jump-start type of training, ASPs often provide online classes (using the software that has just been purchased) and online help.

Opportunities for Collaboration Hosted services can provide a good infrastructure for libraries pursuing collaborative real-time reference services. For independent libraries that lack any cooperative ties or libraries seeking to establish a collaborative venture outside their local network, joining a popular hosted service can make sense. Vendors such as *24/7 Reference* also serve as a facilitator for the subscribing libraries, helping them work together to share virtual desk hours or subject expertise. For example, *24/7 Reference* helps coordinate schedules and develop knowledge bases of local resources such as library services, catalogs, and databases for digital librarians to rapidly access when fielding questions from users of libraries other than their own. LSSI actively encourages collaborative partnerships among clients, as illustrated in the following statement taken from the company web site.

> It is also possible to share your seat or seats with other libraries. For example, three libraries might want to work together to offer a 24-hour online reference service. During normal business hours, each would staff the service itself, using its own seats on the network, but they might share their seats for after-hours service, with each library taking a turn in handling the late night traffic from all three. This is a common arrangement, particularly in a library consortia. (Library Systems & Services, LLC 2000)

Reference Outsourcing Specialized library ASPs also provide outsourced reference services and operate reference centers with digital librarians to answer questions. LSSI *VRT* has a general reference service, a business reference operated by the James J. Hill Reference Library in St. Paul, Minnesota, and a Spanish language reference service called "Referencia en Espanol." Many libraries take advantage of this type of service to extend their virtual hours of service or to back up their librarians during peak hours of usage.

RUNNING A CHAT SERVICE LOCALLY

Why would anyone want to bother operating a chat system locally when you can get a company to do it all for you? There are some significant advantages to running the chat software locally. "If local server expertise and hardware is available, you will always be able to provide more reliable service locally than will be possible for a provider which is accessed over the open Internet," says Bill Covey (2002), Head of the George A. Smathers Systems Department. Situating your service locally facilitates faster system response and reduced expenses over time. It also affords librarians complete control over policies, service hours, the interface, and data.

Most vendors of call center software and courseware offer a local option, as do companies selling web-based chat programs that incorporate IRC. Some popular examples are *ConferenceRoom* (WebMaster), *VRLplus* (Docutek), *eLibrarian* or *Groopz* (Digi-Net), *RightNow Live*, *VRD* (divine), *Live Web* (eGain), *OnDemand* (Convey), and *ChatSpace*. This is not an exhaustive list, because new products are constantly coming on the market. Let's examine the issues in hosting a service yourself, beginning with the issue of system performance.

Reliability and Response Time

If you host your service with an ASP, you are totally dependent on the ASP's system reliability, speed, and service schedule; you are also dependent on the Internet. This means that during periods of peak Internet usage users and librarians may have trouble connecting and then experience lag once connected. Lag and connection problems are deadly for a chat service, because most users will not tolerate delays in this type of communication. Such problems may also be due to the performance of the server handling your chat service. Some libraries, such as that of Cornell University, have had trouble with hosted services such as *LivePerson* being sluggish (Constantine 2000). Choosing to run the service locally circumvents some potential for lag because there is less transfer of data over broad expanses of the Internet between the triangle of the user, the ASP's server, and the librarian. Although transfer of packets of data on the Internet is generally fast when all points are functioning, congestion, crashed routers, cut lines, and other communication problems have an exponential impact on the speed of transfer the greater the geographical expanse. Such issues have a less noticeable impact on activities such as e-mail but become very noticeable when trying to chat, instant message, download a file, talk using VOIP, or even view a web page. Like chat, these online activities are heavily time dependent. Some vendors may combat lag or outages by operating redundant servers and other strategies. Speed is an important issue. If your institution lacks the computer infrastructure (as discussed in the next section), however, a little lag may be acceptable compared with the problems inherent in setting up a service locally.

Another advantage of a standalone installation is that it is possible to troubleshoot network and chat server problems locally. If you contract with an ASP, there is less control. All you can do is report the problem to the technical support line and hope for a speedy resolution.

When deciding which software to install locally, I recommend that you test the system by logging onto the vendor's site a couple of times and chatting. Be sure to test it via a slower dial-up connection, during a time of peak Internet activity, and with different web browsers. Try the product on an operational site such as a business or other library. Perform a load test. You will also want to test your local system in this way once it is up and running to get a true picture of how fast the system will operate for your users and for librarians working from home. The optimum test of performance is to have an out-of-state colleague or a friend with a slower modem connection log on to your service and assess the speed of the various features, including push and escorting.

Local Infrastructure for Chat

If your library (or affiliated organization) has its own web server(s), e-mail system, relational database system, and so on, then adding real-time reference locally will work. The main concern is having the network infrastructure and staff to support the systems that run in tandem with a chat service, especially one based on call center software. With such a computer complex in place, the costs of adding a new server and the chat software will probably be cheaper in the long run than contracting for services with a vendor. When we were faced with this decision making at the University of Florida, the systems head at the University of Florida calculated that we would recoup the cost of the initial outlay for the chat server and the server software over a couple of years, compared with the recurring costs of hosting an equivalent service. In October 2000, the cost for the NetAgent server software (now divine *VRD*), three seats, on-site training and installation, and the maintenance agreement including software upgrades was approximately $18,000 for the Smathers Libraries. (See the case study by Mimi Pappas and Colleen Seale in Chapter 15 for more details.) There are, of course, less obvious costs. If you are starting from ground zero but want to establish a networked infrastructure in addition to your service, be sure to include in your budget funds for support staff, system backup, space, and ongoing training.

Customization and Policy

Probably the most persuasive reason to consider a locally based real-time reference system is the flexibility in the area of interface, policy making, service hours, and control over security. If you go with a hosted solution, some concessions will have to be made in the area of policies, the manner in which your service is presented, and in how features are programmed into the software. Maybe your library would like to change the colors of the chat window to match your school colors or incorporate a library logo on the banner of the chat web page. Perhaps you would like to try staffing your service with student assistants but can't because a library with which you are collaborating isn't comfortable with the idea. If you are running the chat software locally, you have complete control over policy. The only limit to creative control is you and your staff's technical and design abilities. With a large hosted service such as *QuestionPoint, 24/7 Reference,* or LSSI VRT you will be able to customize some of the appearance, but much of the interface is standard. (You can get an idea of the level of customization on the users' side by visiting various libraries that contract with the ASP.) If you are considering a free or inexpensive chat service such as Yahoo! Chat, you may have to accept some advertising as part of the terms of service.

Privacy

Of more concern to many librarians is the privacy of the data generated from sessions with users. If you are hosting your service locally or with your local institution, it is possible to have much more control over access to and storage of transcripts. With a hosted ASP, it may be unclear who owns the transcripts or data that are stored after each transaction with a user, particularly if the service would like to use transaction information for marketing or other purposes. Library services such as LSSI and *24/7 Reference* are sensitive to these issues, as are educational services such as *Connections* or *Diversity University.* Don't count on ASPs that cater to e-commerce or recreational chat rooms to be overly sympathetic, however. Likewise, even if your ASP has provisions for privacy of transcripts, your transactions with users may be susceptible to snooping at relay points on the Internet, as data travels from the user to the server to the librarian to the host server to the user and back again. If locally operated, your systems staff can install firewalls, for example, to deter this type of intrusion.

As you can see, there are many factors to consider in selecting the best software to facilitate communication in a real-time reference service. The goal of this chapter was to introduce advanced software that makes communication in real-time online possible, as well as to point out the issues in hosting a service with an ASP or with a locally operated model. Chapter 4 offers specific guidelines and a criteria chart to apply in the evaluation of various types of software and vendors.

REFERENCES

Bernett, Howard, and Melissa L. Jaramillo. 2001. "Assessing Web-Enabled Call Center Technologies." *IT Pro* (May–June): 24–30. Available online at http://www.computer.org/itpro/it2001/f3024abs.htm (accessed 4 April 2002).

Carterette, Bob, and Sari Feldman. 2001. "KnowItNow.net in 90 Days—Or Bust!" *Implementing Digital Reference Services: Setting Standards and Making It Real.* New York: Neal-Schuman, 95–102.

Coffman, Steve, Kay Henshall, and Michelle Fiander. 2003. *A Virtual Reference Primer* (working title). Chicago: American Library Association. Draft available online at http://alaeditions.virtualreference.net (accessed 5 February 2003).

Constantine, Paul J. "Cornell University's LiveHelp Service." Paper presented at "Facets of Digital Reference." The Virtual Reference Desk—2nd Annual Digital Reference Conference, 16–17 October, Seattle, WA. Available online at http://www.vrd.org/conferences/VRD2000/proceedings/constantine-intro.shtml (accessed 5 February 2003).

Covey, Bill. "RE: [DIG_REF] Locally Loaded Chat Reference Software." DIG_REF Listserv. Archived online at http://www.vrd.org/Dig_Ref/dig_ref.shtml (accessed 25 February 2002).

Harrison, Laurie. 2001. "Courseware Accessibility—The Saga Continues." Paper presented at "Accessing Higher Ground Conference—Assis[s]tive Technology in Higher Education," November 14–16, University of Colorado, Boulder. Available online at http://snow.utoronto.ca/access/saga/ (accessed 1 March 2002).

Library Systems & Services, LLC. 2000. "Products and Services: Full Seat." Virtual Reference Desk. Available online at http://www.virtualreference.net/virtual/03a.html (accessed 5 February 2003).

WEB SITES CITED

America Online
  http://www.aol.com

Ashtabula County Public Library, *AskUsQuestions.com*
  http://www.askusquestions.com/library/ashtabula.htm

Bryn Mawr, *Live Help*
  http://www.swarthmore.edu/library/reference/vr.html

Cornell, *Live Help*
http://www.library.cornell.edu/okuref/livehelp.html

DIG_REF
http://www.vrd.org/Dig_Ref/dig_ref.shtml

Keystone Library Network, *Virtual Information Desk (VID)*
http://vid.sshe.edu/

Lands' End, *Lands' End Live*
http://www.landsend.com/

University of Pennsylvania (Wharton School of Business, Lippincott Library),
Chat with a Reference Librarian Live
http://www.library.upenn.edu/lippincott/askoption.html

Livereference
http://groups.yahoo.com/group/livereference

McKinley Memorial Library, *AskUsQuestions.com*
http://www.askusquestions.com/library/mckinley.htm

Monster.com, *Monster Live Chat*
http://www.monster.com/contact/

NOLA Regional Library System, *AskUsQuestions.com*
http://www.askusquestions.com/

University of Florida, *RefeXpress*
http://refexpress.uflib.ufl.edu

University of Florida, *GovXpress*
http://govxpress.uflib.ufl.edu/govxpress/

Philadelphia University, *RefChat*
http://www.philau.edu/library/refchat.htm

Walgreens
http://www.walgreens.com

3 THE AUDIENCE FOR ONLINE LIBRARY ASSISTANCE IN REAL TIME

Reference services are undergoing a renaissance as librarians seek to reach users beyond the confines of the reference desk. Some librarians wish to establish an approachable and instantly responsive online presence to find better, more efficient ways to serve the rapidly growing number of people using the Internet for research and leisure. Others see in chat reference a powerful weapon in the competition against seductive commercial information providers such as AskJeeves or Questia. Yet the reality remains that there are pockets of people in the United States and beyond who do not have ready access to computers and the Internet. How does a library know if its user base is ready to chat with a librarian, if real-time reference will be an effective tool to reach their desired audience? This chapter introduces indicators to help librarians gauge if a significant audience exists in their community for real-time reference.

KNOW YOUR AUDIENCE

As with any user service, planning a successful real-time reference operation centers on knowing your library audience and understanding their online research habits. So naturally you will want to begin by performing some type of user assessment. This assessment may be formal, using surveys, interviews, and focus groups, or it might be based on other studies or more informal observations of your users' needs. The questions that you will try to answer are "Does my library have a base of users that would benefit from real-time reference" and "Would my library users be receptive to reference assistance online using chat?"

Several factors support offering real-time assistance to library users. A rapidly growing number of people are online, and a proliferation of web-based information stores are readily available to anyone with an Internet connection. We live in a culture of convenience in which customers expect immediate assistance or gratification at fast-food restaurants, stores, and service-oriented businesses. New types of consumer services are being delivered online to meet this demand. For example, many movie theaters sell tickets online so that viewers need not worry about arriving early to catch a new release. Businesses maintain web sites to provide consumers with rapid access to facts and product inventory. Retailers such as Wal-Mart and Amazon.com offer credit-card shopping online at any hour of the day. Banks offer online checking and bill-paying services, as well as automated teller machines, and more and more employers are delivering paychecks electronically to financial institutions so that employees need not stand in line on payday to cash their checks. Examples of online services are too numerous to attempt to list. The point here is that so many commercial services are being offered online that people are coming to expect instantaneous feedback as a given. These expectations are also applied to library services and information seeking.

Certain types of audiences are doubtlessly more ready for real-time library reference services than others. Sara Weissman, online reference librarian at the Morris County [Public] Library in Whippany, New Jersey, and member of the Virtual Reference Desk AskAnExpert service, emphasizes, "If you serve either college students and/or a business community, e-reference is nearly a must" (Oder, p. 49). These are not the only audiences for chat reference; school children, urban public library users, international students, and researchers in remote centers are other customers ripe for speedy online assistance. Almost every library today has users who would be receptive to chat reference, but the decision to offer it must be made after a close examination of other user needs and priorities. Careful consideration of the following indicators may aid in establishing such priorities.

REAL-TIME REFERENCE INDICATORS

Your library

- has a large percentage of users who regularly use the Internet at home or work,
- serves users who like real-time online communication such as chat or instant messaging,
- supports distance learners,
- provides access to a sizeable number of online databases and information stores,
- supports a geographic area or organization that favors online communication, or
- has a popular e-mail reference service.

If some of these statements describe your library audience, you probably have a base of users who would benefit from real-time reference. Let's consider each of these factors in a little more detail.

Access

As for any online service, user access may be the most important factor to consider. Are a large proportion of your users connected to the Internet? National surveys indicate that they are. A recent report from the U.S. Department of Commerce, based on the 2001 Census, emphasizes that the number of people accessing the Internet is growing rapidly. This report, *A Nation Online: How Americans are Expanding Their Use of the Internet* (2002), indicates that more than half of the nation is online (54%) and that the number is increasing rapidly by 2 million users a month. The Pew Internet and American Life Project (PIP) survey, *Counting on the Internet*, estimates that 60 percent of Americans are now online (Horrigan and Rainie 2002). Rural areas lag behind urban areas, but this gap is narrowing because of the rapid growth of online access. Americans also are increasingly using the Internet for research and daily tasks such as communicating with others (e-mail); to search for information on products, health issues, or services; and to purchase goods (*A Nation Online* 2002). Many people have ready access to the Internet on computers at home or work, indicating that they research, surf, or otherwise collect information from locations outside the library, away from the physical proximity to the traditional reference desk. Only a few U.S. Internet users (10%) rely exclusively on accessing it at libraries (*A Nation Online* 2002, p. 40).

Connectivity

Although access is probably the most crucial factor in determining whether there is an audience for real-time reference services, connectivity has an important role to play in how you implement your service. The quality of networking in your user community affects selection of the most effective real-time reference software for your setting. How do your patrons connect to the Internet? Is the networking fast and reliable in your community and institution? Do most people dial in via a modem, or does your community have high-speed Internet access via DSL (digital subscriber line) or cable? If residents mostly use 54K modems to access the Internet, then it may be wise to choose simpler real-time software that concentrates on text-based chat because advanced features such as whiteboarding or remote control of the user's desktop require a fast connection. If the majority of your target audience uses higher-speed connections such as DSL, cable modems, or Ethernet to reach the Internet, it may be practical to deploy chat software that incorporates advanced features.

College students, faculty, and staff are avid Internet users who tend to have fast Internet access. They are so "connected" that chat reference is a smart way to reach these users. In the college environment, students may have ready access to computers at home and in labs on campus, and professors work online in their offices, in the classroom, and from home. The quality of networking is also excellent; many colleges provide Ethernet access to the campus backbone in residence halls and other student housing. It is also becoming commonplace to offer DSL,

Ethernet, or cable modem access in apartment complexes catering to students and faculty.

Universities and corporate offices are common wireless environments, as are large cities such as San Francisco, Stockholm, and New York City. Wireless systems are also springing up in towns such as Aspen, Colorado, on Indian reservations in Montana, and in Mongolia (Rheingold 2002, 133–156). People in highly wired communities are taking connectivity a step further by using cell phones and PDAs (short for personal digital assistants, or handheld computers) to surf the Web, send e-mail, and communicate with instant messaging. "How will human behavior shift when the appliances we hold in our hands, carry in our pockets, or wear in our clothing become supercomputers that talk to each other through a wireless mega-Internet," Howard Rheingold (2002, xv) asks in *Smart Mobs,* his book examining the emergence of new communication patterns. This means that users with wireless laptop computers or PDAs can access library resources from a greater number of locations than ever before, and they may appreciate online assistance.

Many universities are establishing wireless networking and virtual personal networks to facilitate access to the Internet and authentication in buildings and even outside in open areas where students and faculty congregate. At the University of Florida, it is not uncommon to see a student sitting with a laptop at a picnic table or bench, surfing the Web and reading e-mail during breaks in classes. These students need reference assistance as much as those who come to the library to do their research.

Another wireless device, the PDA, is an immensely popular communication and productivity tool in the medical community. Physicians and medical students use Palms, Visors, or a BlackBerry device to access patient records and for scheduling, as well as for downloading textbooks, web pages, and periodical articles for reading at a more convenient time. Instant messaging, streaming audio, and video applications are the newest developments for wireless PDAs, indicating these highly portable devices may soon be mobile access points for users seeking reference assistance.

You may be able to learn more about the state of your community's computer distribution and networking by examining marketing research and census data as well as the web sites of your local Internet service providers and chamber of commerce. Once you have established that users can access your real-time reference service, it's time to take a look at demographics.

Users

Social acceptance of reference assistance online via chat or other real-time technology is another factor to consider. Social acceptance might be referred to as "critical mass." Computer science professor Jonathan Grudin writes about the social aspects of groupware, or how software designed for group use is accepted in homogenous groups. Grudin (1994) emphasizes the need to achieve a "critical mass" of users to successfully launch a communication system. Does your library have a sufficient number of users familiar with the technology to target? A *Nation Online* and another recent study funded by the Pew Charitable Trusts indicate that Internet users frequently work with synchronous communication in the form of instant messaging and chat. This seems to indicate that—in America, at least—a critical mass has evolved. Let's take a look at some of the user demographics from these studies.

A *Nation Online* (2002, 14) reveals that "computer use is relatively high—about 70 percent in 2001—among people in their prime workforce years (generally people in their 20s to their 50s)." Use among older Americans has also grown as well, albeit more slowly; users in their 50s or older have increased in number by 11.6 percent since 1997. The report further states that 95.9 percent of people between the ages of 18 and 24 who attend school or college, use a computer. The PIP is another source of data on this issue. One of its surveys, *Teenage Life Online*, reports that the Internet has replaced the library as a research tool for 94 percent of online teens (Lenhart, Rainie, and Lewis 2001). This statistic will not surprise librarians who work with this convenience-oriented group. What is more pertinent to our discussion of virtual reference is that 74 percent of online teenagers use instant messaging, and 54 percent have visited a chat room. One might suspect that teens and young adults use instant messaging and chat to socialize, but research indicates that they also use it for academic support or as Teenage Life Online (p. 11) puts it, "Many teenagers use instant messaging to communicate with teachers and classmates about schoolwork or projects." Figure 3.1, taken from A *Nation Online*, illustrates major activities among children and young adults on the Internet.

College students are another group of users that like to chat. Another PIP study, *The Internet Goes to College*, concludes that "college Internet users are heavier users of instant messaging and online chat than those in the overall online population. While about half of all Internet users have sent instant messages, nearly three-quarters of college Internet users have done so, and college Internet users are twice as likely to use instant messaging on any given day compared to the average Internet user" (Jones 2002, 7).

PIP indicates that adults use real-time online communication less frequently; 44 percent of adults who access the Internet use instant messaging (Lenhart 2001). Although a smaller percentage than children or teens, a surprisingly large number of adults are using real-time communication. I suspect that this percentage would be slightly higher in a corporate or professional environment where online conferencing is especially popular. For example, the Boeing Company library has discovered that Boeing employees are receptive to chat. Boeing operates a real-time reference service staffed by twenty-two library employees, spread across four corporate libraries in different time zones. Employees can access librarians from their computers or even kiosks in factory lunchrooms (Martin 2001).

In conclusion, surveys indicate that there is fertile ground for real-time reference among children and young people, as well as in the corporate world. Let's move to another type of user who can greatly benefit by accessing research assistance online, the distance learner.

Figure 3.1. Major online activities among children and young adults, 2001.

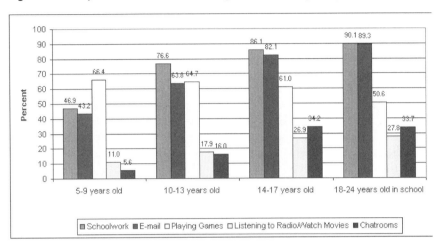

SOURCE: From *A Nation Online: How Americans Are Expanding Their Use of the Internet* 2002, 44. NTIA and ESA U.S. Department of Commerce, using U.S. Census Bureau Population Survey Supplements.

Distance Learners

Support of distance learners is one of the strongest justifications for creating a real-time reference service. Students enrolled in distance learning, that is, taking online or television courses, need remote reference intervention, because they may be unable to come to the library due to geographic distance or time constraints. Barron (2002) talks about these learners' needs for library services, saying, "A student who is taking a class from a residence hall room or an on-campus studio classroom still has a significant advantage over the student who is 70 (or 500) miles away, because he or she can usually walk across campus to the library if necessary. On the other hand, the restrictions on time, etc., that have led a person to choose an online or televised (distributed) course might also limit his or her access to the library every bit as much as physical distance." After all, online education is convenient for people who work full-time.

Most academic libraries recognize the special needs of distance learners and offer unique services to them. College, university, and even public libraries often support distance education programs by offering online databases, specialized interlibrary loan services, or document delivery. For example, the state of Florida has a statewide program to support distance learners in higher education, called the Florida Distance Learning Library Initiative. Public, community college, and university libraries work together to offer reciprocal borrowing, convenient interlibrary loan delivery, and access to FirstSearch databases. These libraries also strive to make access to reference services easier through e-mail or toll-free telephone numbers. The Florida Reference and Referral Center (RRC), which closed in December 2001 because of budget problems, was an interesting experiment in centralized service for distance learners in the state of Florida. When the RRC was open, university students could receive assistance by e-mail, a toll-free number, or via the RRC's chat reference service (ConferenceRoom by WebMaster). Another intriguing example of virtual reference support is the Walden University Library Liaison program. Walden University is a campusless entity that contracts for library services with a brick-and-mortar institution, the Indiana University Libraries at Bloomington. Every summer, Walden doctoral students converge on Bloomington for an intense summer of research and tutelage by university librarians. During the remainder of the year, the students access databases online and receive virtual support from the librarians via a toll-free number and e-mail. Because these doctoral students receive less face-to-face interaction with advisors and professors during the course of their studies, they would likely appreciate the immediacy and intimacy of research consultation in real time.

Another type of user with needs similar to those of the distance learner is the remote user. Many colleges have branch campuses in remote locations that offer special degree programs, continuing education courses for practitioners in the field, or semester abroad programs. These students may rely on the library facilities of the college's main campus. It is also common for graduate students to relocate before completing their master's thesis or doctoral dissertation, finishing their degree in a location far from their institution's library. Librarians strive to meet the special needs of these students or researchers through online services and databases as well as reciprocal agreements with other libraries, but sometimes this system doesn't suffice. Real-time reference service is simply a logical extension of services to this population that may find calling or visiting their library time or cost prohibitive.

Use of Databases Online

Yet another factor in determining the feasibility of launching a real-time reference service is your library's online presence. What kind of resources do you offer online to your users? Many academic libraries with large collections of online databases have noticed a decline in questions at the reference desk. Some observers attribute this decline to an increase in users researching and looking for information from their homes, offices, or other nonlibrary locations. The PIP study, *The Internet Goes to College*, supports this theory: "The convenience of the Internet is likely tempting students to rely very heavily on it when searching for academic resources. In our own research, an overwhelming number of college students reported that the Internet, rather than the library, is the primary site of their information searches. Nearly three-quarters (73%) of college students said they use the Internet more than the library, while only 9% said they use the library more than the Internet for information searching" (Jones 2002, 12).

Preference for convenience over authoritative information is not uncommon among school or college students and adult users. Many users prefer scouring hundreds of vague search engine hits or using commercial services such as AskJeeves to coming to the library or even hanging up the modem to call a librarian. Boeing Corporation librarian Julie Martin notes that "personal contact with users is down—users rarely physically come into the library and even phone usage has decreased....Users get what they need from the Internet, intranet, and library web site" (Martin 2001). "The volume of reference questions is generally down, though use of library e-resources is rising" (Oder 2001). Because of increasing breadth of library information available on the Web, users are beginning to demand phone or chat assistance as a baseline service, along with dial-up access to databases (Bryant 2001).

Online Community

Online or virtual communities are common on the Internet, which means that some library users may participate in one or more of them. Members of virtual communities thrive on chat and e-mail. But what is a virtual community? Howard Rheingold (1993, 5) defines virtual communities as "social aggregations that emerge from the Net when enough people carry on public discussion long enough, with sufficient human feeling, to form webs of personal relationships in cyberspace." People have all kinds of personal relationships online; don't believe the hype in the press that would have you believe it's all dating services or sex. Most online groups exist to socialize, play games (such as Dungeons and Dragons, EverQuest) and even discuss political, professional, or educational issues. Connections is an example of a lively MOO-based community of English professors and graduate students who gather every Tuesday evening to discuss issues in teaching and literature. Probably the most well-known virtual community is the Whole Earth 'Lectronic Link or WELL, which started in 1985 as a small online community based in the San Francisco Bay area but has since expanded to thousands of members across the world. The WELL has many channels devoted to socializing, politics, and just about any area of interest you can name.

There are numerous other virtual communities that congregate in chat rooms, MOOs, on bulletin board systems or message boards, in forums, e-mail discussion groups, or even freenets. Some examples of virtual communities are EnviroLink, the City of Cambridge's (Massachusetts) community net, Diversity University MOO, slashdot, and BUBL (the United Kingdom–based library science discussion forum). Increasingly, even online newspapers and magazines such as the *Washington Post* or the *Atlantic Online* offer venues for joining a community, with threaded discussion forums, chat, and e-mail.

Libraries need to extend reference services to online communities, especially those that reside in their geographic area. The idea that such groups of disembodied users often have a geographic basis may come as a surprise to some librarians, however. Online strategist and e-democracy advocate Stephen Clift, of Publicus.net, says, "One of the biggest under-the-radar trends is the growth of online communities based on local and regional geography. We even have lakes in northern Minnesota with online communities. I predict that far more people will interact in online communities with people who live near them than in more global special interest communities" (Cashel 2002). Participants in online communities should prove receptive to real-time reference because socializing, working, and seeking information online is simply a way of life for them.

E-mail Reference Usage

The final indicator of heightened receptivity to real-time reference is use of e-mail. Does your library, or do neighboring libraries, offer e-mail reference? If e-mail reference is popular and you get a high volume of requests for assistance from your primary clientele, as do the Libraries at the University of Florida, this may indicate a preference as well as a need for online assistance. Examine any transcripts of questions and answers from your e-mail reference service to get a sense of how many users were hoping for immediate assistance or could have benefited from such. (If your practice is to not archive transcripts of e-mail, consider storing them for a limited amount of time for the purposes of researching the types of questions submitted by users. Analysis of transcripts are useful in identifying patterns of user need, as well as in evaluating quality of service as touched on in Chapter 4.) Many of your e-mail users would probably be amenable to an even more convenient reference service with a faster turnaround time like chat real-time reference.

An examination of your library community's online preferences, connectivity, and predilection for chatting will help your planning team define the audience for real-time reference service. Establishing this need is important to gain administrative and financial support for the project. With this underpinning in place, planners may advance to the next steps of the process: selecting the appropriate software to best serve your audience.

REFERENCES

Barron, Brette Barclay. 2002. "Distant and Distributed Learners are Two Sides of the Same Coin: 'Is There a Difference Between Distant and On-Campus Students Anymore? Or Is That Distinction Disappearing in Our Current State of Academic "Wired-Ness?"' (Distance Education and Instructional Services (DEIS) at the University of South Carolina)." *Computers and Libraries* 22 (January): 24–8. Available online at the Expanded Academic Index (accessed 7 February 2003) http://www.galegroup.com.

Bryant, E. 2001. The Changing Face of Reference. *Library Journal*, 125, 11 November, 8.

Cashel, Jim. 2 March 2002. "Interview with Steven Clift, Publicus.net." *Online Community Report*. Available online at http://www.online.communityreport.com (accessed 27 March 2002).

Grudin, Jonathan. (1994) "Groupware and Social Dynamics: Eight Challenges for Developers." *Communications of the ACM.* 37 (January): 92–106.

Horrigan, John B., and Lee Rainie. 2002 (December 29). *Counting on the Internet: Most Expect to Find Key Information Online, Most Find the Information They Seek, Many Now Turn to the Internet First.* Washington, D.C.: Pew Internet & American Life Project. Available online at http://www.pewinternet.org (accessed 7 February 2003).

Jones, Steve. 2002 (September 15). *The Internet Goes to College: How Students Are Living in the Future With Today's Technology.* Washington, D.C.: Pew Internet & American Life Project. Available online at http://www.pewinternet.org (accessed 7 February 2003).

Lenhart, Amanda, Lee Rainie, and Oliver Lewis. 2001 (June 20). *Teenage Life Online: The Rise of the Instant-Message Generation and the Internet's Impact on Friendships and Family Relationships.* Washington, D.C.: Pew Internet & American Life Project. Available online at http://www.pewinternet.org (accessed 5 February 2003).

Martin, Julie. 2001. "Ask A Librarian Service." Paper presented at the 3rd Annual Virtual Reference Desk Conference, Setting Standards and Making it Real, 12–13 November, at Orlando, Florida. Available online at http://www.vrd.org/conferences/VRD2001/proceedings/jmartin.shtml (accessed 27 March 2002).

A Nation Online: How Americans Are Expanding Their Use of the Internet. 2002, February. U.S. Department of Commerce. Economics and Statistics Administration. National Telecommunications and Information Administration. Washington, D.C. Available online at http://www.ntia.doc.gov/ntiahome/dn/ (accessed 8 August 2002).

Oder, Norman. 2001. "The Shape of E-Reference." *Library Journal*, (1 February): 46–50.

Rheingold, Howard. 1993. *The Virtual Community: Homesteading on the Electronic Frontier.* Reading, MA: Addison-Wesley.

Rheingold, Howard. 2002. *Smart Mobs: The Next Social Revolution.* Cambridge, MA: Perseus Books.

WEB SITES CITED

Amazon.com
http://www.amazon.com

AskJeeves
http://www.ask.com/

Atlantic Online, The
http://www.theatlantic.com/

BUBL, the UK based library science discussion forum.
http://bubl.ac.uk/

City of Cambridge
   http://www.ci.cambridge.ma.us/

ConferenceRoom (Webmaster)
   http://www.webmaster.com/main.htm

Diversity University MOO
   http://www.du.org

EnviroLink Network
   http://envirolink.org

Indiana University Libraries, Bloomington
   http://www.libraries.iub.edu

Questia
   http://www.questia.com

slashdot
   http://slashdot.org/

Walden University
   http://www.waldenu.edu

Wal-Mart
   http://www.walmart.com

The Washington Post
   http://www.washingtonpost.com

The WELL
   http://www.well.com/

4 SELECTING REAL-TIME SOFTWARE FOR YOUR USERS AND LIBRARY

Selecting the software for a real-time reference service is difficult because there are so many programs and variables within each program to consider. Choices of software range from simple instant messaging programs such as America Online's *Instant Messenger* (AIM) and Internet Relay Chat (IRC) to course management software and programs used at commercial call centers. If you skipped reading the earlier chapters in this book that discuss the characteristics and virtues of each class of software, you may wish to revisit them because they introduce the wide assortment of programs and systems that enable communication on the Internet in real time. This chapter concentrates on evaluating real-time software in the context of library needs.

SOFTWARE SELECTION CRITERIA

Because there are so many types of programs to consider and examining software takes so much time, it is helpful to identify who will evaluate the software and to establish a list of evaluative criteria to guide the decision making. Depending on the size and scope of your project, there may be a single person or a large team directing the evaluation effort. The planning group may grow at the end of a pilot period, as skeptical colleagues see the value of online reference in action. At the University of Florida (UF), we assembled a planning team of librarians representing various disciplines and expertise across the George A. Smathers Libraries. These members include Ann Lindell, Art Librarian; Mimi Pappas, E-mail Reference Coordinator and Instruction Librarian; Alice Primack, Science Librarian; Colleen Seale, Head of Reference, Humanities & Social Sciences; Suzy Covey, Systems Librarian; and myself, the Program Director for Undergraduate Library

Services (and later the Interactive Reference Coordinator). Libraries seeking to launch real-time reference through a consortium such as ASERL (the Association of Southeast Research Libraries) may work in an even larger team. ASERL formed a software evaluation team and a "virtual reference best-practices" team with representatives from member libraries to guide software selection and service guidelines and practices. For a more in-depth discussion of the role of the planning team in developing a virtual reference service, consult Chapter 5, "The Human Element."

One of the most difficult parts of software selection is balancing a desire for special features, such as escorting and databases of frequently used sayings, with the realities of price, operating system(s) compatibilities, and administrative features. In addition, the software needs to be easy to use for both patrons and librarians. Using a criteria list to rank software will help to compare and contrast features in a logical fashion.

Features can be divided into the following areas for purposes of comparison:

- User interface
- General and administrative features
- Librarian interface
- Cost and licensing
- System

The most important issue to consider is usability, starting with the user interface.

USER INTERFACE

When we were selecting a system at the University of Florida, the RefeXpress planning team agreed that the primary concern was developing an attractive, easy-to-navigate user interface that offered a minimum of restrictions to the user trying to reach a librarian for help. As we examined each software package, we looked at them from a user's perspective, endeavoring to answer the following questions (centered on the criteria given later). Does the chat software have an intuitive interface? What would constitute an intuitive interface for our users, based on their knowledge of computing and the Internet? Would our users be willing to download and install software on their computer to ask a question, or would this deter potential users? Do a large number of our users already use conferencing software, such as *AIM* or *mIRC,* which could be adopted for a real-time reference service? Does the software need to work with a variety of operating systems, such as Windows, Unix, or Macintosh, or does the library exist within a homogenous computing environment? For example, Indiana University at Bloomington "has a very sweeping site license with Microsoft, which gives IU and all the people affiliated with IU access to the major operating systems and applications of Microsoft, free of charge" (Liu, personal correspondence, March 1, 2002). If this is the case in your setting, and the vast majority of your patrons use a common operating system such as Windows, then a proprietary but inexpensive program such as Microsoft's *MSN Messenger* or *NetMeeting* offers a couple of advantages. First, the software comes bundled with the rest of Windows or is easy to download and install with existing computer support. Second, your target audience will be familiar with the conventions of the system. If your library serves an environment in which no single operating system dominates, however, it is important to find software that supports as many of your audience's operating systems as possible. Some vendors are willing to adapt their software to work with a variety of platforms. For example, OhioLINK, a large consortium enveloping the Ohio State Library and numerous academic libraries, recently awarded a contract to Digi-Net Technologies to develop real-time communication software (*eLibrarian*, also called *Groopz*) that will work with Macintosh, Windows, and other platforms ("Digi-Net" 2002).

User Interface Factors:
- Attractive, friendly
- Minimum of instructions needed
- Help feature
- Alert features
- Ability to customize interface
- Java applet or otherwise accessible from web page
- Client installation required
- Single or multiplatform support

Perhaps the most important user interface consideration is whether to choose software that requires users to install software on their computer to reach the service. Many synchronous software packages require nothing more than a web browser to log on. This is usually achieved through the use of Java applets that rapidly transfer from the chat server to the user's computer and that activate with a simple click of an "okay" button. Some software achieves a connection via telnet, but many synchronous communication programs such as *AIM, CUSeeMe,* or *mIRC,* require the installation of a client on the user's computer. In an AOL-rich environment such as SUNY Morrisville College, many students already have *AIM* loaded on their computers. In a diverse computing environment, or one with less confident users, it is wiser to go with an option that requires nothing more on the user's side than *Netscape Navigator, Internet Explorer, Opera,* or another type of web browser.

Another aspect of the user interface to evaluate is the manner in which answers will be presented to real-time reference users. Will answers be delivered strictly by text in the chat window as with *ConferenceRoom* or *AIM,* or is an accompanying web browser incorporated into the program's interface along with the chat window (eGain *Live Web* or divine *Virtual Reference Desk [VRD]*). If the program is strictly text based, will your users be able to handle multitasking while communicating (so that they can cut and paste URLs into a separate web browser to see an answer on a web page)? Does the software support "clickable" URLs, as does *ConferenceRoom?* Clickable means that when a user clicks on a URL given in the text of the chat, a web browser launches, displaying the page independently of the chat program. One important feature to examine in programs that incorporate a web browser is how the web browser works. Are the web browser and chat

Figure 4.1. User's view in divine *Virtual Reference Desk.*

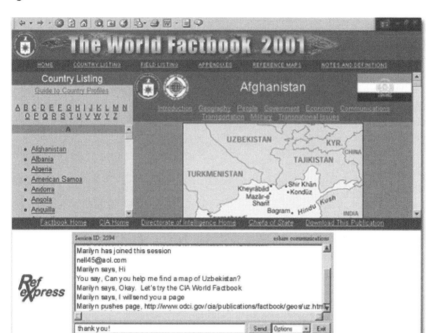

window presented in frames, so that both are always visible on the screen (as does divine *VRD*, Figure 4.1), or does the chat session reside in a separate small window that floats above the main web browser window (*LiveAssistance*, Figure 4.2). How will users know when new information is sent to them? This is an issue even when chat and web browsing are integrated on the user interface because when working with a multitasking user, it's possible to lose contact if the user is surfing in another window while waiting for you to respond with an answer. Look for built-in alert features that ring the computer bell or move the chat window to the foreground of the computer screen when new comments are posted.

Automated responses for users are another aspect of the user interface to critique. While evaluating software, examine the type of response users get while trying to log on or waiting in a queue for their turn to talk to the librarian. Of particular importance are the first messages a user sees. If users see an unfriendly or confusing message or experience a total lack of response when they try to log on, they may not return a second time. Programs that offer some type of message indicating the status of the user's connection are preferred. Many call center software packages allow librarians to edit preprogrammed messages such as "next in queue" to make messages more specific to the library setting, or friendly in tone.

Customization is another important issue to consider. Does the software offer the latitude to customize the interface and incorporate local library links or

Figure 4.2. User's view in *LiveAssistance*.

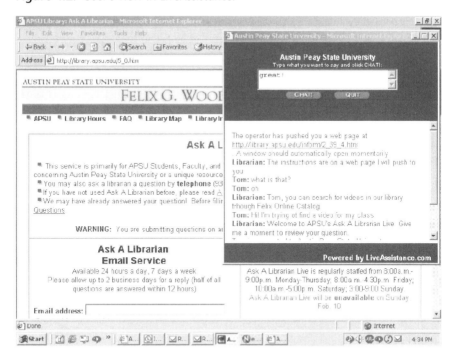

graphics or alter the design to serve users better? This is important when evaluating hosted services. Some services, such as *24/7 Reference*, allow a great deal of customization. If you look at the interface for the Boston Public Library, you can see that it is possible to customize the welcome page and program in local links (see Figure 4.3). There may be less latitude with services of a more commercial or recreational nature such as *Yahoo! Chat* or *Lycos Chat*. Free hosting may be attractive because of the cost savings, but these services often feature advertising that can be distracting or disruptive in the case of pop-up ads.

Another feature related to customization is that of built-in help. If users must master commands to navigate the software, it is important to have easy and well-written instructions. For example, *mIRC* has commands embedded in pull-downs as well as a help feature where users can search for instruction without bothering their chat session. Libraries will also want to create customized help links, as well as pages explaining policy and other avenues for obtaining help when the service is closed.

GENERAL AND ADMINISTRATIVE FEATURES

Now that we have discussed the user interface, it is time to turn to more general features that help librarians deliver answers effectively, as well as manage the

Figure 4.3. Boston Public Library 24/7 Reference (*24/7 Reference*).

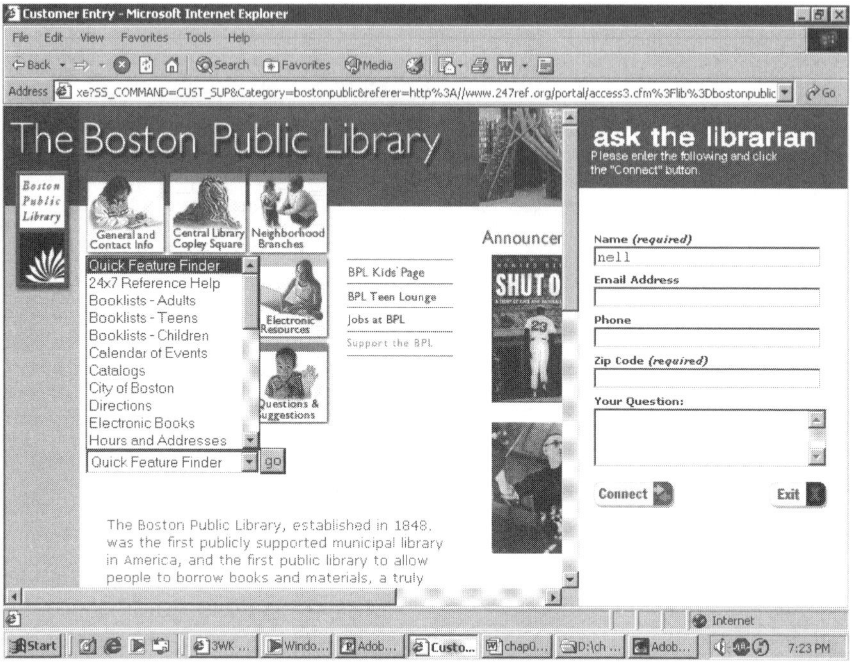

day-to-day operations of the service. I've listed below a few features that are useful to compare.

General/Administrative Features:
- Ability to control number of users
- Ability to disconnect or ban users
- Environment: number of rooms/channels, privacy
- Private messaging
- Clickable URLs
- Push page
- Escorting (co-browsing)
- Productivity features
- Site restrictions based on IP address
- Statistical reporting
- Transcript management

User Management

User management features vary widely across real-time software and are important in establishing "crowd control." Crowd control measures include the ability to control the number of users that can be connected at one time, to restrict connections, and to disconnect or ban users, as well as communication or navigation commands. Let's start with attendance.

Do you plan to allow large numbers of people to log on simultaneously in your real-time reference service, or do you prefer to limit log-ons to one person per librarian? You can manage either approach through choice of software or management features in the software. For example, instant messaging software is based on a one-on-one communication model, whereas call center software can be set to allow a certain number of users to log on, based on the number of librarians online or the level of each librarian's computer ability. Call center software gives real-time reference managers the latitude to enable multiple sessions for experienced virtual librarians, at the same time limiting connections to one-on-one for new hires or less dexterous staff. divine *VRD*, for example, can be programmed for a ratio of anywhere from one to six users working simultaneously with each librarian. Digi-Net's *eLibrarian* and LSSI's *Virtual Reference Toolkit (VRT)* also allow librarians to work with more than one user at a time. How does this work in practice? If librarian accounts are programmed to work with a maximum of two users each and three librarians are online to answer questions, a maximum of six users could be actively engaged and communicating in the real-time reference service. Each librarian would be juggling two users; any additional people logging on for help would be instructed to wait in a queue until someone logged off.

Some systems such as IRC or MOO are based on a model in which large numbers of people are online simultaneously. With software such as this, easy commands are important for creating private rooms or channels where a user and librarian can go when the main channel or room gets too busy. In some systems, such as MOO, administrators manage the number of connections by limiting guest accounts. Other software restricts usage by authentication or by IP address. Another strategy would be to choose software that requires users to install client software that is commonly available to your users but would deter people outside your client base. Lastly, whether the virtual environment is large or intimate, it is crucial to have the ability to disconnect users if they forget to log off or to even ban users for disruptive behavior. Misbehavior hasn't been a problem with UF's chat reference service, but we have experienced difficulties with users who either forget or don't know how to log off. The disconnect feature allows the librarian on duty to "free the line" so that other users can get to the service.

Communication and navigation features also help achieve crowd control. If your service will be operating in an environment such as IRC or a MOO that allows multiple log-ons but does not use queuing, it can be difficult to hold a coherent conversation with a patron when several users are logged on. As everyone starts "talking," the text starts rolling by quickly on the screen, and it can be difficult to follow the comments that one user posts. When a librarian encounters such a situation, it is helpful to move to a secluded room or channel. Usually there is some type of command to easily lead or transfer a user to a quiet space such as "/invite" (IRC), or "@join" (MOO), so that the user need not learn complicated navigation commands. Also look for commands that allow librarians to "back channel" or consult privately with a user or other librarian outside the main conversation in the channel or room. This is achieved in a number of ways, ranging from a "whisper" command that sends a message to a specified user to separate built-in instant messaging features as often implemented in call center software. Back channeling also helps make reference shift changes seamless, so that librarians share administrative information without disturbing the flow of reference service.

Clickable URLs, Push Page, and Escorting

Features that enable librarians to converse with and manage users are important, but so are features that help transfer information and compose speedy answers. Two handy features in web-based chat software are push and escorting. Push, simply defined, enables a librarian to show a user a web page. Let's say you are helping a user search for a phone number for the Coca-Cola Company in Atlanta, Georgia. A fast search of *Switchboard.com* is confusing, because there are several listings for Coca-Cola. You could continue chatting with the user to get more information such as a street address, or you could use the push feature to send him the listings of the companies, so that he could evaluate the information directly. Push page ensures that users see what you want them to see on their computers, clarifying communication. Another popular feature is called escorting, also known as co-browsing, or collaboration. Escorting automates the push page feature and allows the user to see every step of the librarian's search as the librarian looks for information in web-based sources. If you wanted to show the person asking for the Coca-Cola phone number where *Hoover's Online* is located in the library and how to use it, turning on the escort feature would let him follow your steps through the web pages. Some software even lets the user see the librarian filling in forms and making selections from pull-down menus in certain databases, such as the software used at the University of Florida, divine *VRD*. Other software relies on clickable URLs, which are hyperlinks that launch pages of content when a user clicks on them in the text of the chat window. In the case of the Coca-Cola question, the librarian would copy and paste the URL with the answer from Switchboard.com into the chat and instruct the user to click on the URL to see the page of listings.

Productivity Features

Just like at the reference desk, librarians are sure to find themselves repeating certain things time and time again and encountering certain commonly asked questions. Software with productivity features allows librarians to program greetings or phrases they often use, URLs of heavily used web pages, and even things such as PowerPoint slides or screen snapshots. Software varies widely as to how productivity features are input and accessed, involving programming "know-how" in some cases. Many have administrative modules that make programming productivity features as easy to use as pasting a URL or typing "Have I answered your question?" into a blank. In addition, some systems offer chat reference staff the latitude to program their favorites locally, in addition to the stock answers available to every librarian. This is an extremely important feature in hosted systems where large numbers of libraries may be participating. Some programs such as IRC or MOO even offer robots or "bots," automated features that are programmed with phrases or instructions to feed to users. Others have automated diagnostic features that, when set in motion by the librarian, lead a user through a series of questions presented in floating windows. Called autopilot, the librarian can see the user's responses as she selects answers and break in when appropriate to deliver an answer. Autopilot is a good diagnostic device and helps minimize typing.

Transcripts and Statistics

Access to statistics and transcripts of sessions with users is critical to providing users a follow-up after a chat session and to assist in evaluation of the quality of the reference service. Unfortunately, some real-time software does not offer these features, although sometimes they can be programmed or added through separate software modules. Many software programs have a transcript feature built into the program that stores the proceedings in a database and even automatically sends copies to users at the conclusion of a chat session. Although transcripts do bring up privacy issues, users seem to enjoy receiving the record of instructions or information provided by the librarian in a transcript. Transcripts are also useful tools to analyze the types of questions that users are asking and to identify needs for staff training.

One clear advantage of online reference in real time is the ability to collect statistics automatically. Look for software with a built-in statistical feature or develop a "home-grown" system to automate statistics keeping. Although it is possible to tally transactions the old-fashioned way with "tick sheets," why burden librarians with this cumbersome task? One goal of your project should be to automate as many repetitive functions as possible to free up librarians to concentrate on the more intellectual aspects of reference. Automated statistical features also make it easier to produce reports and ensure greater accuracy. Be aware that software varies widely in the level that statistics are gathered, ranging from recording log-ons and the length of time users are online chatting with a librarian to categorization of questions for analysis with reports and graphs. When programming the categories, the questions seem to fall within the following areas: reference, circulation, interlibrary loan, directional, full-text article, connectivity problems, and referral.

LIBRARIAN INTERFACE

We have now moved to a point in the software evaluation process where all of the indicators we have examined earlier in this chapter should be assessed again, in light of how they address the online librarian's needs. The main ones to consider are listed in this section. First, consider whether the system you are evaluating offers the librarian and the user the same interface or if an enhanced interface is available, as is often the case in web-based chat and call center software. If an enhanced interface exists, is it generated from a software client that must be loaded on librarian's computers, thus necessitating certain hardware, or is it web based? How does the interface automate repetitive tasks, offer productivity features that are easy to find and use, or alert the librarian to log-ons or new messages? Are e-mail, statistics, and a web browser built-in, or will librarians need to multitask to record statistics or look in a database? Are statistics and transcripts easy to access? Some interfaces even offer spell checking and a graphical presentation of commands for easier access.

Librarian Interface:
- Easy to navigate, find features
- Integrated with web browser or requires multitasking
- Help feature
- Spell checker
- Alert feature
- Productivity features
- E-mail support

PRICE AND SYSTEM FEATURES

Thus far, discussion has centered on interface and software features. But now we move to a significant consideration in the software evaluation process: critiquing the software in the areas of cost and system functionality. The factors summarized next concerning cost, licensing, and system software and hardware should be helpful whether you are evaluating an inexpensive software program with simple features or a fuller-featured selection such as that used in web-based corporate call centers. Incidentally, don't feel pressured to purchase an expensive software program right away. Bell (2001) says that many libraries start on a small scale with a pilot of real-time reference service using free or modestly priced chat programs such as *HumanClick* (LivePerson) and move to more expensive products such as LSSI *VRT* as the need arises. Yatsko (2001) said it well, when she noted on the virtual reference e-mail discussion group DIG_REF that librarians should "certainly try several methods of providing service, because no one system will provide the best medium for service to all patrons in all situations." It is not unusual for a library to move to a different type of real-time software after a year or less in operation. For libraries that lack computer support, one attractive option is to try a free or inexpensive commercial service to host a trial. For example, you could create a library channel on *Yahoo! Chat* at no charge or establish a more controlled environment using Backpack or one of the less expensive options from *WebMaster* (under $1,000). If you want to start with more full-featured, real-time software, you may be able to arrange a trial with a hosted service specializing in libraries such as *24/7 Reference* or LSSI *VRT*. Pursuing a hosted trial with a vendor has the advantage of freeing you from some immediate technical issues so that you and your staff can concentrate on learning how to provide reference services synchronously.

Cost and Licensing Issues:
- Cost per user
- User expense
- Advertising (for free services)
- Software trial or demonstrations available
- Technical support and documentation
- Training

Expense

When selecting software, it is important to choose a medium that will allow users to access your service as easily as possible (see the user interface section earlier in this chapter) and at the least cost to the individual. When thinking about cost to the user, what immediately comes to mind are costs associated with connecting to the Internet or buying software to access the library reference service. If you set up a real-time reference service based on software, equipment, or an Internet service provider that the typical user in your library district doesn't have, hidden costs associated with your service may set it up for failure. For example, setting up a real-time service based on *CUSeeMe* assumes that a large number of your library audience owns computers with cameras, microphones, sound cards, and an Internet connection fast enough to use videoconferencing effectively. Another example, hosting a service on the network of a popular Internet service provider such as America Online or Road Runner, may seem like a good idea but would a user's lacking an account prove a barrier to him accessing the virtual reference desk? Other things to consider are the presence of advertising (a big issue when considering hosted software), the ability to preview the software before purchase, and the quality and extent of technical support and documentation. A final consideration is the level and quality of vendor training. The more complex the chat-based software, the more training that is required to install, administrate, and use the system. Vendors offering sophisticated software often bundle onsite instruction for librarians staffing the service or, at the very least, training for the real-time reference administrators.

SYSTEM SOFTWARE AND HARDWARE

User interface, features such as push page and transcript management, the administrative module, and price are all important considerations in the selection of a real-time reference system. Computer and network interoperability, hardware requirements, and other technical issues often drive the choice of software in the end, however. The reader will find several points listed in the next section that will speed along this stage of the software evaluation. One note: if you have not yet involved your local computer support team in planning for the new service, it is particularly critical to do so at this step in the software evaluation process. This is true even when considering systems such as *24/7 Reference* or *QuestionPoint*, which are hosted on a vendor's computer system.

Figure 4.4. Checklist of features and specifications for real-time software.

☑ User's Interface:	Comments:
Attractive, friendly	
Minimum of instructions needed	
Help feature	
Alert feature	
Ability to customize interface	
Java applet or otherwise accessible from web page	
Client installation required	
One or multi-platform support	
General/Administrative Features:	
Ability to control number of users	
Ability to disconnect/ban users	
Environment: number of rooms/channels, privacy	
Private messaging	
Embedded URLs	
Push page	
Escorting (co-browsing)	
Productivity features	
Site restrictions based on IP	
Statistical reporting	
Record transcripts of chat sessions	
Librarian Interface:	
Easy to navigate, find features	
Integrated with Web browser or requires multi-tasking	
Help feature	
Spell checker	
Alert feature	
Productivity features	
Email support	
Cost/Licensing Issues:	
Free or relatively low cost per user	
Advertising	
Demo version available	
Level of technical support and or documentation	
Training	
System Software and Hardware:	
Hosted or local	
Operating system (UNIX, Windows NT, etc.)	
Requires additional software	
Relational database (SQL, Oracle, etc.)	
Web server	
Compatible with email system	
Ram, CPU load, bandwidth, disk space requirements	
Firewall configuration	
Logs: access, content, server activity	
Integrate with RealMedia, MS Netshow, Shockwave	
Client platform: Java, IRC, HTML, ActiveX, etc.	
Speed (lag)	
Level of programming required	

System Software and Hardware:
- Hosted or local
- Operating system (UNIX, Windows NT, etc.)
- Requires additional software
- Relational database (SQL, Oracle, etc.)
- Web server
- Compatible with e-mail system
- Ram, CPU load, bandwidth, disk space requirements
- Firewall configuration
- Logs: access, content, server activity

- Integrate with RealMedia, MS Netshow, Shockwave
- Client platform (Java, IRC, HTML, ActiveX, etc.)
- Speed (lag)
- Level of programming required

As can be seen from this list, the key factors to examine are compatibility with the library's local operating system(s) as well as Web and e-mail system. Other issues that may influence your decision are additional requirements for supporting the system, such as hardware, need for a relational database or other software, and how the system establishes a connection for the user at their end (through Java, HTML, etc.).

The software must be compatible and work with the library's local operating system, whether hosted or locally situated on a library server. Happily, there are many chatlike programs on the market or available on the Internet for Unix and Windows operating systems, as well as others. It should also work with your clientele's operating systems. If you have an existing network server complex (Web, mail, etc.) located at your library, hosting chat software locally will not require undue additional overhead. If you do not, it may be wise to choose remote hosting with a library vendor or chat vendor to avoid the costs of establishing the other network services needed to support a local chat system. This is all subject to local circumstances. Be sure to get a detailed list of the features and specifications for any program that you are evaluating for your library setting.

In conclusion, several factors have been introduced that typically play a role in selection of real-time reference software. Figure 4.4 pulls together all of these features in a reproducible checklist to assist in decision making. Because real-time software is rapidly evolving, I urge readers to continue their investigation past the pages of this book to articles and reviews in library and computer science magazines and journals, as well as business publications devoted to covering developments in e-commerce.

REFERENCES

Bell, Lori. 2001. "Re: Demand for Live Reference." *Livereference Listserv* (4 December). Archived online at http://www.yahoo.com/group/livereference; livereference@yahoogroups.com

"Digi-Net and OhioLINK Partner to Create Virtual Reference Desk Software: Virtual Reference Desk to Connect Ohio's Entire Academic Library System" (press release). *Yahoo! Finance,* 11 June 2002. Available online at http://biz.yahoo.com/bw/020611/110044_2.html (Accessed 28 August 2002).

Yatsko, Laurel. 2001. "Re: Demand for Live Reference" (4 December) *Livereference Listserv.* Archived online at http://www.yahoo.com/group/live reference; livereference@yahoogroups.com

WEB SITES CITED

AIM (America Online Instant Messenger)
    http://www.aim.com/

Association of Southeast Research Libraries, ASERL
http://www.aserl.org/projects/vref/default.htm

Backpack, WebMaster
http://www.conferenceroom.com/products/backpack.htm

CUSeeMe
http://llic2.cuseeme.com/

eLibrarian, Digi-Net Technologies
http://www.digi-net.com

HumanClick (LivePerson)
http://www.humanclick.com/

Indiana University at Bloomington
http://www.iub.edu

Live Web, eGain Communications Corp.
http://www.egain.com/

LiveAssistance
http://liveassistance.com

Lycos Chat
http://clubs.lycos.com/live/ChatRooms/ChatHome.asp?Area = 1

MSN Messenger
http://messenger.msn.com/

NetMeeting
http://www.microsoft.com/windows/netmeeting/

OhioLINK
http://www.ohiolink.edu/

RefeXpress, University of Florida
http://refexpress.uflib.ufl.edu

Talk to a Librarian, SUNY Morrisville College
http://www.morrisville.edu/library/talk.html

24/7 Chat Reference, Boston Public Library
http://www.bpl.org

Switchboard.com
http://www.switchboard.com

Road Runner
http://www.rr.com/rdrun/

Yahoo! Chat
http://chat.yahoo.com/

5 THE HUMAN ELEMENT

When planning a new real-time reference service, establishing an effective model of staffing is essential. It may be tempting to concentrate on sexy software with exciting features such as push page and databases of preprogrammed responses. But don't overlook the important human side of the equation—the people who will be answering the questions. "Regardless of whether a user is interacting with an unseen human miles away or standing before the reference desk, the sense of connection to another being is an important part of the reference experience" (Parsons 2001). It's possible to spend thousands of dollars purchasing software and marketing a service, but when it comes to user satisfaction, a virtual reference service such as real-time chat or e-mail is only as good as the person answering the question at the other end.

Initially users may be impressed by the novelty of a library-based chat room, or high-tech features such as escorting or white-boarding. It's important to remember, however, that users connect to chat reference services for prompt, capable assistance at their point of need. If the service appears unresponsive, or if they don't receive help within what they consider to be a reasonable amount of time, they won't return for guidance a second time. When I say unresponsive, I am referring to dead air time, or time when the user is waiting for feedback from the chat service. The longer the time with no feedback, such as a greeting, a status report, or a new web page to look at, the more likely it is that the user will become anxious, frustrated, or will even log off.

To meet users' needs rapidly, identify real-time competencies and train staff in these skills. Chat reference competencies include good typing skills, mastery of online information sources, effective reference interviewing skills, and the ability to solve problems. These skills are more fully discussed in Chapter 6.

E-commerce offers some insight into staffing a real-time service operation. Managers of web-based call center operations continually examine user data such as session length, demand, and the amount of time users wait in queues before engaging with a service representative. Managers often apply mathematical formulas (such as Erlang C) to determine the typical amount of time a representative can spend with a customer before the customer wants to log off or there is a demand to work with a second customer. Although standards vary from call center to call center, depending on the type of product being supported or level of service, many call centers work on the assumption that the average customer will wait up to 120 seconds for resolution of his or her question.

This is not to say that all answers can or need be delivered within two minutes flat, or even that users expect this from a library service. Reference transactions are, by their nature, much too varied to apply a rule such as the 120-second rule, which was formulated for a setting where 80 percent of the answers are delivered from pages on the service's Web site. Think of the types of questions customers might ask at *1-800-FLOWERS*, <www.800flowers.com>, or at the Web site of the office supply giant *Staples*, <www.staples.com>. I do think that the 120-second rule may apply to a reference transaction in the following way, however. It is reasonable for users to expect to be greeted within a few seconds of logging in for assistance, to get some assurance that the librarian understands their question, and to be advised as to the time frame for getting an answer and how that answer will be delivered. To provide this type of reference service, you must have staff members who are computer savvy, who can think on their feet, who know their reference sources, and who are not afraid to experiment and try something new.

SELECTING STAFF

In an ideal world where budgets are plentiful, staffing a real-time reference service would be a simple matter of hiring librarians with the requisite reference and technical skills and paying them lucrative salaries to work swing shifts in plush reference command centers with comfortable chairs, fast networking, and a core reference collection. You would have an expert team of librarians vying to cover the red-eye shifts during evening and the weekend hours for overtime pay and other perks. The service would be available twenty-four hours a day, seven days a week. Well, it would be nice if staffing were this easy, but realistically speaking, it may be one of the more problematic areas in getting your service up and running. In many libraries (such as mine), funding issues or competing reference priorities often dictate starting with shorter service hours or a smaller number of librarians to get the new service in operation.

The hours of service and base of operations will be determined by who will be staffing your chat service. If you feel strongly that professional librarians should staff the service, then will your budget support hiring or reassigning librarians to work the service? Will you recruit subject specialists in addition to reference generalists? What if librarians are not available for staffing after 5 P.M.? Using library professionals or even library school students is one strategy to increase the number of staff members working in the service, but support staff in many libraries are just as busy, if not busier than, librarians; will you add more hours to their work-week? If so, will you have to worry about overtime pay or union limitations on working more than forty hours a week? There are many questions regarding staffing to be answered.

Many institutions are using library professionals or library school students to field chat-based reference queries. At the University of Illinois, Urbana–Champaign (UIUC), there is "a mix of young and experienced librarians working on providing real-time reference assistance. Some of our staff have been working in the Library since [the] 1970s, some have only one or two years library experience, and some are still studying at library school" (Henry 2001). UIUC operates 130 hours a week and has as many as five chat reference staff online at one time (Ronan and Turner 2003). If you are uncomfortable with using staff with this level of experience, you can always test your service with professional librarians. Starting with a pilot will allow you to get a sense of your library's online audience and an examination of the questions that users are submitting may support extending staffing to library professionals, or not. If your library is experiencing a decline in questions at the reference desk, administrators may see real-time reference as an "add-on" to existing reference desk duties. Piloting the service will give some indication whether this is a workable model for your library. At the University of Florida, we staffed *RefeXpress* the first year using only professional librarians but soon extended staffing to use library assistants. This is because when we launched our service in 2000, the concept of real-time reference assistance was so new that we were unsure what level of reference questions we would get from users. Members of the planning team changed their minds about this issue after an analysis of session transcripts revealed that many questions were of the type that library professionals routinely handle at the reference desk, such as verifying bibliographic citations, locating online databases, and advising undergraduates on research basics. We now follow a practice of assigning library assistants to hours where backup assistance is readily available from professional librarians in the office or from librarians at one of our many reference desks.

Once you have decided on the type and level of competencies that you require from your chat workers, there are a variety of ways to accomplish the actual staffing. You can hire new staff, reassign existing reference staff or recruit volunteers. Outsourcing late night hours or the complete chat operation to your local consortium or a commercial service such as *24/7 Reference* or LSSI *Virtual Reference Toolkit (VRT)* is also an option. A few libraries have created new job positions to administer and staff their new chat services, whereas others have recruited existing personnel to "moonlight" for extra pay. Two large public library consortia, the NOLA Regional Library System in Ohio (Oder 2001) and the Suffolk Cooperative Library System in New York state (Hoag and McCaffery Cichanowicz 2001), recruit staff from member libraries as independent reference contractors to cover evening chat hours. These late night chatters get paid an hourly wage above and beyond their library salaries as a reward for moonlighting. The general pattern in most organizations (or at least among academic libraries), however, seems to either recruit volunteers from existing reference staff or to adjust librarians' reference duties to incorporate virtual reference desk hours. For example, the library administration at SUNY Buffalo requests that librarians contribute one hour a week to staffing *Instant Librarian* (Foley 2002); the Smathers Libraries requires public service reference librarians to work two hours a week in *RefeXpress*, in addition to other regularly assigned duties.

If your independent library is just getting your service off the ground and human resources are scarce, use volunteers to test chat reference in a pilot program or trial. A successful pilot can lead to administrative (and staff) support to either hire new positions or incorporate chat duties into existing job descriptions. Because it can be difficult to foresee user needs in such a new type of service, running a pilot also gives librarians the opportunity to learn the many creative ways patrons will use the medium. And keep in mind that where you physically base staff operations while answering chat reference questions can make participating more attractive for some librarians, especially if working at home is an option.

WHERE TO CHAT?

When setting up a virtual reference service such as chat, you can structure the work environment in a variety of ways. Some libraries employ a centralized model in which every staff member is physically situated in one location, such as one particular reference desk or a special "command center" chock full of reference books, scanners, computers, and telephones. Real-time reference services at other organizations are more decentralized and staff works in a variety of places limited only by computer hookups. Also key to choosing a location is whether you choose to operate the service independently from other public services such as e-mail reference or the information desk, or if you will add answering chat-based questions to reference desk duties.

The Centralized Model

InfoChat, the real-time reference service at the Auburn University Libraries, operates using a centralized organizational model. Just before the rollout of *InfoChat*, Auburn consolidated its four subject area reference desks into "one centralized reference services desk in the main library and installed the chat software "at one of four computer terminals at that centralized service point" (Sears 2001). As many as four librarians, professional staffers, and graduate students work at this desk, but no fewer than two are available at all times to answer chat, telephone, and walk-in questions. Another example of the centralized model is the "off-site services desk" at the North Carolina State University Libraries, where all telephone, e-mail, and real-time questions are handled. The off-site services desk is located in a room adjacent to the reference desk and collections, equipped with extra phone directories and schedules, as well as a computer dedicated to diagnosing remote access problems through various ISPs (Anderson, Boyer, and Ciccione 2000).

Using a centralized design has certain advantages. If staff members all work in one location, it eliminates the need to duplicate and maintain client software, computer hardware, and peripherals such as scanners. It also makes it easier to develop a comprehensive collection of ready reference sources to use in answering questions either by situating chat workers near the reference collection or by establishing one location to gather directories, encyclopedias, style guides, and other ready reference tools. The centralized chat operation may also be easier to administrate in some ways. If staff are all working in one location, librarians see each other when changing shifts and will be more likely to pass on technical problems or the "hot questions of the day." Centralization also makes it possible to fold chat scheduling into the existing reference desk or telephone reference services schedules. This is a popular model for staffing large commercial call centers where chats, e-mails, and VoIP transactions number in the thousands a week, because it is easier to administrate and keep workers productive. Library reference desks do not operate like call centers, where customer representatives work exclusively with online or telephone queries. Placing real-time reference at the traditional reference desk means that the staff must work with people calling on the phone and walking up to the desk as they chat online with users. Centralizing a real-time service at the reference desk may increase dead time and delays in answering online calls for assistance because staff are often pulled away from the desk or are interrupted. In addition, strict adherence to a centralized model where librarians and staff work only at the designated chat reference area may not be conducive to recruiting staff for late night or other hard-to-cover service hours. A decentralized model allows staff members to work in a variety of locations where they can pursue other projects while waiting for calls during slow shifts. You may have more luck in recruiting coverage of late-night hours, for example, if you encourage telecommuting and lend staff laptops to use at home as we do for *RefeXpress*.

The Decentralized Model

The decentralized staffing model seems to be the most popular across all library types, probably because it offers the most flexibility. With this type of organization, librarians may be working from a variety of different locations in the same building, in branch libraries on campuses or across a city, or even dispersed geographically or organizationally in the case of large cooperatives, across several cities, states, and even countries. At the University of Florida, librarians from eight branches work out of their offices, homes, and, on rare occasions when we are short of staff, at the reference desk. Another example of a decentralized operation is the *Ready for Reference* service of the Alliance Library System in Illinois, where each of the eight participating Illinois college and university libraries staff the service at least eight hours a week, and the remaining weekend and late-night hours are outsourced to LSSI (Sloan 2001). The Boeing Company's *Ask a*

Librarian service is staffed to follow the sun, starting with the librarians at the St. Louis location in the morning, moving to Arizona, California, and Puget Sound as the day progresses (Martin 2001).

Probably the chief advantage of approaching staffing in a decentralized manner is that you can tap into expertise and staff from a variety of locations. It also enables your library to explore cooperation with other libraries or systems and to share a chat reference service, an attractive option for smaller libraries. For staff an advantage is to have the latitude to work in an environment where they know the layout and feel comfortable. The main disadvantages of a decentralized staffing model are coordinating personnel and procedures and the increased amount of training required. Managing a decentralized service demands more effort to keep up with staff, especially when there is a complicated schedule of staff working from a variety of locales and even organizations. It's important that the chat coordinator set up special communication channels and strategies. Drawing on personnel located in a variety of collections and branches of a library system means that they will have different comfort levels outside their areas of specialty. Some librarians or library professionals may wish to have colleagues nearby for referral or assistance as they learn to function in the new service. It is also necessary to establish easy-to-access service schedules and clear procedures for covering vacations, shift trades, and absences due to illness, forgetting a shift, or tardiness.

Chatting at the Reference Desk

Is it a good idea to base chat out of a reference desk? There are definitely pros and cons to working with remote and walk-in clientele at the same service point. Many real-time reference services currently operate from the traditional reference desk, such as *Ask A Librarian Live* at Austin Peay State University (see the case study in Chapter 12) and *TalkNow* at Temple University (Stormont 2000). Some librarians prefer to cover chat at the reference desk because of convenience of scheduling, proximity to collections, and the built-in backup from other staff. For others, it may be a necessary compromise because a lack of personnel makes it difficult to offer a reference service separately from the reference desk.

Basing a real-time reference service at a reference desk demands answers of certain operational questions. For example, what about the logistics of who actually answers the online questions when librarians are taking questions from the phone, in-house users, and the chat service? Will any staff member be open for a call, or will one be assigned to take chat users? How will the person chatting handle walk-in visitors? How will chat-based questions be handled at desks structured around tiered or differentiated service models, or where librarians are encouraged to rove? What are the priorities in answering in-house, telephone, and chat users? How does it work when librarians from several branches or libraries at different locations are logged on? These are just a few of the questions that may need to be answered in the quest to deliver effective service, which are discussed in Chapter 8 on policies and reference interviewing.

REAL-TIME REFERENCE IN PRACTICE

Let's take a look at some actual practices. At the chat service of the UIUC Libraries, answering responsibilities are distributed to any staff member working at the desk at that time (Kibbee, Ward, and Ma 2002). Normally, at least three librarians and staff members are on duty at any time. The person who is free takes the question from the remote user. Other services designate one person to field online questions, while coworkers focus on in-house users. In other libraries, several librarians may be logged on to take questions simultaneously. At Temple, "staff from several different libraries can log onto *TalkNow* simultaneously," increasing "the odds that when one desk is busy, another has staff available to answer a particular question" (Stormont 2000). The advantage of sharing staffing across several locations is that numerous staff members are logged on, so more librarians are monitoring the question queue, increasing the odds that a librarian will be free for virtual users. This is the most decentralized approach of all. But what happens with this type of organization when an unattractive question is posed. It could be a difficult reference question or a query from a client with a reputation for being challenging. How long does one librarian wait for the others to respond before picking up the chat? It seems to me that unless one staff member is assigned ultimate responsibility for picking up virtual calls within a set length of time, there is a real danger that users would log off before being helped because of the lack of a timely response.

Many libraries experiment with locating the chat librarian(s) at the reference desk but soon move to chatting in offices or other nonreference desk locations. Why? A frequent complaint from librarians trying to do both is that the environment at the reference desk is too boisterous and that "communicating in a virtual environment is labor intensive" (Antonelli and Tarlton 2000). Often during a chat reference transaction, the librarian is jumping between conducting a reference interview, searching in databases to find answers, and sending or pushing information to a user. It is intense, especially when first learning how to communicate in chat. Likewise, it is easy to become distracted and frustrated by interruptions from nearby in-house users or colleagues. SUNY Buffalo moved chat away from the reference desk because librarians found working at the desk was distracting, their software (AOL Instant Messenger) gave inadequate user log-on cues, and there was no way to notify online visitors that librarians were busy if the librarians were away from the desk (Foley 2002). Librarians using call center software seem to have more success in combining services because of inherent features such as automated responses that notify users a librarian will be online shortly and the multitude of alert features to cue librarians.

Perhaps the Lippincott Library of the Wharton School at the University of Pennsylvania has achieved a balance in the debate over whether to chat at the reference desk. Librarians at Lippincott cover some hours at their reference desk but move chat services to a quieter locale during busy hours (Eichler and Halperin 2000). Some libraries may find it productive or necessary to work at the reference desk, but it is likely that working in offices, an off-site services desk or other quiet location helps ensure that virtual users receive the same level of service as in-house users and that in-house users are not frustrated by trying to ask questions of a librarian who is on the computer.

Comments from the Front Lines
Taken from a Thread on the DIG_REF Listserv,
Thursday, November 1, 2001
Subject: Live reference or chat at the reference desk?

At Carnegie Mellon we already have in-person and phone reference at our traditional reference desk. Our reference traffic is heavy enough that our service would really suffer if we tried all three at once. We do try to watch the chat reference as well in a pinch, but it's a bit much.

Matthew R. Marsteller, Physics and Math Librarian
Carnegie Mellon University

I staff the chat reference while serving the public reference [desk]. Most times, both are slow during my time slot. With the live reference beginning to pick up it is becoming more difficult to do both. Most live patrons don't understand that if you are working at a computer you are not available to work with them. (It reminds me of when my daughter was two and would climb on my lap while I was reading.)

Sarah Haman, Mendocino County Library

When we are not busy, it really is no problem servicing all of them at the desk. In fact, I just had a seven-minute dig ref transaction, two in-person patrons (easy questions), and one phone call. Of course, if more than one of the questions becomes too complex, then that's it. Something has to give; usually it's not the in-person patron. We just use our best judgment. Phone patrons are usually happy to let us call them back, but sometimes we have to tell the dig patrons to hang on while we help someone in the library.

Kelly M. Broughton, Reference Coordinator
Jerome Library, Bowling Green State University

We do live reference, telephone reference and email at the reference desk. It sometimes takes a bit of juggling between the telephone and the person in front of you but we always try to answer those who have come into the library first. We sometimes have to take a telephone number and call a patron back, but they are usually very understanding.

Roxann Silbaugh, Rapid City Public Library

GENERAL SERVICE OR SUBJECT EXPERTISE SERVICE

Staffing a virtual reference desk does offer a great deal of flexibility in how librarians are presented to users. You can set up a general help desk or structure it so that users may select a librarian based on subject or expertise. With the generalist approach, all users enter their service through one entry point, and users don't know who will be answering their questions. For example, when users log on to *RefeXpress*, *Ready for Reference*, or the *Q and A Café*, the software connects them to a librarian that happens to be on duty that hour. Other libraries have their log-ons set up so that users select a librarian based on subject expertise or availability. Call center, courseware, web-based IRC, and even MOO software all have the potential to facilitate a subject approach because the service can be structured into "queues," "channels," or "rooms" devoted to a particular subject, where users may go to obtain specialized help. For example, if there is more than one librarian on duty on *RefChat*, at the Gutman Library of the University of Philadelphia, the user can choose from the list of librarians currently online, based on descriptions of librarians' hours and their backgrounds. The listings notify the users as to each librarian's hours. At *KnowItNow 24X7*, users are presented with a variety of subject areas when logging on. If they select the general reference option, they are routed to the main question queue in the software where generalists work with the user. If a *KnowItNow* a user selects "science," her question is either fed to or drawn from the queue by the librarian on duty with the most science expertise. Staffing one way or the other depends on the mission of the service and, in large part, on the way in which traditional reference services are structured.

HOURS

There are three basic factors that come into play when establishing your chat service hours. These factors are the number of personnel and hours of availability, hours of user activity, and the feasibility of extending hours via outsourcing or shared staffing. One limitation that many libraries face in launching a new service is the number of staff and the actual hours that each staff member can devote to chat reference, unless your institution can afford to outsource real-time reference completely to a vendor.

The most important thing to consider in establishing your service is when users are asking questions and are online; this information should have been gathered in the needs assessment prior to your project, as discussed in Chapter 3. The goal is to cover periods of peak user activity, juggling all the staffing variables to provide optimal service to your online users. It may help to identify patterns of high user activity, moderate or low activity, and finally hours where there is little to zero activity. What is meant by a pattern of activity? Activity refers to users 1) e-mailing reference questions, 2) searching library databases or the library web site, and 3) asking questions at the library reference desk. Variations in activity from high to low to zero occur throughout the day and form typical patterns that influence the design of your service. Most of these statistics should be available from your local webmaster or reference services coordinator. Once you identify user patterns, strive to cover, at the very least, hours when usage is high. With luck, you will be able to establish a "core" of chat reference hours that can be satisfied by your new real-time reference team. Figure 5.1 summarizes service hours

Figure 5.1. Summary of service hours by library type.

Public Libraries*		Academic Libraries**	
Weekdays		**Weekdays**	
9 a.m. - Noon	2	9 a.m. - Noon	43
Noon - 5 p.m.	103	Noon - 5 p.m.	59
5 - 9 p.m.	75	5 - 9 p.m.	34
9 p.m. - 1 a.m.	72	9 p.m. - 1 a.m.	6
1 a.m. - 9 a.m.	0	1 a.m. - 9 a.m.	9
Weekends		**Weekends**	
9 a.m. - Noon	0	9 a.m. - Noon	11
Noon - 5 p.m.	3	Noon - 5 p.m.	16
5 - 9 p.m.	72	5 - 9 p.m.	9
9 p.m. - 1 a.m.	72	9 p.m. - 1 a.m.	3
1 a.m. - 9 a.m.	0	1 a.m. - 9 a.m.	2
Libraries open 24/7	66	**Libraries open 24/7**	28
No Posted Hours	14	**No Posted Hours**	0

across library types for libraries listed on the *Index of Chat Reference Services* (Francoeur 2002), as listed June 2002.

What if you can't cover even the highly active hours, given the resources that you have to work with? Start small and work your way up to your goal of complete coverage during regular reference desk hours (Horn 2001). The public library of Logan, Utah, piloted real-time reference in 2001 with one librarian, whereas the *Sunday Night Live* project was open Sunday evenings for a three-month pilot (Hoag and McCaffery Cichanowicz 2001). It's common for libraries to start with service hours as low as ten hours per week, as did the Libraries at Vanderbilt University and to work up progressively to broader hours of service over several semesters or months of operation. *Ask a Librarian Live* at Vanderbilt moved to twenty hours a week after one semester (Porter 2002).

Lack of personnel is a good reason to consider joining a cooperative where you can divide up hours or stay open later through partnerships with libraries in other time zones. If your budget allows, another strategy is to contract with a library vendor to cover problematic hours such as late nights and weekends.

Large libraries or shared services with lots of chat traffic may find it challenging to match staff to the volume of chat questions that come in during certain hours. One option is to use a formula that is popular in business call centers to calculate staffing levels. "Erlang C is a calculation for how many call agents (answerers) you'll need in a call center that has a given number of calls per hour, a given average duration of call, and an acceptable level of delay in answering the call" ("Erlang" 2002). Given the "substantial body of evidence documenting how call centers, whether inbound or outbound, exploit and degrade workers" (Dilevko 2001, 226), it's debatable whether the use of Erlang C is advisable in a nonprofit service setting such as a library. Some libraries are exploring it as an option, as are outside sources such as LSSI. For more about how the formula works, consult "Staffing for the Customer Service Center" (Reynolds 2000). Erlang C is not the only strategy that can be used to set levels of staffing. There are also several web-based calculators such as the online *Workforce Calculator,* maintained by a company called Preferred Solutions, where it's easy to plug in numbers and calculate staffing levels. In addition, there have been many excellent articles written to guide librarians in setting hours for reference services, including a recent one in *RQ* based on the types of questions posed by users in person and via telephone at a college reference desk (Dennison 1999).

REFERENCES

Anderson, Eric, Josh Boyer, and Karen Ciccone. 2000. "Remote Reference Services at the North Carolina State University Libraries." *Facets of Digital Reference*. Paper presented at the Virtual Reference Desk 2nd Annual Digital Reference Conference, 16–17 October, Seattle, WA. Available online at http://www.vrd.org/conferences/VRD2000/proceedings/boyer-anderson-ciccone 12–14.shtml (accessed 16 January 2002).

Antonelli, Monika J., and Martha Tarlton. 2000. "The University of North Texas Libraries' Online Reference Help Desk." *Digital Reference Service in the New Millennium*. New York: Neal-Schuman.

Dennison, Russell F. 1999. "Usage-Based Staffing of the Reference Desk." *Reference and User Services Quarterly* 39 (winter): 158–65.

Dilevko, Juris. 2001. "An Ideological Analysis of Digital Reference Service Models." *Library Trends* 50 (fall): 218–46.

Eichler, Linda, and Michael Halperin. 2000. "LivePerson: Keeping Reference Alive and Clicking." *Econtent* 23: 63–6.

"Erlang." *Whatis?.com*. 2002. Available online at http://searchnetworking .techtarget.com/sDefinition/0,,sid7_gci212073,00.html (accessed 26 July 2002).

Foley, Marianne. 2002. "Instant Messaging Reference in an Academic Library: A Case Study." *College & Research Libraries* 63: 36–45.

Francoeur, Stephen. 2002. "Index of Chat Reference Services." *The Teaching Librarian* (11 March). Available at http://pages.prodigy.net/tabo1/chatlibrary types.htm (accessed 25 April 2002).

Henry, Marcia. 2001. "The Future of the Academic Reference Desk in Virtual Library Services: Responses from University, Public, and Community College Libraries." Paper presented at Internet Librarian Conference 2001, 6 November, Pasadena, CA. Available online at http://library.csun.edu/mhenry/il2001. html (accessed 25 April 2002).

Hoag, Tara J., and Edana McCaffery Cichanowicz. 2001. "Going Prime Time with Live Chat Reference." *Computers in Libraries* 21: 40–4.

Horn, Judy. 2001. "The Future Is Now: Reference Service for the Electronic Era." Paper presented at the Association of College and Research Libraries Tenth National Conference, 5–18 March, Denver, CO. Available online at http://www.ala.org/acrl/papers01/horn.pdf (accessed 21 January 2002).

Jacobs, Sally J. 2001. "[DIG-REF] 24/7 'live person' service." DIG_REF Listserv. Archived online at http://www.vrd.org/Dig_Ref/dig_ref.shtml (accessed 19 May 2001).

Janes, Joseph. 2002. "Digital reference: Reference librarians' experiences and attitudes." *Journal of the American Society for Information Science and Technology* 53: 549–66.

Kibbee, Jo, David Ward, and Wei Ma. 2002. "Virtual Service, Real Data: Results of a Pilot Study." *Reference Services Review* 30(1): 25–36.

Martin, Julie. 2001. "Ask A Librarian Service." Paper presented at the 3rd Annual Virtual Reference Desk Conference, Setting Standards and Making It Real, 12–13 November, Orlando, FL. Available online at http://www.vrd.org/conferences/VRD2001/proceedings/jmartin.shtml (accessed 27 March 2002).

Oder, Norman. 2001. "The Shape of E-Reference." *Library Journal* 1: 46–50.

Parsons, Ann Marie. 2001. "Digital Reference: How Libraries Can Compete with Aska Services." Digital Library Federation (DLF) Newsletter (2 January). Available online at http://www.diglib.org/pubs/news02_01/ (accessed 25 April 2002).

Porter, Katherine. "Re: [DIG_REF] Scheduling Chat Services." DIG_REF Listserv. Archived online at http://www.vrd.org/Dig_Ref/dig_ref.shtml (accessed 1 May 2002).

Reynolds, Penny Cole. 2000. "Staffing for the Customer Service Center." *Center-Force Technologies*. Available online at http://www.cforcetech.com/direct-staffing.htm (accessed 25 April 2002).

Ronan, Jana Smith, and Carol Turner. *Chat Reference* SPEC KIT 273. Washington, D.C.: Association of Research Libraries, 2002.

Sears, JoAnn. 2001. "Chat Reference Service: An Analysis of One Semester's Data." *Issues in Science and Technology Librarianship* 32. Available online at http://www.istl.org/istl/01-fall/article2.html (accessed 11 April 2002).

Sloan, Bernie. 11 July 2001. *Evaluating System Use*. Available online at http://alexia.lis.uiuc.edu/~b-sloan/r4r.final.htm (accessed 19 July 2002).

Stormont, Sam. 2000. "Interactive Reference Project—Assessment After Two Years." Paper presented at *Facets of Digital Reference*, the Virtual Reference Desk 2nd Annual Digital Reference Conference, 16–17 October, Seattle, WA. Available online at http://www.vrd.org/conferences/VRD2000/proceedings/stormont.shtml (accessed 31 Jan. 2002).

WEB SITES CITED

Chat with a Reference Librarian Live, Lippincott Library of the Wharton School, University of Pennsylvania
http://www.library.upenn.edu/lippincott/RefDeskLive/

RefChat, University of Philadelphia
http://www.philau.edu/library/refchat.htm

KnowItNow 24X7, CLEVNET Library Consortium
http://www.cpl.org/vrd/learnmore.html

Ask A Librarian (chat no longer functioning) Logan Library, Logan, Utah
http://www.logan.lib.ut.us/ginfo/askalibrarian.html

Sunday Night Live, Suffolk County Public Libraries, NY
http://www.suffolk.lib.ny.us/snl/

Ask a Librarian Live, Vanderbilt University
http://www.library.vanderbilt.edu/heard/librarian.shtml

Workforce Calculator, Preferred Solutions
http://www.prefsolutions.com/html/calc.htm

6   TRAINING

REAL-TIME REFERENCE COMPETENCIES

There has been a lot of debate on the DIG-REF and the Livereference discussion lists concerning the characteristics or competencies of an effective real-time reference worker. It is a given that knowledge of online reference sources ranging from proprietary databases to search engines is important, but what about education or computer skills? Some librarians feel strongly that only trained professionals possessing a master's of library science or similar level of education should be staffing a library chat service, as is the practice of *Ask a Librarian*, the real-time reference service of the Santa Monica Public Library (Jacobs 2001). Others feel that with training, professional staff and beginning library science students are well suited to take simple questions from chat users, as is the practice of *Ask A Librarian* at the University of Illinois, Urbana–Champaign or *USF Reference Chat* at the University of South Florida. Then some real-time reference services even outsource certain kinds of questions to other Internet information services or are drawing subject specialists outside the field of librarianship to provide information. For example, the CLEVNET Library Consortium's *KnowItNow 24X7* and *Brarydog.net*, a portal for elementary and middle school users of the Public Library of Charlotte and Mecklenburg County, North Carolina, both contract with Tutor.com to deliver real-time homework tutoring (Bryan 2002). In addition, *KnowItNow 24X7* users may pose questions to registered nurses from Cleveland's MetroHealth Line, "a free telephone referral and health information service" (MetroHealth 2002).

Although there is no real consensus about level or focus of education to staff a chat reference service, it is clear that computer skills such as typing and a familiarity with Windows-like systems and multitasking are essential for working as a chat librarian (Fiander 2001). After examining user and librarian behavior over two years of administering a chat reference service, I have reached the following conclusions. Slow typists experience problems engaging users and getting them to stay online long enough to get a full answer to their question. Also, the ability to multitask, or run more than one program or web browser window at a time, is essential and helps the librarian understand the user's behavior. College students and younger users are masters of computing multitasking and typically run multiple web sessions or other programs while surfing the Internet. This means that if a user does not immediately respond to a librarian's question, it may be because he or she is temporarily occupied with another activity. Just as multitasking entertains users while waiting for an answer to a question, it also shortens the amount of time needed to find answers for users. Multitasking also can increase librarian satisfaction with providing chat services. Librarians can attend to other tasks such as reading e-mail or writing reports during slow periods while waiting for calls from users.

Getting staff with experience in chatting is of course desirable, but it's difficult to require this of staff if you hope to recruit from the existing reference desk ranks. Chatting is a relatively recent innovation in the library world. A recent survey distributed to more than 1,500 public and academic librarians reveals that 68.2 percent of 648 librarians that responded have never instant messaged and 65 percent have never even recreationally chatted (Janes 2002). This indicates a lack of experience with real-time communication technology among librarians in the field, although this should change with the current interest in chat reference. Happily, chatting can be learned fairly easily if one can type and is comfortable with computers, but it does require practice and training in online synchronous communication basics.

Some organizations have compiled extensive lists of "staff skills, abilities, and aptitudes that lead to effective virtual reference services" (Ross, n.d.). The Washington State Virtual Reference Project compiled a comprehensive list, illustrated here.

Washington State Virtual Reference Project: Skills for Effective Virtual Reference

1. Ability to derive professional satisfaction from virtual reference transactions
2. Keyboarding proficiency
3. Online communication skills and etiquette, for chat, e-mail, and other online communication
4. Ability to conduct an effective reference transaction in online environments, including the creation and use of prescripted messages
5. Internet searching skills, in particular, the ability to choose the best starting points for online searches
6. Ability to search effectively and demonstrate searching of library databases
7. Ability to assist online users in developing critical thinking skills in locating, using, and evaluating information
8. Ability to effectively conduct a collaborative browsing session with a patron

9. Evaluation of online reference transactions and identification of improvement strategies
10. Multitasking and managing multiple windows; effective use of Windows keyboard commands and shortcuts
11. Technical troubleshooting skills and ability to explain technical problems to information technologies staff to facilitate diagnosis and solution
12. Ability to apply reference transaction policies in an online environment (e.g., time limits, obscene callers, harassment)
13. Commitment to continuous learning and motivation to improve skills in all areas of reference services

> *Washington State Virtual Reference Project,*
> *Mary B. Ross, Training and Development Managing Librarian,*
> *Seattle Public Library. E-mail: mary.ross@spl.org*

As you can see, many of these skills are already part of an accomplished reference librarian's repertoire. Other skills, such as conducting an effective reference transaction online, probably will require training and practice. Another list of competencies is available in *Q and A NJ*'s online librarian's handbook.

STAFF TRAINING

> "Even the most savvy reference librarian needs to learn new skills and develop new habits or behaviors to be successful in the virtual environment—especially when using chat technology or other synchronous communication medium."
>
> *Anne Grodzin Lipow*

Many libraries setting up chat services are working with reference staff whose sole experience with the medium has been shooing teens away from AOL IM or Yahoo! Chat sessions on public-access computers. A good training program will help orient staff to chat-based reference and the potential that the medium holds to reach out to remote users.

No matter how much experience your reference staff has had in online searching in FirstSearch and Google or in using e-mail, most will have difficulties carrying on a conversation via chat. You may find some librarians are anxious at the prospect of using what is to them a foreign computer system to communicate with users. There may be "generational problems" because many "post tenure librarians resist learning new technology" (Oder 2001). Trainers must work to empathize with trainees because this will be a difficult transition for many; trainers need to work at a pace that is slightly challenging yet comfortable for the reference staff. My own experiences as a neophyte are still fresh in my mind. I can remember logging on to MOOs and IRCs a mere five years ago, fumbling to remember commands to talk to people or to move to a new room, but mostly "lurking" because I didn't understand how to behave or what was expected of me in a virtual environment. Many of my coworkers expressed similar feelings while they were learning how to communicate in real time in our chat service. It seems surreal at first. More than one colleague has said to me after working with his or her first online clients, "I wasn't sure it was a real user. But I went ahead and answered their question anyway." It is important to realize that these are normal responses and will pass with time and practice.

Worth noting is the fact that librarians with recreational experience in IRCs or instant messaging naturally caught on faster to the medium but still had issues with reference interview techniques in chat. The main issue in training is not learning the bells and whistles of fancy software packages or how to chat, but teaching librarians and library professionals to transfer the techniques taught in library school to communication in real time.

Skills

How does one start when setting up a training program for real-time reference? Identifying skill sets that your staff will need to provide real-time reference is a logical place to begin. You could conduct a formal assessment of each staff member, but it's safe to say at this early point in the development of real-time reference that most reference staff need at least some help in learning how to use your chat software to communicate with users, followed by computer literacy skills and online reference sources. The ability to multitask is vital, because many call center or web-based chat software programs are based on the concept of multiple concurrent web sessions. It is also helpful to be able to jump between your chat program and a session in a database such as your catalog or a periodical index while working with users. Although most librarians and staff should have mastered multitasking at the reference desk, don't assume that they have or that the skills will be easily transferred to an environment where almost every keystroke is a communication.

Besides computer skills, staff must also learn how to apply traditional reference skills in the online environment. What are these skills? In the popular library school textbook *Reference and Information Services,* Woodard (2001) suggests that "reference interview techniques," "knowledge of information sources," ability to manipulate online information, teamwork, and "sharing knowledge in a constructive way" are the skills most needed at the information or reference desk. These abilities translate into the chat environment as the ability to conduct an effective reference interview in real time without nonverbal or auditory cues; knowledge of the library's or organization's reference infrastructure, including subject guides to the Internet and core proprietary databases; learning how to deliver answers to users online and handle questions demanding answers that are not possible or practical to deliver in chat; and finally, learning to function as a team with other library public service points. One mistake that many beginning real-time reference librarians make is thinking that every query must be answered as rapidly as possible, with answers being delivered online. Not every user wants an answer in five minutes or less; *RefeXpress* sessions average eight to ten minutes. Even if one wants an immediate online resolution, it may be unreasonable to attempt to fulfill this desire. New chat librarians tend to forget in the heat of the moment that they can follow-up a question via e-mail, that they may need to refer certain questions, and that sometimes answers are only to be found in the print collection. Training and practice in these skills are crucial to a successful service.

If some of your staff are drawn from the ranks of subject specialists or branch libraries with a focused collection, these librarians and support staff may need training in general reference resources as well as databases and information sources outside their area. As University of Florida science librarian Pam Cenzer puts it, "Chat services require generalist skills" (personal communication, 2002). In a strictly physically oriented reference service, some filtering of questions happens by the way in which the local library system is structured. A small public library in one building with one reference desk will receive all kinds of questions, across a variety of subjects from business to readers advisory. But in larger systems, often the physical layout of the library itself helps to steer users to the appropriate reference service point. For example, the central library of the Chicago Public Library (CPL) system, the Harold Washington Library Center, is an enormous, nine-story edifice with each floor devoted to particular subject areas. People can ask questions at the first floor information desk, but chances are that if their question is complex, they will be referred to another department and a librarian who specializes in the area. Patrons can also go directly to a subject collection for assistance. A user with a business-related question can look at the CPL directory, locate the floor with the business collection, and go there (or telephone) with the query. University libraries often have branch libraries devoted to a subject area, geographically located close to the academic department being served. In this case, location is a strong filtering device. At the University of Florida, we have separate branches for science, education, journalism, music, and so forth. Librarians and staff in these locations get some general questions, but most reference queries are focused in the subject discipline.

Staff members used to working in specialized environments may be challenged when joining a chat service where anyone with an Internet account or a library card is a customer. Because subject specialists can expect to get a much broader range of questions working in a real-time reference service, they may need special preparation. General reference workshops or generalist-led updates covering heavily used reference tools such as encyclopedias and directories, search engines, and general periodical indexes are useful.

Duration and Depth of Training

When establishing a timeline for training for a new service such as chat, there's a need for intensive training at start-up, followed by a more relaxed, ongoing training program to hone chat, reference, and research skills.

Jump-Start Training

Let's start with the intensive training to launch the service. No matter what the skill or experience level of your staff, trainees will need to learn the specifics of the software, such as how to log on, to push a page, and so forth. In addition, it may be many of your trainees' first experience with using instant messaging or text-based chat. It's important to provide hands-on training in groups for this first part of training so that staff can practice chatting themselves and exploring the basic software features. The logistics of this will be defined by the number of people staffing your service, the training facilities, and the number of librarians who are licensed to simultaneously log on to your service.

When limited to a certain number of log-ons, one rule of thumb is that you can train twice as many people as the number of seats by using role-playing. With role-playing, staff pair off, and one plays the librarian while the other pretends to be a user. Not only do you double the number of people you can have in a training session, but librarians learn what the experience is like for users, which strengthens their reference skills. If you use external trainers from your vendor, the company usually bumps up the log-ons to accommodate anyone who wants to attend. In addition, some vendors may be willing to temporarily lend more connections to libraries doing their own start-up training. If this is not the case and your institution has only one or two seats or accounts and limited training facilities, it also works to repeat the initial orientation sessions several times. Working with smaller groups can be more effective because the trainer can spend more time with individuals, and attendees may feel more free to contribute to the discussion. In addition, your local head of reference or coordinator may also find it easier to cover the reference desk and phones while staff are training if the sessions are staggered.

External Trainers

Some vendors such as LSSI or divine offer online remote training through the software package itself. Vendor training is a good option to start your staff chatting; many companies offer "jump-start" training as part of the software contract to get services up and running quickly. Do keep in mind that trainers for *QuestionPoint* and LSSI *VRT* offer some coverage of chat reference techniques along with software basics, whereas nonlibrary vendors such as *eGain* or *LiveAssistance* cater to e-commerce applications of synchronous technology. It is difficult to find outside trainers for the more basic types of chat software. Unless you are working with a friendly IRC or MOO coordinator such as at *Diversity University*, there aren't many opportunities. If you are using MOO software, the *Connections* MOO holds an excellent online workshop, where educators volunteer their time to teach new users how to build rooms and describe the virtual environment, as well as to build interactive objects such as bots or message boards that talk or display information.

Do It Yourself Jump-Start Training

Here are some tips for starting a local training program. When designing your training, it's best to first address basic computer proficiencies such as the interface and commands of your real-time reference software to build a solid foundation for training in higher-level interpersonal and information seeking skills. In addition, starting with the chat software will also defuse anxiety for first-time chatters. Try to make learning the software fun, and concentrate on the bare basics the first session or two. Concentrating on the most basic commands is especially important if you are using complex software such as call center software. Start librarians with simple tasks such as logging on, accepting a session with a user, chatting, and logging off. Scaffold, or build on, these rudimentary commands in later training, teaching staff members to push pages, use canned responses, and so on. In our training at the University of Florida, we established a "hierarchy of skills" to share with trainees, in which we listed the most important skills to master, followed by more advanced skills. Providing staff members with a hierarchy, or list of tasks to master, accomplishes two vital educational objectives. First, the chat reference staff has a concrete list to take away from the training and to master. Second, and of equal importance, a list demystifies the process of learning chatting and complex software for those who tend to be anxious by breaking down the learning into discrete manageable steps. These skills are listed in order of difficulty, starting with the most crucial skills and ending with advanced tasks such as escorting a user during a search.

Hierarchy of Skills: Test Your Skills with These Tasks

1. Logging on, and logging off
2. Accepting a call from a user
3. Converse with a user using the chat feature until you feel comfortable chatting
4. Acquaint yourself with the software's built-in browser (if it has one), finding the home button, the back and forward buttons, and the location box to input a URL
5. Multitask
   a. Open a Web browser (separate from your real-time reference software)
   b. Practice switching back and forth between the browser and the real-time reference software
6. Send the user a preprogrammed response
7. Send the user a bookmarked Web page from the real-time reference software's internal browser
8. Push a web page to a user
9. Transfer a user to another librarian
10. Message another librarian using back-channeling or the instant message feature
11. Cut and paste text or URLs into the real-time reference software's chat, then cut and paste information from a chat conversation into a database or search engine (to search)
12. Escorting
    a. Escort a user through a Web search
    b. Follow a user through a search in a database or on the Web

In the first training sessions, we concentrated on the first four objectives, and then built upon these in later sessions. As you can see from the hierarchy, the most rudimentary skills are logging in, chatting with someone, and logging off. From there, one learns to navigate databases, to push or transmit pages or files to the user depending upon the software that you are using, and so on. I recommend from experience that you supply as much hands-on training as is possible. Consider following up the training by supplying staff members with tools to evaluate their performance. The Q and A NJ online manual (New Jersey Library Network 2002) supplies their virtual librarians with a reference session evaluation checklist, to help them gauge their progress in learning to communicate online (Figure 6.1). Some points address software and navigational skills.

If your library is hosting real-time reference through LSSI *VRT*, the service's training manual, *Establishing a Virtual Reference Service* (Lipow and Coffman 2001), takes librarians through a guided tour of the software, feature by feature. Librarians not using *VRT* may wish to consult the manual as a model for establishing their own local training, or consult Anne Lipow's (2002) new book, *The Virtual Reference Librarian's Handbook*. The *Handbook* provides many engaging training activities for new real-time reference staff.

Ongoing Training

Once you have completed the basic training on the chat software, it is time to plan sessions on reference interviewing and online information resources. Chapter 7 is devoted to the subject of the online reference interview, including strategies for teamwork across reference services. Sessions are also needed to practice software commands or skills that might not be used every day, because newly learned skills tend to atrophy if not put into immediate use. For example, many of our librarians may not have had the opportunity to transfer a user to a second librarian during a semester and have forgotten how the command works in the *RefeXpress* software. A refresher helps to remedy this.

One truth concerning virtual reference is that "librarians must be trained (and retrained) to cope with this fast-changing field" (Oder 2001, 47). Chat librarians need to be kept abreast of new authentication procedures, changes in online library services such as interlibrary loan or document delivery, as well as new databases or changes in interfaces. Happily, this is an area in which training for chat dovetails with continuing reference desk training.

TRAINING EXERCISES

I'd like to share some exercises that I have found helpful in training coworkers to chat. You will notice that these exercises focus on easing trainees into online communication in real time through demonstration and play. Remember that this training session may be the first experience some of your staff has with chat. Make the first encounter as pleasant as possible to demystify the technology and create a positive tone that can be expanded on in later training.

Figure 6.1. Q and A NJ evaluation checklist.

 Library Info | Reference | Support | Service Guidelines | Schedule | Staff | News | Login

Reference Session Evaluation Checklist

			Software/Technical
Yes	No	N/A	
			The librarian sent a web page and not just a URL
			The librarian sent what she/he announced
			The librarian successfully sent files or screenshots
			The librarian successfully used proprietary databases
			Research/Search Skills
Yes	No	N/A	
			The resource or item sent answered or partly answered the question
			The librarian sufficiently evaluated the item before sending it
			The librarian checked if the resource (e.g., a web site's search facility, links, etc.) was functional before sending it
			Appropriate resources were used in answering this question
			A Resolution Code was properly assigned
			Communication and Model Reference Behavior
Yes	No	N/A	
			The librarian used open-ended probing questions to elicit the customer's specific question
			The librarian maintained a steady dialog with the customer
			The librarian kept the customer informed of her/his activities
			The librarian communicated what next steps were expected of the customer
			The librarian made appropriate use of scripted messages
			The librarian informed the customer before sending an item
			The librarian explained to the customer what she/he sent
			The librarian provided instruction in the resource sent, if needed
			The librarian explained where to find the answer in the item sent
			The librarian appropriately referred the call
			The librarian appropriately took responsibility for getting back to the customer.
			The librarian asked the customer if she/he has completely answered the question
			It was clear from the customer's point of view that the librarian was ending the session

Show and Tell

This exercise begins with a demonstration of a chat session from the users' perspective and is followed by a second brief demonstration as viewed by the librarian. This means that at least two trainers are needed, so that one trainer represents the librarian and the other portrays the user during a demonstration. Select a common reference question that is easy to answer online. Using the question, demonstrate a complete but simple reference encounter. Project the session as the user experiences it, on a screen for the whole class to see. The trainer playing the librarian should be sure to interview the "user" to give attendees an opportunity to observe a real chat in action.

After the first demonstration, show a chat session with a new question, projecting the librarian's perspective. Try to get feedback from the audience about how to answer the question. Once again, have the trainer who is posing as a user ask a question that can be answered rather easily from an online source. Use one of those ubiquitous questions from real reference desk experience to loosen up the audience and generate some laughs. Another technique to create a playful, lighthearted mood is to have the second trainer log on using a famous personality's name and ask a question in character. For example, in December 2000 and in early 2001, it was possible to evoke laughs from audiences by logging on as "Al Gore," "George W. Bush," or "Ralph Nader" and then asking for presidential election results.

Explore Some Commercial Web Centers

If you are training librarians and staff that have never chatted before, a fun way to introduce them to the medium is to ask them to go to commercial web sites and chat with customer service representatives. Pair up the librarians, give them a list of web sites outfitted with live help that appeal to a variety of interests (such as fashion, sports) and ask each team to initiate a chat. Try to team up fast typists with slower ones. Having staff work in teams is an effective teaching technique for learning chat. Research indicates that this type of pairing when learning a new form of synchronous communication appears to "decrease the cognitive load created by having to pay simultaneous attention to content and a new technological process" (Murphy and Collins, 1997). Watch the tension drain from the training room as attendees start having fun chatting with customer representatives about a new dress in stock or next year's automobile models. After ten or fifteen minutes, ask each team to report back on their experiences to the rest of the class, and even critique each other's communication skills.

Role-Playing

This activity designed for use in a computer classroom is good to help new chatters explore the characteristics and limitations of online communication in real time. It accommodates twice the number of trainees as there are simultaneous accounts for logging on to your chat service (you may also be able to get the number of accounts expanded temporarily). Incidentally, role-playing exercises work best when the attendees have at least a rudimentary understanding of how the chat reference system works. Trainers should model how the system works as a user and as a librarian if there are any neophytes in the group. The "show-and-tell" activity is a good prelude to a role-playing session. Divide attendees into two groups and explain to them that they will be role-playing. Half the group on one side of the room will pretend to be library users, while the other half of the group will play librarians. Try to separate the "users" from the "librarians" so that the participants will be forced to rely exclusively on the textual chat to communicate. Ask the "users" to pose a typical but fairly easy reference question to one of the "librarians."

When facilitating a role-playing exercise, schedule enough trainers to be able to rove around the room and answer individual questions. Trainees will typically exhibit some initial frustration as well as amusement as they struggle to chat with each other. Even groups of six new trainees will keep two trainers busy answering questions and pointing out system features. It is important that participants experience each perspective, so after approximately fifteen to twenty minutes, ask the class to log off and then switch roles. Role-playing is useful because it forces staff to communicate online in a supportive atmosphere with a support group of peers, where they can peek at another person's screen to get ideas for what to do next if they are stuck or ask questions. It also generates discussion among staff about how chatting with a user is different from face-to-face or telephone communication, paving the way for exploration of the online reference interview.

Buddy System

Another useful exercise pairs up librarians and staff to work together as teams, in a formal, hands-on training session and for self-guided instruction or support. You can ask staff to choose a buddy with whom to practice, although the trainer should be prepared to assign participants to work in pairs. Ask the buddies to role-play during the in-class training session but to also practice with each other online as they start to cover actual reference shifts. Ask each team to work through the hierarchy of skills (customized for your chat software) starting with the most basic skills and moving to the most advanced skills.

The buddy system also bestows confidence on librarians as they start to work with actual users. Before my colleague Mimi Pappas and I realized that pairing up staff members was an effective strategy, we noticed that many of the *RefeXpress* staff gravitated toward working in pairs or even in threes at a computer during the first few online shifts they worked. Certain call center software such as divine's *VRD* and IRC-based chat allows librarians to work in teams online, sharing a session with another librarian and user. More familiar technology can be employed in the buddy system as well. For example, many *RefeXpress* staffers use the phone to consult with their buddies if they need help with a question or a software feature, or even e-mail. Working with a "buddy" is a natural and comfortable way for some people to learn new skills and techniques.

ONLINE MENTORING

One of the most effective ways a chat reference coordinator can help train staff is to work with them one-on-one while they are online. This training is time-consuming at first but has large payoffs in terms of increased staff proficiency and confidence after two or three hours of training. Here are some training suggestions to employ when mentoring online.

Safety Net

Notify staff members that you will be online and working with them during their first shifts, and get their permission. Most staffers are only too happy to have an experienced person online as they start. It is important to ask for permission, because the aim is to serve as a resource, not a critic hovering and observing their fledgling attempts at chatting. Two basic activities are simulating a user to give the trainee some practice and feedback and assisting the trainee in answering an actual call. During slow periods, role-play. To simulate a question, log on to the real-time reference service as a user does and ask questions that lead the trainee through using various software features or databases. It's useful to base questions on problem areas for the trainee or from a review of service transcripts.

Coaching

Another way to mentor the trainee online is simply to lurk until an actual user logs on and asks a question. Lurking is an online activity in which one connects to a real-time environment and observes the proceedings without posting any comments. Lurking is possible in software that supports groups of chatters or session sharing in which two or more librarians can work with one user. Although call center software, courseware, and IRC supports groups and sharing, lurking is not an option supported by instant messaging or some types of chat software. This teaching technique allows the trainer to coach or take over the session with the user, modeling skills as needed. Coaching involves monitoring a trainee's session with a user, and giving private feedback as needed.

Another option for coaching is private messaging. Many software packages enable private messaging between librarians while online. Sophisticated software such as LSSI VRT (eGain Live), and divine VRD have a built-in instant messaging feature that is independent of the chat feature for working with users. For libraries using instant messaging for chatting with users, trainers can initiate a second IM session with the trainee to give instructions on working with the user. This support strategy is best for confident staff members with good computer skills. When coaching a new staff member, do be sensitive to his or her grasp of chat skills; maintaining an independent IM session with you while working with a user may be too difficult a level of multitasking for some people. Using the buddy system may be a better alternative for less confident chat reference staff.

If your library is using one of the more basic software programs such as web-based IRC or MOO, the trainer will have to use back channeling such as "whispering" or "xxirc" to talk to the trainer. Back channeling is holding a private conversation outside the main chat forum. Most staff will require some classroom training to master back-channeling communication. This is an important point concerning coaching: regardless of the coaching strategy used to support staff members while they are online, be sure to practice with them in a training setting before assisting them while live.

CONTINUING TRAINING

The last part of preparing a training program to get your real-time reference service up and running is to plan for continuing education. Once your institution has completed the initial training program for all staff, you will need to develop strategies for training new librarians as they join the service, as well as refresher sessions where existing staff members can hone their skills. You may wish to offer regularly scheduled workshops at convenient times during the year, such as once a month on Fridays (when it is slow in the library) or at the beginning of the semester in an academic setting. Trainers may also opt to hold classes on demand, as new personnel join their service or challenges arise. These challenges may present themselves in the form of new databases that need to be mastered or skills that need work. Although in actual operation, real-time reference coordinators will doubtlessly identify areas in which librarians need more practice. Sometimes this becomes apparent while examining session transcripts or through similar requests for assistance in a task from staff. At the University of Florida, we have discovered that it's easy to forget how to use some less intuitive software features during slow periods when there aren't many users. Because of this, we hold periodic refreshers on basic commands such as transferring users to another librarian. These continuing training opportunities also allow staff to share experiences and to voice common problems that librarians and support staff were reluctant to report individually. Training personnel to provide reference assistance online is truly an ongoing task.

REFERENCES

Bryan, Robin. 2002. "Brarydog.net: A Homework Assistance Portal for Students." *Public Libraries* (April): 101–3.

Fiander, Michelle. 2001. "Re: [DIG_REF] Pre-employment Testing." DIG_REF. Listserv (15 December). Archived online at http://www.vrd.org/Dig_Ref/dig_ref.shtml (accessed 16 December 2001).

Jacobs, Sally J. 18 May 2001. "[DIG-REF] 24/7 'Live Person' Service." DIG_REF Listserv (18 May). Archived online at http://www.vrd.org/Dig_Ref/dig_ref.shtml (accessed 19 May 2001).

Janes, Joseph. 2002. "Digital Reference: Reference Librarians' Experiences and Attitudes." *Journal of the American Society for Information Science and Technology* 53 (March): 549–66.

Lipow, Anne Grodzins. 2002. *The Virtual Reference Librarian's Handbook*. New York: Neal-Schuman, forthcoming.

Lipow, Anne Grodzins, and Steve Coffman. 2001. *Establishing a Virtual Reference Service: VRD Training Manual*. Berkeley, CA: Library Solutions Press.

MetroHealth Online Tour. 2002. *The MetroHealth System* (Cleveland, Ohio). Available online at http://www.metrohealth.org/tour/page12.asp (accessed 24 Apr. 2002).

Murphy, Karen L., and Mauri P. Collins. 1997. "Development of Communication Conventions in Instructional Electronic Chats." Paper presented at the Annual Convention of the American Education Research Association, March 24–28, Chicago, IL. Available online at http://disted.tamu.edu/aera97a.htm (accessed 9 Nov. 2001).

New Jersey Library Network. Q and A NJ. 21 May 2002. *Librarian's Online Manual*. Available online at http://www.qandanj.org/mANUAL/ (accessed 29 May 2002).

Oder, Norman. 2001. "The Shape of E-Reference." *Library Journal* (February 1, 2001): 46–50.

Ross, Mary. n.d. "Skills for Effective Virtual Reference." Washington State Virtual Reference Project. Available online at http://libweb.uoregon.edu/orbis/staff home/vrtf-skills.htm (accessed 2 Aug. 2002).

Woodard, Beth S. 2001. "Reference Service Improvement: Staff Orientation, Training and Continuing Education." *Reference and Information Services*, pp. 210–44. Englewood, CO: Libraries Unlimited.

WEB SITES CITED

Ask A Librarian, Santa Monica Public Library
http://www.smpl.org/library/

Ask A Librarian, University of Illinois, Champaign-Urbana
http://www.library.uiuc.edu/ugl/vr/

Brarydog.net, Public Library of Charlotte and Mecklenburg County, NC
http://brarydog.net/

Connections MOO
http://web.nwe.ufl.edu/~tari/mooshop

Diversity University
http://www.du.org/

eGain
http://www.egain.com/

KnowItNow 24X7, CLEVNET Library Consortium
http://www.knowitnow24x7.net/

LiveAssistance
http://www.liveassistance.com/solutions.html

QuestionPoint Collaborative Reference Service, Library of Congress and OCLC
http://www.questionpoint.org

RefeXpress, University of Florida
http://refexpress.uflib.ufl.edu

Tutor.com
http://www.tutor.com/

USF Virtual Reference Chat, University of South Florida
http://www.lib.usf.edu/virtual/services/index.html

Virtual Reference Desk (VRD), Divine
http://www.divine.com/vrd

Virtual Reference Services (VRS), Library Systems and Services, L.L.C. (LSSI)
http://www.lssi.com/

7 EVERYDAY ADMINISTRATION OF A REAL-TIME REFERENCE SERVICE

To understand some of the issues in administering a real-time reference service, it's helpful to examine the structure and roles of each person involved in the service, from the user up to the administrator. Michael McClennan and Patricia Memmott (2001, 143) of the Internet Public Library provide a useful outline in their article "Roles in Digital Reference."

> Many of the decisions that go into building a digital reference service are ones with which librarians are already familiar: developing an efficient staffing schedule, offering a tiered versus non-tiered service, setting up a system for keeping usage statistics, and so on. Librarians, in particular, have developed a great deal of expertise over the years in creating reference service models that match the available resources and the needs of their community. Making the transition to the digital environment involves building on this expertise, while at the same time keeping in mind that the new environment imposes radically different conditions and raises important new questions.

Although McClennan and Memmott are talking primarily about e-mail reference, these functions also fit real-time reference.

McClennan and Memmott identify five roles of participants in virtual reference: the patron who asks the question; the filterer who weeds, answering repetitive and ready reference questions; the answerer or reference librarian; the administrator who tends to daily operations; and the coordinator who oversees the entire operation. Depending on the size and complexity of the operation, sometimes the function of filterer and answerer are blended, as are the roles of administrator and coordinator. In small libraries or systems, or in settings where librarians are implementing basic software such as instant messaging or hosted web-based chat, the administrative and coordinator functions may be taken care of by one librarian, while in a larger environment such as a consortium or in a library using complex software, these responsibilities may be divided among several people. At the University of Florida where we use complex call center software, administrative responsibilities are divided among a computer systems coordinator who takes care of any software, server, or networking issues; a service coordinator, an assistant service coordinator; and a planning team made up of librarians from various units. The software we use is divine's *NetAgent*, now marketed as *Virtual Reference Desk (VRD)*. The interactive reference planning team sets policy and procedures and advises on training, hours of service, publicity, and future plans, whereas the two service coordinators manage the day-to-day operations of the service, maintain the chat web site, provide statistical reports, and perform other routine duties. At the *Q and A NJ* project (New Jersey Library Network 2002), a real-time reference cooperative also using call center software hosted by the LSSI *Virtual Reference Toolkit (VRT)*, a central project manager works with project managers at member libraries to plan and coordinate services, supported by another level of administration at the LSSI.

What does administrating a chat service involve? For services run locally, as at the University of Florida, there are technical issues such as maintaining hardware, software, networking and a web site. The staffing issues involve recruiting or hiring, scheduling, planning, training, and facilitating development of policies and procedures. Many libraries outsource the technical demands by subscribing to hosted systems such as *24/7 Reference*, *VRD*, or *QuestionPoint*. Unless the service is entirely outsourced, however, including the answering of questions, there will still be things to coordinate locally. You still have to make sure all staff has access to computers and the right software and attend to personnel issues. I've found that to keep a real-time reference service running smoothly, it's wise to heed certain duties as listed in the following section. There are details that need attention on a daily basis, whereas some duties need to be addressed less frequently. In some organizations, one person may take care of all of these responsibilities in addition to software and hardware issues; in others, these duties may be split up among two or more positions.

DAILY ROUTINES

- Check to see that the service is accepting calls.
- Check to see that the service is closed at the end of day (unless it operates twenty-four hours a day, seven days a week).
- Check to see that the automated greeting feature is working.
- Troubleshoot personnel problems (such as forgetting a shift, tardiness, difficulty logging on).
- Assist staff with difficult reference questions or software features.
- Monitor chat e-mail, listserv, or telephone for staff reports of trouble.
- Monitor the system for downtime and inform staff.
- Forward trouble reports to library systems staff or vendor.

DUTIES AND ROUTINES PERFORMED MONTHLY OR AS NEEDED

- Run, analyze, and share usage statistics.
- Compile, analyze, and share evaluative feedback from users with staff and planning team.
- Follow-up trouble reports forwarded to vendor or library systems to see that technical problem has been resolved.
- Create and maintain chat web site.
- Update service hours as needed (for holidays, special events).
- Customize librarian interface (add preprogrammed greetings, files, web pages).
- Customize user interface.
- Troubleshoot network outages and other problems.
- Negotiate with vendor or library systems to fix minor technical issues or glitches.
- Create, revise, and distribute policy and procedures as needed.
- Create, revise, and distribute an online chat reference handbook.

Because many of the more technical duties are specific to the type of online real-time software being used, I concentrate here on the more general issue of coordinating staff to provide chat reference services.

PERSONNEL AND SCHEDULING

Managing personnel is an ongoing task. One issue is supervisory responsibility. In some organizations, the project coordinator may directly supervise staff working in the real-time reference service, but in other settings, the coordinator's relationship with librarians or professional assistants may be less direct. In settings where chat duties are combined with reference desk responsibilities, the person who supervises staff performance at the reference desk will also be monitoring their progress in providing reference assistance via chat. In services where staff is recruited from a variety of departments or separate libraries, the role of the coordinator may be to simply train, schedule, and monitor the chat service to make sure that it is covered during open hours, without any supervisory responsibilities. For example, in a distributed service in which large libraries or groups of libraries are cooperating to provide a service, individual libraries may be assigned specific desk hours on certain days and a local coordinator manages scheduling for that time period. This is how *Q and A NJ,* the real-time reference service of the New Jersey Library Network (2002), is administered. Figure 7.1 illustrates the myriad of ways staffing can be approached in a single library or in a cooperative venture.

The flow chart pictured in Figure 7.1 illustrates the ways in which a supervisor of a single library's chat service or a consortium's service can manage personnel. The choices for either setting are essentially the same: to staff the service entirely with the institution's own librarians; to schedule some hours locally and outsource some to a consortium, a vendor, or freelancers; or to outsource the service entirely to a consortia, a vendor, or freelancers. If you follow the chart from the single

Figure 7.1. Staffing possibilities for real-time reference.

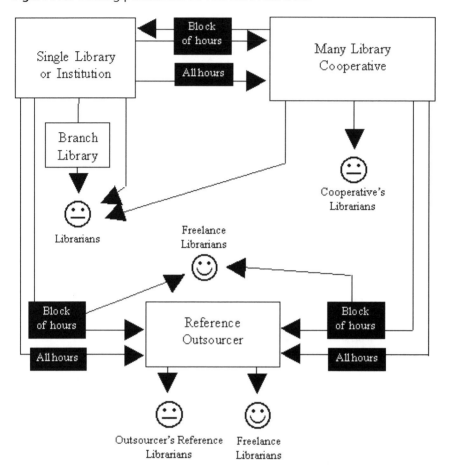

library or institution at the top left, the chart presents the choices for staffing; the process for a consortium is pictured at the right. In a consortium, the real-time reference coordinator could directly schedule each librarian from each member institution, use personnel hired at the consortia level, ask member libraries to commit to blocks of hours and handle the scheduling locally (a common practice), outsource some or all coverage out to a freelancing vendor such as LSSI, or hire independent contractors, as is practiced at the Suffolk Country Library System (Hoag and Cichanowicz 2001). Many consortia use a combination of these techniques, as do *Q and A NJ* and *24/7 Reference*. In a single library or institution, a real-time reference coordinator could be assigned the responsibility to schedule each staff member. Another option is to ask the head of reference or heads of branch libraries or collections to manage parts of the schedule. A recent survey of academic libraries indicated that this is the most prevalent mode in this type of library setting (Ronan and Turner 2002). The library or organization may also decide to outsource some or even all chat service hours to a library network or consortium or to a vendor.

Regardless of whether a central coordinator or a local coordinator has supervisory responsibility over staff working in the real-time reference service, each type of coordinator will be performing certain functions with staff to keep the service operating smoothly. A listing of these concerns follows.

Personnel
- Schedule staff.
- Coordinate scheduling with other reference units (to avoid conflicts).
- Make special schedule for holidays, special events.
- Manage staff absences and tardiness.
- Facilitate shift trades.
- Plan and implement training (ongoing and for new staff).
- Provide evaluative feedback (computer skills, reference performance).
- Facilitate interstaff communication through meetings, workshops, online communication, and so forth.

Q and A NJ is a good model of the many ways in which a distributed service can be managed through a well-designed web site. Much of the coordination for the service is facilitated electronically through an online manual, which aids the central project manager in working with local project managers and staff at member libraries. Central Project Manager Marianne Sweet (personal communication, April 30, 2002) assures me, however, that she still makes lots of site visits to train and work with the 200 odd staff that provide real-time reference assistance. The *Q and A NJ Librarian's Online Manual* includes scheduling guidelines and tools, training tips, policies and procedures, competency checklists, and many other valuable staff tools.

Tips for Scheduling a Real-Time Reference Service

Establishing a schedule for a new service is a time-consuming process. The first schedule is the hardest to set, but once a template or pattern is established, it becomes much easier. The duration of the schedule will vary depending on your institution. A perfunctory examination of public library chat services revealed that schedules do not vary much from month to month, save during the holidays or summer when staff are on vacation. This may also be the case with special libraries. For libraries serving a school, college, or university environment, hours of service are often tied to the academic calendar, which means that the schedules vary from semester to semester. Virtual reference services even may be suspended during intersessions as students and faculty take a break from classes or go on vacation. A survey of Assocation of Research Libraries revealed that most reduce or eliminate service hours during such periods (Ronan and Turner 2002).

The first attempt at scheduling may involve negotiation between local librarians and support staff at member libraries, supervisors, and schedulers coordinating other public service operations, depending on the size of the organization. Allow plenty of time to accommodate this communication. If you have never set up a service schedule before, it's a good idea to consult with the person who manages your local reference desk schedule for ideas on how to approach it. This also helps to lay the groundwork for coordination between schedule keepers, because you will likely both be scheduling and even competing for time from the same personnel. Also, if you are not directly supervising the staff members who you are scheduling, it's a good idea to work with local supervisors to keep them in the loop and get scheduling support.

It often takes time to iron out problems in a permanent schedule (especially when scheduling large numbers of people). It's a good idea to start off with a short-term schedule for a couple of weeks or a month until the permanent schedule gels. The coordinator(s) need to be prepared to cover vacant slots and troubleshoot until an equilibrium is established. I recommend recruiting volunteers to cover problematic hours and that coordinators clear their personal calendar. Coordinators of services that are hosted have an additional option: talk to your vendor about arranging temporary coverage from the vendor's reference center to cover unexpected demand or gaps.

Despite your best efforts, busy librarians or professional staff may forget shifts as they get used to working in real time. After all, there aren't any visual cues—such as a reference desk—to jog the memory. Although the coordinator will want to be on hand to resolve staffing problems when launching and testing the service, it's a good idea to set up a procedure for personnel to handle this independently among themselves. The procedure would give strategies for smooth shift transitions, such as requiring the person who is to be relieved to telephone or e-mail a reminder to the librarian assigned to the next shift. Even the best system is not foolproof, however. Until the service and schedule settles into accepted routine, the coordinator should be prepared to remind staff gently about upcoming shifts with e-mails or even phone calls and call on backup support as necessary.

Scheduling in Action

Scheduling at a Single Library So how do different libraries approach the task of scheduling? One way is to simply merge the virtual reference schedule with the one for the reference desk, as is the practice at the North Carolina State University (NCSU) Libraries. Not only does this reduce the number of schedules for the reference staff to monitor, but also a combined schedule encourages better coordination of reference desk shifts and real-time reference shifts, especially if desk and online duties are seen as separate. Amy VanScoy, Assistant Department Head of Research and Information Services at the NCSU Libraries, handles scheduling for their off-site services desk (OSS) in this way:

I create a schedule at the beginning of each semester that assigns one to three staff for the Desk and one staff (with perhaps a backup) for "OSS." On the printed schedule, an asterisk designates that staff member for the OSS. This responsibility is like the Desk. The hour has to be covered if a staff member is sick, and the staff member has to trade it if he/she has a conflict. All reference staff spend some time in OSS although I take into account their preferences—some like more OSS hours than Desk, others prefer the in-person contact. I prefer to schedule staff in two-hour blocks. The pace is very hectic in OSS, but each staff member must log into the chat and email software, so the two-hour blocks just make things run a little more smoothly. I deal with unpopular hours for OSS the same way as I do for the Desk. Everyone gets some unpopular hours during the week. (personal communication, 2002)

When working with personnel who will be juggling real-time and reference desk duties, shift transitions will be easier if librarians are not scheduled for back-to-back reference desk and chat reference shifts. If a librarian gets involved with a user at the reference desk at the end of the shift, as often happens, she or he may be delayed in logging on for the chat shift. The same scenario is possible for staff members working with online users. This may not be a problem if the chat is paired at the same reference desk with traditional or phone service; other staff members can see what is going on and either wait or ask another colleague to take over until the librarian in question is free. If chat personnel are working from different physical locations, such as another branch library in the city or a department on another floor, the librarian looking to be relieved after two hours of duty online may have no idea why a colleague is late. Back-to-back scheduling may also affect the quality of the reference encounter if the librarian feels pressured to break off the encounter with a user so as not to inconvenience a colleague waiting to be relieved at the reference desk.

Scheduling across Branches or Libraries A combined desk and chat schedule may work for a small or one library operation, but what about larger libraries staffing across branches such as at the University of Florida, or sharing a service with other libraries in a cooperative such as *Q and A NJ*? You can either develop a master schedule working individually with each librarian or staff member or pass on some of the scheduling responsibilities to member libraries by asking each branch or library to be responsible for covering a block of hours. The next decision is whether the coordinator will distribute hours to the staff or member libraries on a first-come, first-serve basis; by time zone; or attempt to distribute the hours equitably to rotate unpopular hours. Librarian Margaret A. Demien of the Boeing Corporation describes scheduling in this way: "Our multisite corporate library's Chat service is available from 6 A.M. PDT to 4 P.M. PDT M–F. We divide the time between various locations with the most eastern library taking the earliest hours. Each library location then assigns individuals to a particular day for certain hours. This varies by staff size and numbers of hours per location" (Demien 2002).

At the University of Florida, we set a new schedule each semester, allowing staff to rotate unpopular hours such as evenings or Friday afternoons. At the end of each semester, the coordinator polls staff members for their desk preferences for

the next semester and recruits "pinch hitters" or staff that serve as backup if someone is ill or misses a shift. The interactive reference coordinator then establishes a
semester schedule, which is posted in the *RefeXpress* staff handbook and on the
library web site. This web-based schedule also includes hyperlinked e-mail addresses as well as the telephone number of each staff member. But because librarians
and staff often need to trade shifts because of meetings or other commitments,
we have established a "working calendar" using Microsoft Outlook, where the
RefeXpress staff members record trades on a day-to-day basis. We use an internal
e-mail list to facilitate shift exchanges. When a trade is needed, personnel simply
post a request to the *RefeXpress* list, and colleagues respond to the person seeking
the trade directly. After the person finds a substitute to cover the chat reference
shift, he or she posts a final message to the entire list so that the coordinator and
the rest of the staff know that the shift has been covered. Then the staff member
responsible for the reference shift records the name of the substitute on the working calendar. *RefeXpress* personnel can access the working calendar either at their
desktops through Outlook, or through a web site when not in their offices. Establishing a working calendar is essential because it eliminates the need for the coordinator to constantly monitor desk trades. It also improves communication
among staff. When someone is late logging on, the librarian who is to be relieved
of duty can check the working calendar to see if there is a substitute scheduled,
then call or e-mail the substitute. If this system breaks down for whatever reason,
librarians can call one of the two coordinators, who will either log on and cover
the desk shift or find a pinch hitter. Finally, special schedules are established for
weeks affected by attendance at the American Library Association annual and
midwinter conferences.

Consortia Scheduling Scheduling is especially challenging for libraries sharing a real-time service across institutional boundaries, but it can be done. One
group that has developed a workable system is the *Q and A NJ* project, involving
more than twenty-nine public, two academic, and two special libraries. Each of
the member libraries commits to covering certain blocks of online real-time reference hours. Local project managers handle the actual scheduling of local librarians to answer the questions and work with users. To facilitate this process, *Q and
A NJ* developed a "Scheduling Norms" policy that charges member libraries with
the responsibility of covering their scheduled shifts, asks libraries to solicit trades
via the project listserv, and requires reporting of shift trades to the project coordinator (South Jersey Regional Library Cooperative 2001). Late-night hours and
any question overflow during busy shifts are covered by librarians at the LSSI online reference center. Figure 7.2 is a screen snapshot of a recent *Q and A NJ* Virtual Reference Desk Schedule.

The *24/7 Reference* consortium schedules in a similar manner, using subject
specialists and generalists alike on the virtual reference desk. *24/7 Reference* maintains the complete password protected web-based ColdFusion schedule on its web
site; administrators at member libraries are authorized to make changes. The

Figure 7.2. Virtual reference desk schedule, *Q and A NJ.*

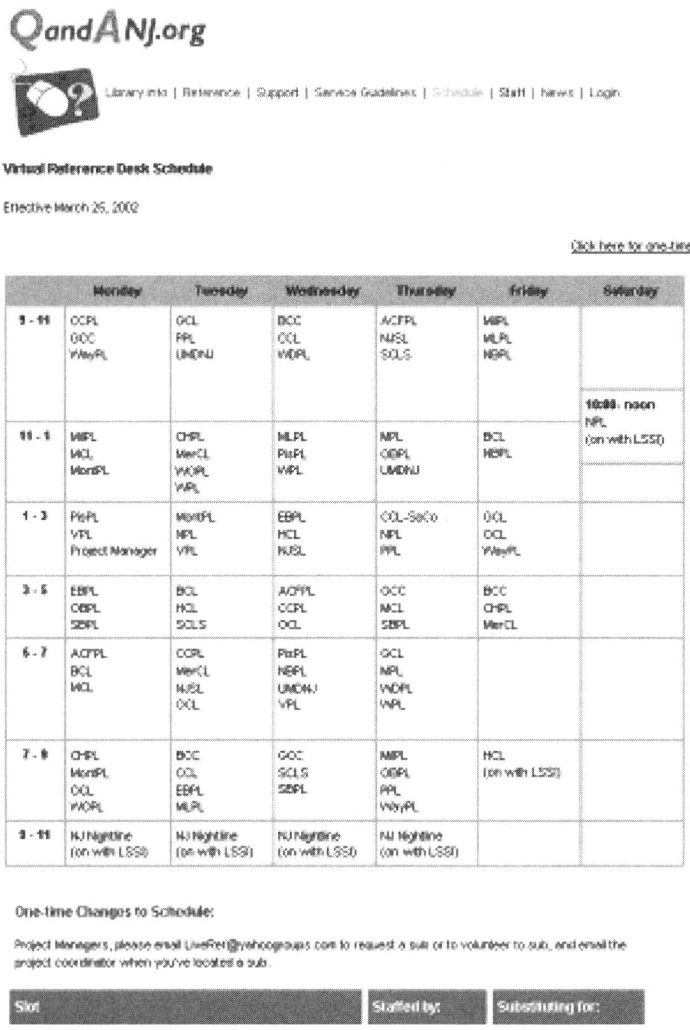

QandANJ.org

Library info | Reference | Support | Service Guidelines | Schedule | Staff | News | Login

Virtual Reference Desk Schedule

Effective March 25, 2002

Click here for one-time changes to the schedule

	Monday	Tuesday	Wednesday	Thursday	Friday	Saturday
9 - 11	CCPL GCC WayPL	GCL PPL UMDNJ	BCC CCL WDPL	ACFPL NJSL SCLS	MIPL MLPL NBPL	
						10:00 - noon NPL (on with LSSI)
11 - 1	MIPL MCL MontPL	CHPL MerCL WOPL WPL	MLPL PisPL WPL	NPL OBPL UMDNJ	BCL NBPL	
1 - 3	PisPL VPL Project Manager	MontPL NPL VPL	EBPL HCL NJSL	COL-SaCo NPL PPL	OCL OCL WayPL	
3 - 5	EBPL OBPL SBPL	BCL HCL SCLS	ACFPL CCPL OCL	OCC MCL SBPL	BCC CHPL MerCL	
5 - 7	ACFPL BCL MCL	CCPL MerCL NJSL OCL	PisPL NBPL UMDNJ VPL	GCL NPL WDPL WPL		
7 - 9	CHPL MontPL OCL WOPL	BCC OCL EBPL MLPL	GCC SCLS SBPL	MIPL OBPL PPL WayPL	HCL (on with LSSI)	
9 - 11	NJ Nightline (on with LSSI)	NJ Nightline (on with LSSI)	NJ Nightline (on with LSSI)	NJ Nightline (on with LSSI)		

One-time Changes to Schedule:

Project Managers, please email LiveRef@yahoogroups.com to request a sub or to volunteer to sub, and email the project coordinator when you've located a sub.

Slot	Staffed by:	Substituting for:

schedule facilitates communication among a large number of personnel with some clever design features that make finding contact information easy. For example, colleague's e-mail and AOL Instant Messenger addresses are packaged in rollovers; to access this information, one simply holds a cursor over the person's listing on the schedule. Figure 7.3 is a snapshot of the *24/7 Reference* schedule, which can be accessed online at <http://www.247ref.org/schedule/libschedule.cfm>. As you can

Figure 7.3. *24/7* reference schedule.

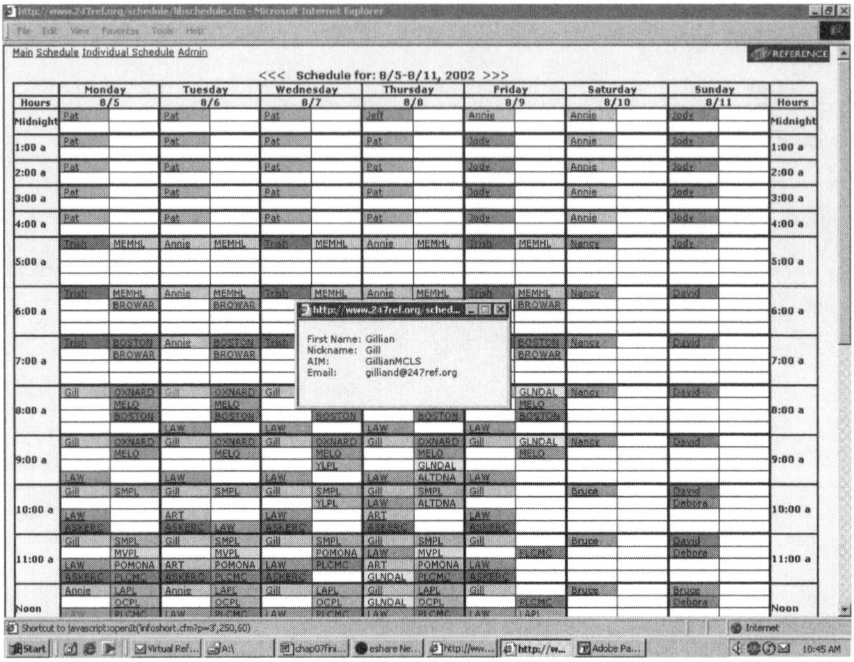

see from the schedule, many of the member libraries maintain fluid local schedules, signing up for blocks of time and scheduling the hours locally.

Other Scheduling Strategies Other strategies for scheduling might be a tiered model, in which library assistants or even student workers are assigned to be online and triage incoming questions. Although assistants or students can be trained to handle certain directional and ready reference questions such as locating a database on the library web site, more in-depth questions could be transferred easily to a second staff member, a librarian standing by in another service queue or chat room. Or perhaps generalists could be enlisted to staff the front lines and could call subject specialists to log on and assist with questions in their specialties. These are just a couple of the scheduling models out there for consideration.

As you can see, there is a great deal of flexibility and many creative options to staffing a real-time reference operation. Staffing a real-time reference service involves a great deal of planning, particularly in the early stages of the project, but it soon settles down, requiring primarily attention to ongoing tasks such as identifying and planning new training opportunities and facilitating staff communication.

REFERENCES

Demien, Margaret. 2002. "Re: [DIG_REF] Scheduling Chat Services." DIG_REF Listserv (29 April). Archived online at http://www.vrd.org/Dig_Ref/dig_ref.shtml (accessed 30 Apr. 2002).

Hoag, Tara J., and Edana McCaffery Cichanowicz. 2001. "Going Prime Time with Live Chat Reference." *Computers in Libraries* 21: 40–4.

McClennan, Michael, and Patricia Memmott. 2001. "Roles in Digital Reference." *Information Technologies and Libraries* 20: 143–48.

New Jersey Library Network. *Q and A NJ*. 21 May 2002 *Librarian's Online Manual* http://www.qandanj.org/manual/ (29 May 2002).

Porter, Katherine. 2002. "Re: [DIG_REF] Scheduling Chat Services." DIG_REF Listserv (30 April). Archived online at http://www.vrd.org/Dig_Ref/dig_ref.shtml (accessed 1 May 2002).

Reynolds, Penny Cole. 2000. "Staffing for the Customer Service Center." *Center-Force Technologies*. Available at http://www.cforcetech.com/direct-staffing.htm (accessed 25 April 2002).

Ronan, Jana, and Carol Turner. 2002 (December). *SPEC Kit 273: Chat Reference*. Washington, D.C. Office of Leadership and Management Services, Assocation of Research Libraries.

South Jersey Regional Library Cooperative. 2001. Live Online Reference: Project Managers Meeting #5. Available at http://www.sjrlc.org/ProjMan_minutes7_17.PDF (accessed 31 August 2002).

8 GUIDELINES AND POLICIES FOR REFERENCE IN REAL TIME

Policies! Best practices! Guidelines! Standards! Where does one begin when starting up a real-time reference service? When I started writing this book in 2002, there were no established guidelines to help librarians, but guidelines should become available in either late 2003 or early 2004. By the time this work hits bookstores, the ad hoc Virtual Reference group within the Machine Assisted Reference Section (MARS) of the Reference and User Services Association will have distributed a draft set of guidelines for general comment. Look for the *Guidelines for Implementing and Maintaining Virtual Reference Services* on the MARS web site.

Why not simply stick to existing reference policies designed to support in-house users or e-mail? It's a good idea to consider existing policies or unwritten practices when developing a new real-time reference project, if only because chat policies need to complement and support your library's other public service practices. Chat reference should not be treated as an independent entity, but as an innovative tool to extend reference services to new populations. Be aware, however, that virtual reference introduces some new wrinkles into issues that we face at the reference desk every day. As Bill Katz and Anne Clifford (1982) state in the introduction to their survey of policies and practices, the *Reference and Online Services Handbook*, "Who comes first when the telephone rings, the person standing at the desk or the individual with a question on the phone?" Now you can add to the clamor the sound of the computer bell dinging, signaling there is yet another person "queued up" waiting for assistance. It's difficult to know what to do in this situation without some type of preparation. Without at least some rudimentary policies and procedures, gridlock can occur and services to users will suffer.

Clearly defined and stated policies serve two important functions. Policies communicate the type of services that you are providing while communicating library expectations to users, and they guide staff in providing a more uniform standard of reference services. Drafting policies and publicizing them need not be an onerous task. Many libraries incorporate brief policy statements at pertinent points on their web site, such as a sentence on the login page stating who may use the service and the hours. Real-time reference services such as *Q and A NJ*; *Ask a Librarian* at the University of Illinois, Urbana–Champaign; or *Ready for Reference*, include more extensive policies on their site. Many libraries have policies that are circulated in-house and are not posted on library web sites. A survey of public and academic library chat reference services revealed that most libraries develop some type of publicly posted policy in the following areas: a definition of authorized users, the level of reference services to be offered, behavior, and confidentiality or privacy concerns. Let's look at users first.

AUDIENCE

Probably the most critical policy issue for your new chat service is defining the audience for your project. Real-time reference touches a much broader audience that we are accustomed to with more traditional reference services, given that services are no longer sequestered by geography. Reference services situated at a desk, designed for face-to-face interaction with people, are restricted to users who can find the front door to the library or the number in a phone book, and even the location of the desk within the library. Online reference services are accessible much more easily. Although your local library patrons will probably discover your real-time reference service via a link on the library web page or through local promotion, people from all over the world may find it using a search engine, from e-mailed recommendations from friends or other librarians, and even linked on other web pages or listed in directories of Internet resources such as Yahoo! Define the primary audience for your service.

Some services welcome questions from anyone on the Internet, but others restrict access based on membership or affiliation. For example, the primary clientele for the *Ready for Reference* service is "students, faculty, staff, and others associated with the academic communities served by the eight participating libraries," followed by "clients within the broader communities served by the participating libraries, Illinois residents living in the 14,000 square mile region covered by the Alliance Library System, and Illinois residents at large" (Alliance Library System 2002) in that order. Other libraries, such as the Felix G. Woodward Library (serving Austin Peay State University), extend services to outsiders that would like information about a local collection or about the institution.

Sample User Policies

Following are examples of user policy statements from the web sites of several types of chat reference services:

- **AskUsQuestions.com** (Morley Library)

"Due to licensing restrictions we must require that you are a patron of the Morley Library with a valid library card to access this service. To continue please enter the barcode number from the back of your library card in the box below and click the connect button."

- *Ask a Librarian* (Carnegie Mellon University 2002)

"Carnegie Mellon users only."

- **LiveRef** (Virginia Polytechnic Institute 2002)

"Priority is given to Virginia Tech students, faculty, and staff, and to questions pertaining to Virginia Tech library collections."

- **AskUsNow!** (Baltimore County Public Library 2002)

"This service is available free to Baltimore County residents and/or Baltimore County Public Library card holders. It is designed to provide information primarily to elementary, middle, and high school age students working on homework related assignments in the hours after school."

- **Ask a Librarian** (Department of Energy Library)

"Priority given to US Dept. of Energy users."

- **Ask Librarians Online** (New York Public Library)

"Anyone can browse the Q & A Archive. At this time, however, only New York Public Library cardholders can submit questions. See the eligibility requirements for obtaining a library card."

- **KnowItNow 24X7** (Cleveland Law Library)

"CLEVELAND LAW LIBRARY MEMBERS: Get answers to your reference questions live through the Library's KnowItNow24x7 service. Click on the *KnowItNow24x7* link below to access this service.

NON-MEMBERS: Our first priority is service to our membership. However, we will attempt to provide reference assistance via email only to non-members as time and staffing permits. Please E-mail your request to the address below and be sure to include your name as well as return E-mail address. Or if you wish, you may go to the Cleveland Public Library's free *KnowItNow24x7* Reference service."

Suggestions for Handling Outside Users

Once you have defined the users whom you will serve with your chat reference service, you need to decide how you will handle log-ons from people outside your user base. If you don't mind answering questions for people not affiliated with your institution, it is not a problem. Many academic libraries, such as the University of Florida, encourage contact from outside scholars seeking information concerning unique collections. Some libraries simply refer outsiders to a more appropriate library or services such as the *QuestionPoint Collaborative Reference Service*. The *Librarian's Online Manual* (Q and A NJ 2002) even has a procedure to handle transactions with visiting librarians. "We expect that traffic will also include interested librarians and people from out of our service area. These users will be answered using pre-scripted messages or web pages that describe the project or be offered links for Internet reference help."

If your library would prefer that outside users do not log on to your chat service, publishing a user policy statement on your log-on page deters some (but not all) people outside your patron community. Using authentication is the surest way to restrict access. This is often done by restricting connections to IP addresses at academic institutions or businesses, by library card barcode at public libraries (Avon Free Public Library, the NOLA Regional Library Network), or by requiring users to provide some type of user id and password. Some services such as *KnowItNow 24X7* appear to have authentication; *KnowItNow 24X7* requires users to type in a CLEVNET district zip code for entry. Using barcodes, zip codes, and user ids also serves another purpose in large shared operations, where the software uses these data to route the user to the appropriate library queue or to gather usage statistics.

Priorities in Working with In-House and Virtual Users

As at the reference desk, chat librarians will experience times when several people will be beckoning for help simultaneously, and it will be difficult to work with them if no guidelines have been established. It could be two users logged on at the same time, one a library member, one a nonmember. In a real-time reference service based out of your reference desk, the telephone could be ringing, an in-house user standing in front of you, and the bell on the chat service chiming to let you know someone is waiting for help. Who gets priority? Establishing priorities relieves stress for library staff, while facilitating better quality of service for users.

Some libraries feel that in-house users have precedence over remote users. Policy at the University of Illinois, Urbana–Champaign states, "When staffing *Ask a Librarian* from a public service point (i.e., Information or Reference desk) in-house users take precedence over remote users, who may need to be put on hold, called back, asked to send an e-mail, or asked to try later. Users should not be asked to wait longer than 5 minutes" (Henry 2001). The policy of the Benjamin F. Feinberg Library (SUNY 2000) states that "Patrons physically present in the library take precedence over I-Ref users."

Other libraries seek to provide high-quality reference services for remote users by operating their chat reference service separately from in-house reference services. The Libraries of North Carolina State University (NCSU) have a policy that states, "The Research and Information Services Department considers the research needs of off-site patrons and those of patrons who come into the library to be equally important" (Anderson, Boyer, and Ciccone 2001). NCSU's real-time reference service, *Ask A Librarian*, is situated in a unique center handling e-mail, chat, and telephone queries to ensure full attention is paid to remote users.

Some libraries combine virtual and physical reference services but give equal priority to remote and in-house users. In this scenario, librarians handle requests in the order they are received, regardless of the user's location. Whatever your priorities are for handling face-to-face and online users, it's important to articulate them as policy and to make that policy accessible to patrons and librarians. It is also helpful to develop procedures to guide librarians through sticky situations such as working with virtual and in-house users at the same time.

SERVICE

The level of services a library wishes to provide to remote users significantly affects the parameters of a real-time reference project. Some issues to consider are whether time limits will be placed on chat sessions and the actual level of assistance to be offered. For example, will librarians accept or refer questions involving extensive research? How will you handle users looking for help processing an interlibrary loan or renewing a book? How will referrals be handled? Will librarians seek to instruct users in use of information sources or simply provide answers? These are all situations you will encounter, so think through how to handle each of them. Many of these questions may have already been addressed in telephone and e-mail reference policies and can be extended to your new reference service.

Level of Questions

Will your real-time reference service offer the same level of assistance as the reference desk of your library? Or will the focus be on ready reference questions and assistance in locating and searching online databases? In my experience working with *RefeXpress*, the University of Florida Libraries chat reference service, users ask all kinds of questions—from connectivity questions and requests for facts to requests for assistance in ongoing research. Because many users do not realize the depth of research that may be required to give answers to certain questions, some libraries stipulate up front the types of questions that are answered in the effort to guide users. *AskUsNow* has a policy on their web site that states, "We will provide answers to brief, factual questions such as the verification of a bibliographic citation, spelling or definitions of a word, or addresses of companies. We will also provide a brief introduction to starting research-related tasks, as well as brief instructions in using the catalog, databases and other library resources" (University of Tennessee 2002). Other services such as the *Q and A Cafe* provide examples of the types of questions they answer (see Figure 8.1). Many services do not appear to restrict the level of questions asked online, however, if the lack of such a policy stated on the services' web sites is any indication.

Referrals

Not every question asked in a real-time reference service can be answered immediately online, or even online at all. Depending on your library's staffing model

Figure 8.1. *Q and A NJ* examples of questions.

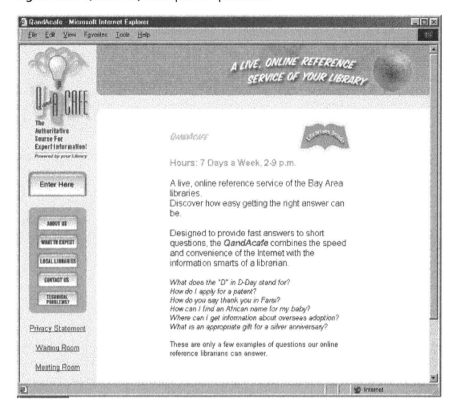

(as discussed in Chapter 5) staff may have a varying range of subject expertise and reference ability. Users may also submit questions that are difficult to answer without some research or consultation with other departments. For example, it's easy to answer a basic question about borrowing a book by pushing a web page with the library's circulation or interlibrary loan policy to a student, but a pointed question about a fine or an interlibrary loan is probably best referred to the appropriate department. With detailed questions requiring some research, it is often necessary to follow up with an answer via e-mail or even to ask the user to come into the library for assistance. Because not everything can be answered online, it's helpful to have a policy in place to explain to users the need for referral in certain instances. Policies and procedures also aid chat-based librarians in understanding the limitations of the medium so that they route or refer such questions to the appropriate librarian or service desk. In the *Virtual Reference Services* (VRS) manual, Lipow and Coffman (2001, module 2-1.6) recommend clarifying "the limits of the service you are giving, how it fits with other services and what the alternatives are that you can offer to the client."

Sample Referral Policies

Here are some examples of referral statements taken from various libraries' chat web sites:

- **Morris Messenger** (Southern Illinois University, Carbondale, n.d.)

"If your question will take time to research, or if it is a toughie, we may refer you to e-mail or ask you to visit the library."

- **Ask Us Live** (University of Minnesota Libraries, n.d.)

"If your question is too complex to answer through chat, or if it requires the attention of a subject specialist, we will have to answer it by email. (We'll discuss this with you at the time.)"

- *Ask a Librarian* (University of Illinois 2001)

"If a question becomes lengthy or complex (e.g., a difficult bibliographic verification), offer to get back to the user by phone or e-mail (see policy on Confidentiality) instead of having them try back or remain on hold for a long time."

- *Q and A Cafe* (as noted in Lipow and Coffman 2001)

"Questions that cannot be answered within the specified time limit, and the patron has indicated continuing interest, can be emailed, faxed or mailed within 48 hours. Specialized inquiries that take longer to answer might require a visit to the library or a referral to appropriate resources (law libraries, medical libraries, community agencies.)...For requests that require extensive searching in printed texts, back issues of periodicals and newspapers that are not online, requests for an online search, or Internet instruction, patrons should be referred to their local library."

Length of Transaction

Many services limit the length of time for sessions, a policy that may be needed to assist staff in handling heavy volumes of traffic. The *Q and A NJ* service has an objective of seven to fifteen minutes for a transaction but qualifies this policy: "This is not a hard and fast rule, however, customers tend to get impatient if they are kept waiting longer than that. Librarians may use their own judgment in this area. If there is nobody in the queue waiting and the patron is willing to stay connected, the transaction may go longer" (*Q and A NJ Reference Policies*). *Ready for Reference* does not stipulate a time limit but suggests up to ten minutes for a ready reference question and notes that "Reference providers should keep their side of the dialogue brief and use message scripts whenever possible. This will help minimize the length of the session" (Alliance Library System 2002). Libraries establishing new chat services may find it difficult to arrive at an optimal session duration statement. It may be useful to follow the examples cited here and then assess transaction lengths after a semester or a couple of representative months of service, with input from the librarians who are staffing your project.

Inappropriate Queries

After defining the breadth of questions that may be posed to your chat service, plan how to handle potentially problematic questions such as legal, medical, and genealogical queries. Rude and inappropriate behavior should also be clearly explained as cause for refusal of services.

Samples of Policy Statements Concerning Content of Questions

• **Ask a Librarian** (Ryerson University)
"We reserve the right to refuse to answer questions we find offensive and inappropriate (profanity, racial epithets) and intrusive personal questions."

• **AskUsNow!** (University of Tennessee)
What will we not provide? This service will not provide the following:

• UT salary information.
• In-depth research, such as compiling a bibliography, searching multiple issues of a periodical, or a lengthy research consultation.
• Genealogical searches.
• Book renewals, holds, and other circulation requests. Please see the *Circulation Department* instead.
• Delivery of electronic full-text of articles (see *copyright* for more information).

• **Live Librarian** (Suffolk County Public Libraries)
"The Live Librarian Reference Librarians do not provide technical support. Patrons with technical questions should contact their home library of SuffolkWeb Tech Support at techsupp@suffolk.lib.ny.us.

The Live Librarian Reference Librarians do not provide legal, medical or tax consulting."

INFORMATION LITERACY

Many academic and other libraries have an educational mission, which means that they seek to encourage users to learn how to research and be "information literate." How does this translate into the online environment? "Is the idea of instructing users like we do at the reference desk still valid online?" (Horn 2001). Will librarians endeavor to instruct students in use of information sources or simply provide answers and referrals? In *RefeXpress*, the policy is to teach users such as undergraduates how to search periodical indexes or the catalog, if appropriate. A special library catering to engineers or lawyers may have a different mission and seek to deliver all of the material needed by the client.

In services where policy suggests an average session length of seven to fifteen minutes, instructing a user how to search a complex database may not be practical. *Q and A NJ* suggests that in a situation such as this, "librarians may use their own judgment" during slow periods when no one else is waiting in a queue for assistance. The policy manual elaborates, "Questions that require more in-depth work can be referred to the Camden County Library" or librarians may choose to complete the question offline (*Q and A NJ Reference Policies*).

Sample Instruction Policies

Here are another couple of examples of policy from two other real-time reference services:

- **Ask a Librarian** (University of Illinois)

"It is not easy to use the software to deliver instructions on 'how to search.' Encourage the user to come in if the user's request involves a lot of library instruction."

- **24/7 Reference Service** (General Guidelines for Interactive Reference)

"Queries that require instruction (e.g., how to use a search engine to locate information or how to use the Library online catalog) are exceptions to [the] quick and factual guideline. Interactive digital reference provides an excellent vehicle for such instruction. Librarians may also make virtual appointments with clients to continue the instruction during the librarian's off-desk time."

BEHAVIOR

Although most users who log on to chat reference services are polite and grateful for help, real-time reference staff may encounter a person who wants to play or who is rude or disruptive. Prepare for problem users by defining what is considered inappropriate use and determining how to respond so that staff know how to handle such a situation.

Inappropriate behavior can be defined as abusive or offensive language, harassing another user, and disruption of communication between two users by a third user. These modes of conduct are often considered grounds for chastisement, disconnection, and even being banned from an online community. Just as profanity, graphic language, and sexual comments are not tolerated at the reference desk, neither are they acceptable online. *A Short IRC Primer* (Pioch et al. 1997) defines harassment as simply, "behavior towards another user with the purpose of annoying them." This would include a range of behaviors from smart aleck remarks or suggestive language to violent emoting and threats and already may be addressed in policies that you or your parent institution has established for e-mail and computing. "Disruption of communication" is a behavior unique to synchronous communication. Let's say that you are using IRC or chat software that enables multiple log-ons at one time. A librarian could be in the middle of a conversation with a user about a research matter, only to have an additional person log on and disrupt the conversation. If the second person is unwilling to wait for assistance and continues to post messages or has logged on to play, the quality of the communication between the librarian and the first user will be seriously denigrated.

Once you have defined inappropriate behavior, the next step is to state the consequences for conscious and repeated breaches of conduct, as well as to outline the procedures for the library staff. Consequences typically involve a warning, then expulsion or "booting" from the chat service. The most extreme consequence would be to bar a user permanently from the service after repeated violations of the code of conduct. Many software programs allow library staff accounts to be set so that they can "boot" or disconnect users; permanently barring a user usually is managed by the software administrator.

Sample Policies Concerning User Behavior

Following are some examples of policy statements relating to online conduct (see also the section on inappropriate queries):

- *Ask a Reference Question* (St. Louis County Public Library)
"Inappropriate behavior or use of profanity will result in the termination of your phone call or chat session."

- *AskUs.Now!* (University of Tennessee)
"Abusive, obscene, threatening or harassing messages will not be tolerated. We reserve the right to terminate the chat session."

CUSTOMER SERVICE GUIDELINES

Computer-based real-time communication may be a new concept for librarians, but educators and hobbyists have established norms that can be adapted to reference work. Real-time coordinators can encourage librarians and staff to familiarize themselves with online social norms or netiquette by including them in their policies for librarians. This could be as simple as including a brief section on service tips or by including links to netiquette sources on the web. A good resource on the subject is the aptly titled online book *Netiquette*, by Virginia Shea (2000). Another option would be to include a more extensive section on working with patrons in real time. The *Q and A NJ Librarian's Online Manual* (2002) has a section devoted to service guidelines that includes policies and a variety of tools for librarians. These tools include a checklist to evaluate a reference session (see Figure 8.2), a decision tree for handling in-depth questions, habits of effective chat librarians, and a section on tips for quality service.

Another set of extremely useful guidelines to consider including in a real-time reference manual are the *RUSA Guidelines for Behavioral Performance of Reference and Information Professionals* (RASD Ad Hoc Committee 1996). The *Guidelines* encourage librarians to think about how the behavioral attributes of approachability, demonstrating interest, listening and inquiring, searching, and follow-up impact librarian-user rapport so as to promote successful reference transactions. Although the *Guidelines* concentrate on effective communication in face-to-face reference encounters, they translate well to a textual chat environment (Ronan

Figure 8.2. Reference session evaluation checklist, *Q and A NJ.*

 Library Info | Reference | Support | Service Guidelines | Schedule | Staff | News | Login

Reference Session Evaluation Checklist

Yes	No	N/A	Software/Technical
			The librarian sent a web page and not just a URL
			The librarian sent what she/he announced
			The librarian successfully sent files or screenshots
			The librarian successfully used proprietary databases

Yes	No	N/A	Research/Search Skills
			The resource or item sent answered or partly answered the question
			The librarian sufficiently evaluated the item before sending it
			The librarian checked if the resource (e.g., a web site's search facility, links, etc.) was functional before sending it
			Appropriate resources were used in answering this question
			A Resolution Code was properly assigned

Yes	No	N/A	Communication and Model Reference Behavior
			The librarian used open-ended probing questions to elicit the customer's specific question
			The librarian maintained a steady dialog with the customer
			The librarian kept the customer informed of her/his activities
			The librarian communicated what next steps were expected of the customer
			The librarian made appropriate use of scripted messages
			The librarian informed the customer before sending an item
			The librarian explained to the customer what she/he sent
			The librarian provided instruction in the resource sent, if needed
			The librarian explained where to find the answer in the item sent
			The librarian appropriately referred the call
			The librarian appropriately took responsibility for getting back to the customer.
			The librarian asked the customer if she/he has completely answered the question
			It was clear from the customer's point of view that the librarian was ending the session

2002). The *Guidelines* are being adapted to include online communication. See Chapter 9, "The Reference Interview Online," for more in-depth coverage of application of the *Guidelines* to online real-time reference.

Sample Customer Service Policy Statements

The "Service Guidelines" section of the *Online Librarian's Manual* from *Q and A NJ* (2002) includes excellent guidelines for customer service:

Service tips to ensure customer satisfaction

Providing quality customer service via real-time interaction over the Internet is similar to providing quality customer service via interaction in person or over the telephone. In all three real-time modes, it is important to be professional without being overly formal or impersonal, and to be friendly without being overly informal or chatty. As friendly professionals, we strive to

- Treat each customer individually
- Get straight to the point, but do an effective reference interview to be sure you GET the question
- Keep sentences brief
- Let the customer know what you plan to do
- Avoid one-word responses, since these fell terse in written exchanges.

PRIVACY

Maintenance of user privacy has always been of great concern to librarians, even prior to the passing of the USA Patriot Act (HR 3162 RDS, October 24, 2001). The American Library Association Council says, "The ethical responsibilities of librarians, as well as statutes in most states and the District of Columbia, protect the privacy of library users. Confidentiality extends to 'information sought or received, and materials consulted, borrowed or acquired,' and includes database search records, reference interviews, circulation records, interlibrary loan records, and other personally identifiable uses of library materials, facilities, or services (American Library Association 1991). Privacy is a real concern in the area of chat reference because it is so easy to record, keep, and share full transcripts of real-time reference encounters. In addition to conversations, many software packages also collect and store personal information such as e-mail addresses, originating URL, the user's operating system, the type of web browser they are using, and their internet provider address. Although librarians use much of this information in an altruistic manner to evaluate how their service is operating, it is essential to establish a policy that articulates what the user's rights are, what the librarian's rights are, and how the data compiled from the reference encounters will be used and the length of time the data will be kept. A policy of sanitizing transcripts—removing any identifying user and staff names—may assist in maintaining privacy. Deletion of transcripts, however, is the best way to ensure confidentiality. Libraries that are outsourcing services should keep in mind that the vendor's privacy policy will also have an impact on local guidelines. With the broad authority provided by the USA Patriot Act, law-enforcement agencies could conceivably work directly with real-time reference vendors to monitor user activity without consulting the subscribing libraries.

Sample Policy Statements Relating to Confidentiality

- **Ask a Librarian** (New York University)

"Is our chat saved anywhere?

Yes. The transcript of the entire chat session is saved and archived by Live Assistance. At the end of the session, we will email a complete transcript of the chat to you, which you may wish to keep for future reference."

- **AskUs.Now!** (University of Tennessee)

"Is my question private?

The University of Tennessee Libraries respects the privacy of users, but cannot guarantee the privacy of files, electronic mail, or other information stored or transmitted electronically. Any research use of transactions will have all identifying information removed."

- **Ask a Librarian LIVE** (Ryerson University)

Who has access to this information?

The information collected by the Library is only accessible to librarians associated with the Ask a Librarian pilot project.

Who does the Library share the information with?

Individual chats are not shared with anyone outside of the Ryerson Library. Statistics generated from chat logs, as well as excerpts, may be used for reports or publications. However, information about specific individuals (e.g., IP address, E-mail, names, phone numbers, etc.) that might be included as part of a chat transcript will never be shared outside of the Ryerson Library.

What choices do users have … ?

Any patron that wants to have a record of their chat deleted may email *dgranfie@ryerson.ca* to request the deletion of their chat transcript from the Ask a Librarian Live database. Users will need to know the date and exact time their chat started in order to be sure the exact chat can be found.

- **AskERIC Live**

"Our ERIC experts will routinely send you to other sites on the Internet. These other sites have their own privacy and data collection practices. AskERIC has no responsibility or liability for these independent policies. For more information regarding a site and its privacy policies, check that site."

24/7 Reference's General Guidelines for Interactive Reference has an extensive section concerning privacy. The table of contents follows.

- 24/7 Reference Service
- What information does 24/7 Reference gather about you?
- How does 24/7 Reference use your personal information?
- How do we use cookies and IP addresses?
- Will 24/7 Reference disclose any of your personal information?
- What kind of security measures do we take to protect your information from accidental loss or disclosure?
- How can you deactivate your account or correct or revise information that we have about you?
- How will you know if 24/7 Reference privacy policy has changed?
- What else should you know about your privacy?

HumanClick (2000) collects this type of information about users:

a) Data that users provide through optional, voluntary participation in chat sessions with HumanClick agents;
b) Data HumanClick collects through aggregated tracking information derived mainly by tallying page views throughout our site;
c) Data is collected through our Contact Us / Support page on a form that visitors may fill out to receive technical support; and
d) HumanClick will never divulge information about an individual user to a third party (except to comply with any applicable laws).

COPYRIGHT AND PROPRIETARY DATABASES

The last area in which a real-time reference service may wish to add a policy is in the area of copyright and use of licensed databases. It may be as simple as adding the copyright notice we habitually post above photocopy machines on the web site or programming the same statement into a canned response for librarians to send to users before pushing them a scanned document (as is the practice at *KnowItNow 24X7*).

Samples of Intellectual Property Statements:

- *Ask a Librarian* (University of Illinois 2001)

Bibliographic citation verification; database searches; requests for online articles, etc: These questions fall outside the scope of service to non-affiliated users and licensing restrictions prevent sending information from proprietary databases. These resources can be used by patrons onsite, but we can't serve as intermediaries in sending citations to non-affiliates. You can inform the user directly or send the canned "Out of Scope" message.

- **Live Librarian** (Suffolk)

"As part of their service mission, the public libraries in Suffolk County, New York provide the information contained on this web site, including reproductions of certain items, for NON-COMMERCIAL, PERSONAL, RESEARCH USE

ONLY. Any other use, including but not limited to commercial or scholarly reproductions, redistribution, publication or transmission, whether by electronic means or otherwise, without prior written permission is strictly prohibited. Granting or withholding of permission is determined on a case by case basis, and a usage fee may be required depending on the type of proposed use.

Users should be aware that materials made available through this web site may be subject to additional restrictions including but not limited to copyright and the rights of privacy and publicity, of parties other than the Libraries. Users are solely responsible for determining the existence of such rights for obtaining any permission, and paying any associated fees, which may be necessary for the proposed use.

Copyright infringements should be reported to Gerald Nichols at cpyright@suffolk.lib.ny.us.

The system administrator reserves the right to terminate accounts and remove all files of repeat violators of copyright law.

For additional information on copyright visit the U.S. Copyright Office on line."

In conclusion, when developing policy and procedures for a new real-time reference service, it is helpful to look at established services to identify issues. Although it is my hope that this chapter provides basic underpinnings for libraries developing a new service, I encourage readers to look for articles in the library literature, consult with colleagues, and search the Web for more examples of policy statements on the web sites of functioning real-time reference services.

REFERENCES

Alliance Library System, IL. Ready for Reference Virtual Reference Desk. 2002. *Guidelines for Service Provision* (April). Available at http://www.alliancelibrary system.com/projects/readyref/Guidelines.doc (accessed 31 August 2002).

American Library Association. ALA Council. 1991. *Policy Concerning Confidentiality of Personally Identifiable Information about Library Users* (July 2). Available at http://www.ala.org/alaorg/oif/pol_user.html (accessed 21 January 2002).

Anderson, Eric, Josh Boyer, and Karen Ciccone. 2000. "Remote Reference Services at the North Carolina State University Libraries." Paper presented at Facets of Digital Reference. Virtual Reference Desk, 2nd Annual Digital Reference Conference, 16–17 October, Seattle, WA. Available at http://www.vrd. org/conferences/VRD2000/proceedings/boyer-anderson-ciccone12–14.shtml (accessed 16 January 2002).

AskERIC Live! n.d. *About Our Service.* Available at http://askeric.org/Realtime/ (accessed 29 May 2002).

Baltimore County Public Library, MA. AskUsNow! *About AskUsNow!* (7 June 2002). Available at http://www.bcplonline.org/askusnow/about.html (accessed 29 May 2002).

Carnegie Mellon University Libraries, Pittsburgh, PA. Ask A Librarian. *Ask a Librarian* (11 April 2002.). Available at http://www.library.cmu.edu/Research/ask.html (accessed 31 August 2002).

Cleveland Law Library Association, OH. *KnowItNow24X7*. n.d. Available at http://www.clelaw.lib.oh.us/lawkin.html (accessed 29 May 2002).

Department of Energy Law Library. *Ask A Librarian*. n.d. Available at http://vrl-web2.lssi.com/wcscgi/CDM.exe/doe?SS_COMMAND = CUST_SUP& Category = DOEREF (accessed 29 May 2002).

Henry, Marcia. 2001. "The Future of the Academic Reference Desk in Virtual Library Services: Responses from University, Public, and Community College Libraries." Paper presented at Internet Librarian Conference 2001, 6 November, Pasadena, CA. Available at http://library.csun.edu/mhenry/il2001.html (accessed 25 April 2002).

Horn, Judy. 2001. "The Future Is Now: Reference Service for the Electronic Era." Paper presented at the ACRL Tenth National Conference, 5–18 March, Denver, Colorado. Available at http://www.ala.org/acrl/papers01/horn.pdf (accessed 21 January 2002).

HumanClick. 2000. *Privacy Policy*. Available at http://www.humanclick.com/support/privacy.htm (accessed 29 May 2002).

Katz, Bill, and Anne Clifford. 1982. *Reference and Online Services Handbook: Guidelines, Policies and Procedures for Libraries*. Volume 1. New York: Neal-Schuman.

Lipow, Anne Grodzins, and Steve Coffman. 2001. *Establishing a Virtual Reference Service: VRD Training Manual*. Berkeley, CA: Library Solutions Press.

MARS (Machine Assisted Reference Section). RUSA (Reference and User Services Association). *Guidelines for Implementing and Maintaining Virtual Reference Services*. Chicago: American Library Association, forthcoming (projected date of publication: 2004).

Morley Library, Painesville, OH. n.d. *AskUsQuestions.com*. Available at http://www.askusquestions.com/library/morley.htm. (accessed 29 May 2002).

Morris Library, Southern Illinois University, Carbondale. n.d. *Morris Library Has Several Ways to Get Help Online*. Available at http://www.lib.siu.edu/hp/about/digiref.shtml (accessed 29 May 2002).

New York Public Library. Ask Librarians Online. n.d. *Terms and Conditions for the New York Public Library's Ask Librarians Online*. Available at http://www.nypl.org/branch/ask/about.html#terms (accessed 29 August 2002).

New York University. Elmer Holmes Bobst Library. n.d. *Ask a Librarian Policy Information*. Available at http://www.nyu.edu/library/bobst/research/ask/askapolicy.htm (accessed 31 August 2002).

Pioch, Nicolas, Owe Rasmussen, Michelle A. Hoyle, and Joseph Lo. 1 January 1997. *A Short IRC Primer*. Edition 1.2. Available at http://www.irchelp.org/ irchelp/ircprimer.html#Behave (accessed 21 January 2002).

Q and A NJ. 21 May 2002. *Librarian's Online Manual*. New Jersey Library Network. Available at http://www.qandanj.org/mANUAL/ (accessed 29 May 2002).

———. *Q and A NJ Reference Policies and Guidelines*. n.d. South Jersey Regional Library Cooperative, NJ. Available at http://www.sjrlc.org/policies.PDF (accessed 29 May 2002).

RASD Ad Hoc Committee on Behavioral Guidelines for Reference and Information Services. 1996. "RUSA Guidelines for Behavioral Performance of Reference and Information Services Professionals." *RQ* 36: 200–3.

Ronan, Jana S. 2002. "Adapting the RUSA Behavioral Guidelines to Real-Time Reference." Paper presented at the Reference Interview: Connecting In-Person and in Cyberspace, 2002 RUSA President's Program, 13 June, Atlanta, GA. Available at http://www.ala.org/rusa/presprog2002.html (accessed 31 August 2002).

Ryerson University, CA. Ask a Librarian LIVE. n.d. *What to Expect*. Available at http://www.ryerson.ca/library/ask/what.html (accessed 29 May 2002).

St. Louis County Public Library. Ask A Reference Question. 13 December 2001. *Policy*. Available at http://www.slcl.lib.mo.us/reference/chat/chat.htm#policy (accessed 29 May 2002).

Shea, Virginia. 2000. *Netiquette*. Available at http://www.albion.com/netiquette/ book/index.html (accessed 29 April 2002).

Sloan, Bernie. 1998. "Electronic Reference Services: Some Suggested Guidelines." *Reference & User Services Quarterly* 38: 77–81.

Southern Illinois University, Carbondale. Morris Messenger. n.d. Morris Library Has Several Ways to Get Help Online. Available at http://www.lib.siu.edu/ hp/about/digiref.shtml (accessed 31 August 2002).

[Suffolk County Public Libraries, NY. Live Librarian.] n.d. *Copyright & Permissions*. Available at http://www.suffolk.lib.ny.us/snl/snlcopyright.html (accessed 29 May 2002).

SUNY (State University of New York) Plattsburgh, Benjamin F. Feinberg Library. 8 September 2000. *Welcome to I-Ref*. Available at http://www2.Plattsburgh. edu/acadvp/libinfo/library/iref.html (accessed 31 August 2002).

24/7 Reference Service. n.d. *General Guidelines for Interactive Reference*. Available at http://www.247ref.org/manual/librarianprotocol.cfm?ti = Librarian%20Protocol (accessed 29 May 2002).

University of Florida. RefeXpress. 2002. *RefeXpress Policy Manual*. Available at http://refexpress.uflib.ufl.edu/rxpolicyman.html (accessed 31 August 2002).

University of Illinois at Urbana-Champaign. Ask A Librarian. 2001. *Basic Procedures and Guidelines for Online Reference. HumanClick—Basic Procedures* (25 September). Available at http://www.library.uiuc.edu/ugl/_staff/vr/proc.html (accessed 29 May 2002).

University of Minnesota Libraries. Ask Us Live. n.d. *What Is Ask Us Live?* Available at http://infopoint.lib.umn.edu/ask-us-live.phtml (accessed 29 May 2002).

University of Tennessee Libraries. AskUsNow! n.d. *About E-mail and Chat Reference Services.* Available at http://www.lib.utk.edu/refs/askusnow/policy.html (accessed 29 May 2002).

Virginia Polytechnic Institute and State University. University Libraries. LiveRef. 2002. *Online Reference Service: LiveRef and AskUs* (21 August). Available at http://www.lib.vt.edu/services/liveref.html (accessed 29 May 2002).

WEB SITES CITED

Ask A Librarian, Carnegie Mellon University Libraries
http://www.library.cmu.edu/Research/ask.html

Ask A Librarian, Department of Energy Law Library

Ask A Librarian, New York University
http://www.nyu.edu/library/bobst/research/ask/aska.htm

Ask A Librarian, University of Illinois at Urbana-Champaign
http://www.library.uiuc.edu/ugl/vr/

Ask A Librarian LIVE, Ryerson University
http://www.ryerson.ca/library/ask/

Ask A Reference Question, St. Louis County Public Library
http://www.slcl.lib.mo.us/reference/ask/index.html

AskERIC Live!
http://askeric.org/Realtime/

Ask Librarians Online, New York Public Library
http://ask.nypl.org/

Ask Us Live, University of Minnesota Libraries
http://infopoint.lib.umn.edu/ask-us-live.phtml

AskUsNow!, Baltimore County Public Library
http://www.bcplonline.org/askusnow/

AskUsNow!, University of Tennessee
http://www.lib.utk.edu/refs/askusnow/

AskUsQuestions.com, NOLA Regional Library System, OH
http://www.askusquestions.com/

HumanClick
http://www.humanclick.com

KnowItNow 24X7, CLEVNET Library Consortium
http://www.knowitnow24x7.net/

Live Librarian
http://www.suffolk.lib.ny.us/snl/

LiveRef, Virginia Polytechnic Institute and State University
http://www.lib.vt.edu/services/liveref.html

Machine-Assisted Reference Section (MARS)
http://www.ala.org/rusa/mars/

Morris Messenger, Southern Illinois University, Carbondale
http://www.lib.siu.edu/hp/about/digiref.shtml

Q and A Café
http://www.qandacafe.org

Q and A NJ
www.qandanj.org

QuestionPoint Collaborative Reference Service
http://www.questionpoint.org/

Ready for Reference Virtual Reference Desk, Alliance Library System, IL
http://www.alliancelibrarysystem.com/Projects/ReadyRef/index.html

RefeXpress, University of Florida
http://refexpress.uflib.ufl.edu

9 THE REFERENCE INTERVIEW ONLINE

One of the biggest challenges in providing reference services in real time is learning to communicate with remote users and translate the interpersonal skills used at the physical reference desk into the virtual environment. Library literature abounds with articles and studies on the reference interview in a face-to-face setting and via telephone and e-mail, yet not much has been published concerning working with users online in real time.

This chapter introduces chat communication norms associated with online communities and gives some suggestions for effective reference interviewing in real time based on the RUSA *Guidelines for Behavioral Performance of Reference and Information Services Professionals* (RASD 1996).

THE TRADITIONAL REFERENCE INTERVIEW

Before jumping into a discussion of the way users communicate in text-based chat, it is helpful to establish some common understanding about reference interviewing. Conducting an effective reference interview is a skill. One of the most insightful yet economical definitions comes from Robert Taylor (1968, 180), who describes the reference interview as a complex human interaction in which "one person tries to describe for another person not something he knows, but rather something he does not know." William A. Katz (2002, 129) distills this important interaction with users into four points: "(1) Obtain the greatest, most precise information about what is needed. (2) Understand at what level the material is needed and how much is required. (3) Complete the interview, and arrive at the necessary key data, in as short a period as possible. (4) Maintain a good relationship with the person asking the question." Librarians strive to achieve these goals by first listening to what the user says and encouraging him or her to elaborate, as well as through attention to what is not verbalized. In addition, librarians carefully observe the questioner's behavior for a deeper understanding of the user's information need. Although studies indicate that overreliance on body language or facial expressions is not productive (Katz 2002), some attention to user behavior and characteristics is useful. Librarians also learn to use verbal and nonverbal cues to project approachability, in an effort to put patrons at ease. A colleague of mine at Indiana University–Bloomington, Lou Malcomb, once described—humorously but aptly—the process of reference interviewing as "information therapy." Is information therapy possible in an environment where all the librarian has to go on are the sentences crawling across the screen, punctuated by mechanical beeps and popup windows signaling entry and departure of users? Text-based chat is an "austere mode of communication," in which "there are no changes in voice, no facial expressions, no body language" and little if no "visual/spatial environment as a context of meaning," says psychologist John Suler (1997). Compared with this, the reference desk is a rich, sensual environment, where an abundance of information can be gleaned from watching and listening to users, as well as their questions.

When a patron calls on the telephone or faces you at the reference desk, you employ as many of your senses as possible to gather more information in the endeavor to discover what is it that the user really wants. You listen to the actual question, but often it is possible to derive additional context from the tone of the user's voice, age, behavior, facial expressions, attitude, and so on. To see how this works, let's compare three users asking the same question. The first user, a middle-aged man in a business suit with a briefcase, strides forcefully through the entrance to the library and to the reference desk where he asks, "How do I find the web site for Proctor and Gamble?" The second person, standing over by your business reference collection looking confused, seems to be a student at your local college, if age and the textbooks spilling out of his backpack are any indication. You walk over and inquire if he needs assistance because you have seen him move from the Internet computers to leaf randomly through business reference books, another clue that he may be experiencing difficulty locating something. You try to sneak a peek at the syllabus on the counter in front of him as he asks for help in finding the Proctor and Gamble web site. The third user poses the question in your reference chat service, as illustrated in Figure 9.1.

With chat, there is little information about the user, beyond the question and the name "Chris" displayed on the computer screen. Even if the log-on page to your chat service is set up to gather more information about users as is done at *KnowItNow 24X7* or *LION (LIbrarians Online)* (see Figures 9.2 and 9.3) many of the contextual clues that guide a librarian in a face-to-face interview are absent. It's difficult to determine the user's searching history, level of education or age, the urgency of the request, and language comprehension without the opportunity to see body language or to work with the user in person over a period of time. Returning to our user examples, the businessman is sending cues of being in a hurry, especially when he glances at a clock while you are working on the question.

Figure 9.1. A user poses a question in a reference chat service.

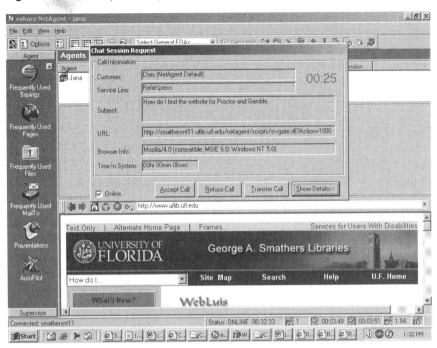

With the second user's general aura of confusion, it wouldn't be surprising if he was struggling with a difficult assignment and is unsure how to proceed. Compare what is known or suspected at the onset of the reference interview with user one and two, to the lack of context for "Chris." In text-based chat, the librarian has to ask users pointed questions to get at the depth and level of need, time frame, and other factors that impact the answer to be given.

LIBRARIANS AND CHAT CULTURE

Librarians are relative latecomers to chatting and instant messaging. Computer users have been chatting and messaging since the 1960s, when you could "finger" a friend on another computer to determine if he or she was online and initiate a private conversation via UNIX talk. A recent study of 648 librarians from small, medium-sized, and large public and academic settings reveals that although librarians may be aware of instant messaging and chat, most do not have direct experience with the technology (Janes 2002). Table 9.1 summarizes the respondents' experiences with the real-time technologies of instant messaging, MOO, chat, and videoconferencing.

This survey reveals that 68.2 percent of the librarians polled had never used instant messaging even for recreation, whereas 65 percent had never chatted.

Figure 9.2. Logging on at *KnowItNow24X7.*

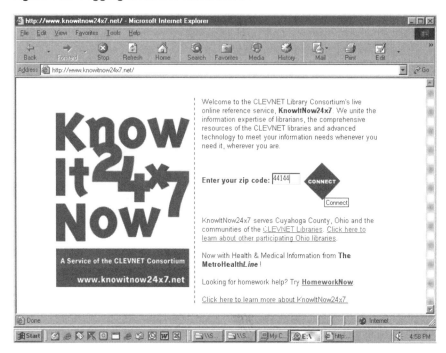

These study results are important in our discussion of the reference interview because they indicate that a majority of librarians in the field lack experience with chat etiquette or culture.

Social Conventions in Chat

Social context is reversed when chatting online. Because social and economic status is not represented virtually as they are in the real world, text-based chat can have an equalizing force. Physical attractiveness has a different impact because how a "user 'looks' to another user is entirely dependent upon information supplied by that person" (Reid 1991), as are age, gender, and emotion. With the absence of the full communication modalities present in face-to-face interactions, particularly intonation of the voice and gestures, it takes some practice to learn how to express oneself strictly in textual terms. You can't just pull a reference book off the shelf and point to a passage, or glance at a person's face while talking to her for feedback. In addition, the rules for proper social behavior in chat are not obvious.

"In the material world, social conventions are built into houses, schools and offices, signaled by modes of dress and codes of etiquette, posture, accent, tone of voice, and hundreds of other symbolic cues that let people guess accurately how

Figure 9.3. Logging on at LION.

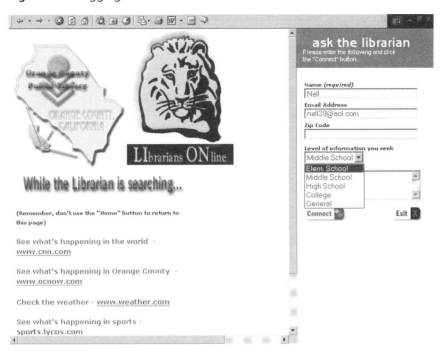

to behave in a particular social situation or society. People learn how to adjust their behavior to conform with a learned mental model of conventional behavior" (Rheingold 1993, 180–1). One example of a setting steeped in social conventions is the library. In the American culture, children are taught from an early age that libraries are places to whisper and keep their voices low. To ask a question, you locate the reference desk; to check out a book, you go to the circulation desk.

Conventions and cues take a different form in the virtual world. Many of the communication techniques that we have codified for use at the physical reference desk do not work when online. Because "language does not express the full play of our interpersonal exchanges," chatters "cannot rely upon the conventional systems of interaction if they are to make sense to one another" (Reid 1991). Even the most skilled reference librarians struggle to answer questions that normally do not pose any difficulty for them in face-to-face encounters because of the unfamiliar conventions of chat and the newly imposed limitations of communicating solely by the written word.

Conventions and Norms in Chat

There are definite conventions for communication and online behavior within chat culture that librarians can draw on in modeling their own online

Table 9.1 Knowledge of and experience with technologies.

	Never heard of (%)	Aware of, but never used (%)	Have used but not for receiving or answering reference questions (%)	Have used for receiving or answering reference questions (%)
Electronic mail	0 (0.0)	3 (0.5)	125 (20.0)	493 (78.8)
World Wide Web forms	39 (6.2)	57 (9.1)	224 (35.8)	292 (46.6)
ICQ, AOL Instant Messager, or other instant messaging software	65 (10.4)	362 (57.8)	163 (26.0)	21 (3.4)
Chat rooms or other chat technology	2 (0.3)	405 (64.7)	180 (28.8)	27 (4.3)
Videoconferencing	5 (0.8)	387 (61.8)	205 (32.7)	20 (3.2)
MOO or MUD	265 (42.3)	294 (47.0)	45 (7.2)	9 (1.4)

behaviors and techniques for reference interviewing. Communication and behavior in chat spaces tend to exhibit the following characteristics:

1. Lack of nonverbal cues, such as body language or gestures
2. Lack of voice intonation or accents
3. Emoting, emoticons, and descriptions of gestures are used
4. Language more like spoken than written
5. Fast paced
6. Typing skills important
7. Writing and spelling skills highlighted
8. Users are actively involved
9. Identity is fluid
10. Reduced inhibitions

Most online communities have unwritten codes of conduct defining appropriate behavior that have been established over many years of interacting together. "On IRC, both topic and tone of discussion is policed only by the participants, with the result that a shared culture has gradually developed that defines communication norms and conventions somewhat differently than they are in face-to-face conversations" (Murphy and Collins 1997, 179). Many are modeled on the same social expectations that guide face-to-face interactions. After all, "people do not enter chat rooms as a blank sheet of paper. Rather they take with them internalized social rules for interacting with others as well as experiences in defining face-to-face situations that are used to approximate the nature of chat room situations" (Bellamy and Hanewicz 1999).

One convention that is not immediately obvious is to talk in short sentences or a couple of words at a time. Abbreviations are also used to speed up the pace of the conversation. Popular abbreviations include "BTW" for "by the way," "BRB" for "be right back," and "LOL" for "laughing out loud." Many chat users use misspelling as a type of shorthand or to indicate slang, as in "ok," or the shorter "k" for "okay," or "kewl" to indicate a distinctive pronunciation of the word "cool." In real-time spaces where three or more users are chatting, the pace of the conversation is fast, and it is difficult to read long missives. Users' postings are constantly rolling off the screen as new responses are added from other participants. Even in one-on-one situations, communiqués are best kept brief. This is because it's difficult to read comments longer than two lines, and because the recipient experiences "dead time," while long messages are being composed.

Some rules of conversational behavior, such as taking turns talking, do not work in chat. In a face-to-face situation, tone of voice and nonverbal cues signal when the speaker is winding down and the next person can interject; it's rude to start to talk before the person who is speaking has finished. In chat, it's not always easy to tell when someone is finished commenting, so exchanges are not limited by this rule. This is in response to the nature of the software, in large part. In most chat systems, including IRC, MUDs, instant messaging, web-based chat, courseware, and call center software, transmission of your comments is not operating in a true two-way synchronous mode in which you can watch character by character what your friend is keyboarding at the other end. Rather, there is "dead time" on your end until your friend finishes writing the message and hits the enter key. At that point, the message is actually transmitted. When groups of three or more people are chatting, the conversation can be disjointed because each person may be simultaneously composing comments to send. This can result in subgroups discussing more than one thread or topic, much as people congregate in small groups at a large party or gathering. One convention used to address a comment to a specific person in a situation such as this is to add the user's name at the beginning of the message: "Chris: the Encyclopedia Britannica is online."

Veteran chatters are used to a high level of stimulation and frequently multitask with other programs while chatting. One librarian learning how to communicate in real time shared the following: "Observing my teenager chat online, I finally began to understand a few things about communicating this way. She was multitasking. She was listening to music, chatting in two or three different conversations and surfing the Web. The time lag didn't bother her at all" (Broughton 2001).

Text-based chat has some interesting conventions to help convey nonverbal cues. Obviously it's impossible to see users smile, frown, or wrinkle their brows with confusion when you are chatting with them. It is possible, however, to add an additional depth of meaning to a message by using an emoticon (such as a smiley face) or to describe what you are feeling or doing in brackets or carets. For example, I could tell a user that I was looking in print reference sources by entering the following: "It will take me a couple of minutes to find the answer. <Jana goes to the reference shelf and looks at a book>." Figure 9.4 lists some common emoticons or symbols that represent actions or emotions.

Figure 9.4. Selected emoticons.

:-)	Smiley, friendly, happy
;-)	Winky
:-(	Sad
>:-(	Angry, upset
:-@	Furious
:-I	Indifferent

Hope that helps ☺

Sorry, we don't have that book. :-(

Unfortunately, it's difficult to gauge the emotional response of another person unless he or she chooses to share it with you in a chat session. Text-based chat is bereft of gestures and other types of body language, as well as the vocal intonations used so heavily in spoken language. For example, think of how many ways a person can pronounce the word, "Oh," to convey interest, disinterest, confusion, anger, understanding, and so on using simple intonation. Consider that an accompanying shrug or frown lends yet a different meaning. Capitalization and underlining are often used in chat to add emphasis. Typing, "DID YOU LOOK IN THE CATALOG," is the equivalent of shouting the same words at a user at the reference desk, so it's wise to make sure the caps lock feature is off on your keyboard when chatting. Underlining is a gentler way of adding emphasis, as in, "Please click on holdings next." In addition, it's hard to tell if you are working with a user who has less than a perfect command of English or whatever language is dominant in your library setting. It's wise to avoid ambiguous words or phrases whenever possible. For nonnative speakers who comprehend the written word better than the spoken word, chatting can be beneficial. In addition to mechanical methods to convey tones such as emoticons, capital letters, or underlining, tone can be conveyed through choice of words or expressions. Consider the difference in tone between "Did you look in the catalog," compared with the softer response, "I wonder, did you look in the catalog?"

In addition to the absence of many nonverbal communication cues, chat can be extremely fast paced and liberating for the user. In chat, the user can use a pseudonym, control the pace of the conversation by asking questions at any point, and even abruptly terminate the conversation by logging off. It's no wonder that "individuals communicating via a computer report feeling more free, uninhibited, and comfortable than in face-to-face communications" (Dietz-Uhler and Bishop-Clark 2001, 271). Dietz-Uhler and Bishop-Clark also write that the reduced focus on self and "concerns about self-presentation" experienced by chat users, lead to "increased contributions to a discussion" as well as "greater disclosure of personal information." This seems to indicate that people who are shy or reluctant to voice certain questions in the public environment of the traditional reference desk may feel more comfortable chatting online privately with a librarian.

Because lack of inhibition can sometimes be taken to an extreme in chat, online communities have developed ways of discouraging or punishing inappropriate behaviors such as swearing, spoofing, and harassing other users. Spoofing in chat is assuming another person's online identity for the purpose of misrepresenting that person to the rest of the online community. When misbehavior approaches a level of harassment or disruption where verbal admonishments from fellow online users are not effective in curbing the behavior, most online groups have guidelines or procedures to manage such users. Sanctions usually consist of first disconnecting the disruptive person with a warning, then restricting access temporarily. For severe or repeated infractions, a person may be permanently banned. Software that has the capability of banning IP addresses keeps disruptive users from logging on again with a new account username; Chapters 1 and 2 discuss this functionality in various types of software.

BEHAVIORAL GUIDELINES FOR CHAT LIBRARIANS

The reader now has some understanding of the social dynamics that characterize chat and some of the norms that exist among online communities. How do these norms and conventions affect a librarian seeking to assist a user in the chat environment? Without specific strategies to determine exactly what is needed, to understand the level and amount of information that is needed, and to maintain a good relationship with the user, there are more opportunities for misunderstanding when working with users in real time. As Katz (2002, 126) puts it, "Misunderstanding is the ghost, which haunts numerous reference interviews." The *RUSA Guidelines for Behavioral Performance of Reference and Information Services Professionals* (RASD Ad Hoc Committee 1996) offer helpful strategies for working with users in the face-to-face environment, based on approachability, interest, listening and inquiring, searching, and follow-up. These guidelines are in the process of being revised to address online synchronous reference technologies such as chat. I offer some adaptation of these guidelines for librarians serving online users via real-time reference services.

Approachability

The *RUSA Guidelines* emphasize being "poised and ready to engage approaching patrons," establishing "initial eye contact," greeting users, acknowledging those waiting for assistance, remaining visible to users and roving. In chat reference, there are three basic components to being approachable for remote users. These are the chat service's web interface, the access points for connecting to your service, and the feedback that the user receives while connecting and chatting.

Interface The interface of your service can assist in luring people in to try your service. Make your service approachable by developing a catchy or memorable name. Some well-known services include, "*KnowItNow 24X7*," "*Q and A Café*," "*Q and A NJ*," and "*TalkNow*." "Ask-A-Librarian" seems to be the most popular name for library real-time reference services. Consider hiring a graphic artist to develop attractive graphics and create a logo for your service. Use of logos encourages "brand recognition," and they can be used as icons on web pages to create links or in posters and advertising. Figure 9.5 features some logos that successful services use.

Another aspect of the service's interface that has an impact on the reference interview is the log-on procedure. Some services require nothing more of the user than filling in a blank with his or her name and e-mail address. Others try to gather more information about the user. This might include the user's institutional affiliation, age or academic status, phone number, and so on. Some librarians advocate using a complex log-on screen as a timesaver and an automated reference-interviewing device, but I suspect that requiring too much information up front probably deters some users who could benefit from online real-time assistance. Researchers will undoubtedly investigate this issue in the future. Some services take the approach of asking a user to pick a subject area when logging on, as does *KnowItNow 24X7*. *KnowItNow 24X7* has a queue for users with general questions or ones that do not fall into their subject categories of business and finance, health and medicine, science and technology, or social sciences.

Visibility on Library Web Site Companies such as the airline search engine *QIXO* and *Nutrisystem* feature prominent links to their live assistance services on the top-level pages of their web sites, as well as links to the service in a persistent position on secondary level pages. If you want to invite users to ask questions, this is a good strategy. On the secondary level web pages, positioning links in a consistent position on each page frees the user from having to scan the page to find the link to the service. It isn't approachable to have one link to your chat service on a web site and burying it a couple of levels below the top page. Users

Figure 9.5. Selected chat service logos.

have to hunt to find it. If your library limits traffic during the pilot of your program by "hiding" the link on secondary level web pages, remember to expand the access points later. Probably the most important places to put links are on the top-level page, in the site map or index to the site, on any reference department pages, and on the general help pages. Many libraries, such as *AskUs.Now!* at the University of Tennessee, Knoxville, and *Ask A Librarian Live* at the University of Utah, combine links to their e-mail reference services with their chat service on the same page, along with information about calling librarians and reference desk locations and hours.

Another suggestion is to put links in databases so that users can access context-specific help without losing their search. Wright State University discovered that its traffic spiked dramatically when links within its online databases were added, indicating that the service was tapping a group of users with a need for assistance at that point (Powers 2002). If you are unsure where to put other links on your web site, examine the types of questions that users are asking to get some indication where links to live assistance might be useful and review statistics on web site hits.

Feedback As at the reference desk where "the first words that come out of the staff members' mouth are very important" (Durrance 1995, 250) in setting the tenor of the ensuing encounter, timely feedback is equally important when working with online patrons. The first step in creating positive rapport is to respond quickly when someone logs on. Chat users expect rapid responses when first logging on. If they have to wait too long for a connection to your service or have to go through a complicated download and installation process, many users will not return.

Greetings The first communication that users should see is some type of welcome followed by an acknowledgment of their question. One way to greet users instantly is to use programmed responses in your software that give speedy feedback as a user connects to the service. If your chat software offers an automated response, set a positive tone with a friendly automated greeting such as, "Welcome to Ask-A-Librarian! A librarian will assist you shortly." Many software programs offer a second programmed greeting for users who are waiting in a queue, as the librarian works with other people. Some real-time reference services even provide users waiting in a queue with a specially tailored web site to browse, featuring frequently asked questions, news, subject listings of Internet sites, and links to popular databases.

Names Another technique to improve approachability is to work the user's name into the conversation. For example, greet a person named Chris with "Hello Chris. How may I help you?" If you know the content of the question already, work in an open-ended question with the greeting: "Hello Chris. So you need information on China?" Strive to be friendly but economical with your words. Just be sure to say hello to the user in some manner. One common error that I've noticed new staff making is immediately starting to search for an answer to the initial question, without greeting the user who has just logged on. "In a text-based chat, presence is manifest only when one is actively messaging: silence is indistinguishable from absence" (Donath, Karahalios, and Viegas 1999, 2). If you do not take time to greet the user, the person has no idea that you are working on their question and may log off, thinking that no one is helping them. The best way to stay visible is keep giving the user feedback. Keep the conversation going.

Self-Revelation One powerful technique to build rapport with an online user is to reveal a little about yourself as you work with them. In chat where little is known about people other than what they choose to share, "disclosure creates a kind of currency that is often spent to keep interaction moving" (Murphy and Collins 1997, 182). Introducing yourself when a user logs on is one way to be approachable. "Hello, I'm Jana. How may I help you?" is much friendlier than "How may I help you?" In services where a generic username such as "librarian" is used, introducing yourself removes the depersonalizing effect and may encourage the user to open up more readily. This is not to say that a generic user name need be impersonal; the New York Public Library chat staff use the names of the sleuths from the Dashiell Hammett novel *The Thin Man* when they chat with users (Shalat 2002). Many people probably do not realize that "Nick" or "Nora" is a pseudonym.

Interest

Of all of the guidelines, conveying interest while online is the most challenging. The *RUSA Guidelines* recommend expressing interest for a user's question by facing the user and listening, maintaining eye contact, establishing a comfortable physical distance, using confirming nonverbal cues, appearing unhurried, and by focusing attention on the person. Almost all of these suggestions are nonverbal in nature. It takes concentration and some practice to get used to expressing in words what is normally conveyed impulsively through gesture or physical action. You can convey interest by working in comments throughout your dialogue with the user indicating that you are listening and are thinking about their question. Frequently acknowledging users is one way to let them know that you are serious in helping them. Pepper your feedback with neutral phrases such as, "I see" or "I understand," or even "yes," or "okay." If appropriate, empathize with comments such as, "That is a tough question," or "Sorry this is taking awhile. Shall we keep going?" Interest and approachability can both be established by making observations too, such as, "Gee, this database is slow today."

Formality and Pacing

Establishing a comfortable physical distance from the user translates into the online interview as using an appropriate level of formality and pace. Take cues from the user, and match your timing and conversational tone accordingly. If you do not know a user, it is always better to say, "Hello John, how may I help you?" rather than, "How's it going John?" or similar informal manner of address, even if the user addresses you in an informal manner. With established users, conversational tone may be more informal, especially if you know the person outside of chat. If the patron uses chat shorthand such as, "u" for "you" or "k" for "okay," it probably indicates that the person is accustomed to instant messaging or IRC. You may need to pick up the pace and message such users more rapidly. Conversely, if a user is responding very slowly, he or she may be a slow typist, have a slow connection, be a new chat user, or be a slow reader, among other possibilities. Slow down your responses to the user's pace if you are a fast typist. Ask the person if you are sending responses too fast, are pushing web pages too quickly and so on. If you are the slow one because your computer is malfunctioning, you are working with two people at once, or you are a slow typist, tell the user. Unless you share such issues, the people on the other end will not know, and they may think you are ignoring them. Finally, because it is difficult to determine if you are conversing with a new chat user, avoid using confusing online abbreviations such as BTW or even the ubiquitous smiley emoticon unless the user indicates a familiarity with such conventions by using them in conversation. Avoid library jargon as well.

Listening and Inquiring

Up to now, the discussion has centered on factors that affect the reference interview when online. Listening and inquiring are the heart of the reference interview. The *RUSA Guidelines* emphasize attention to tone of voice, allowing patrons to fully state their need, rephrasing the question, using open-ended and closed questioning, avoiding jargon and difficult terminology, and maintaining objectivity. In some ways, chat encourages better reference interviewing because users must state their questions word by word in their own vocabulary, thereby revealing their level of understanding and need. In addition, the librarian must rely more heavily on classic questioning techniques.

Because so little can be observed about a person that asks a question beyond what the information they supply about themselves, chat encourages librarians to use all of the questioning techniques in their repertoire. Questions such as, "Please tell me more about your topic" and "How much information do you need" work well in chat. Chat interviews often take longer, because questions that would be ambiguous at the reference desk may be even more confusing online, and there are no visual cues to add understanding. Take, for example, the classic ambiguous question, "I'm looking for something on china" (Katz 2002). Does the user want dishes or did they make a typographic error and need material on the country? Given the verbal ambiguities inherent in language, it is necessary to rephrase users' statements to understand exactly what they mean.

For ambiguous questions, many chat programs offer a powerful feature to help get at a user's problem, the escorting or co-browsing feature. Escorting or co-browsing allows the librarian to follow a user through a search in a database or on the Web or vice versa. So if a user connects and says that he can't find anything on 4-H clubs in *ERIC*, the education database, it's possible to use the escorting feature to shadow the person as they search, to see if they are using the wrong commands, or keywords.

Users take more control of the reference interview when online. Librarians are less of an authority figure online, which can lead to more effective communication. The uninhibited, "talk when you want to talk" environment may also encourage users to break in with their comments more often during the reference interview. Don't be surprised if, while in the middle of a complicated interview, the user interjects abruptly, "No, that is not what I want."

Searching

When the librarian is satisfied that he or she knows what it is the user needs, the next step of the process, searching, begins. The *RUSA Guidelines* offer specific steps for the searching process, which can be summarized as follows: constructing and completing a competent search in the appropriate resource, teaching the process to interested users, meeting the patron's time frame, and knowing when to refer the patron to another library, librarian, or source. Let's take what is required to be an effective searcher.

Reference Sources A chat librarian needs to have a broad repertoire of online reference sources. First and foremost, it is important to understand how to search the local library catalog effectively in the public access mode. Being able to search this important tool will be of great assistance in locating other online tools when working with chat users. After the catalog, familiarity with at least one interdisciplinary periodical index, major proprietary systems such as FirstSearch or Gale Group, major Internet search engines, guides to Internet resources, and the library web site is key. One area in which our library subject specialists have experienced difficulty is general reference resources. Librarians who move from working in a branch library or department where they focus on a concentrated subject area discover that they need to reacquaint themselves with the tools of the reference generalist, such as online almanacs or the *General Academic Index*.

User Limitations One of the most tedious but necessary issues to work through in the area of searching is helping a user who cannot reach a resource. This might be because the user is experiencing a networking problem with her computer, or it might be that the answer to her question is not available in an online format. Then there are people who connect to your service who are not authorized to access certain proprietary information sources.

One approach to this issue is simply to restrict access to your chat reference to library members, as is done at Askyourlibrary.org, a Connecticut-based chat cooperative supported by the Bibliomation network, or *AskUsQuestions.com*. Access to proprietary online databases is a problem for libraries that "provide service to everyone" as well as a problem for "consortium member libraries when the member libraries subscribe to different online databases" (O'Neill 2002). One way to work around this issue if the user needs periodical articles online is to show him how to search in high quality, freely available sources such as *JournalSearch.com* or *Findarticles.com*. Consortium libraries often create reference "consoles" or web sites that enable librarians working with users from other member libraries to connect quickly to the appropriate catalog and to see the list of licensed resources that they have to work with (Tennant 2000). Two examples of a console can be seen in Figures 9.6 and 9.7.

An understanding of how connectivity works at your institution is also important. Will AOL or BellSouth users have difficulty getting into your proprietary databases?

Teaching Searching Skills "One of the advantages of a virtual reference service is the ability to walk somebody through a web search engine or a research database" (Singer 2001). Chat is a wonderful tool for teaching searching techniques. Depending on the software being used, at the very least the librarian can search in tandem with the user in the same database in real time, messaging while they

Figure 9.6. Librarian's console, LSSI *Virtual Reference Toolkit.*

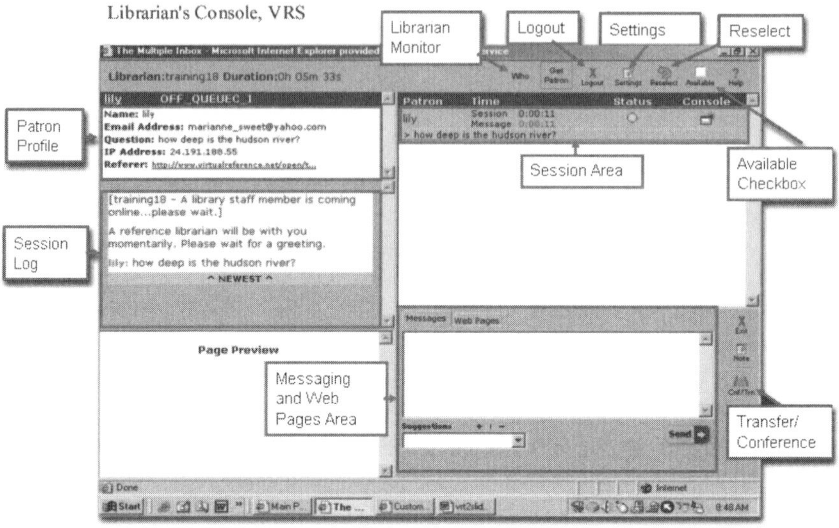

search and sharing insights on effective keywords or ways to apply truncation and proximity operators to improve the search. When using software that enables push page or escorting, the librarian can demonstrate a search from start to finish in search engines such as *Google* and *LexisNexis*. The librarian can also elect to follow the user as she searches by setting the escorting feature to follow. Escorting is especially useful to diagnose what a user may be doing wrong when searching a database or in showing a complicated path on your web site to an information resource three or more clicks away, such as how to connect to *Readers' Guide Abstracts* within *FirstSearch*. When using push or escorting, it is important to keep chatting with the patron, letting them know what you are doing at each step. Ask the user if you can send a page before you push it. Pushing a page without warning can startle a new user or annoy the person on the other end if she is still reading the last page.

If your software offers white-boarding features, it is possible to display a scanned document or a screen snapshot to a user, and then annotate it to explain certain points. For example, you could highlight parts of a citation to a journal article or circle the pertinent part of a long article from a reference book you scanned and transmitted to a user. You could also ask the user to circle parts of a citation that he did not understand.

Time Frame Do not make the assumption that just because users choose to ask a question via chat that they are in a hurry. In this respect, real time is exactly like working with users at the reference desk. Some users need information immediately, but others are happy to work with you for long periods of time. Librarians

Figure 9.7. Librarian's console, divine *Virtual Reference Desk.*

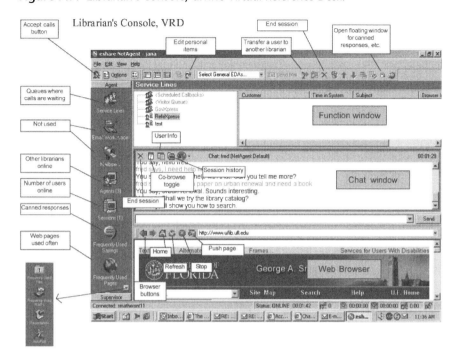

have experienced sessions as brief as a minute and as long as 45 minutes in *RefeX-press*, the chat service of the University of Florida Libraries.

It can be tricky to determine if a person is in a rush when online because of the lack of nonverbal cues. Librarians at a traditional reference desk can tell if haste is of the essence by observing users' body language. Unfortunately, you can't see a person check his or her watch or fidget in chat, so it's important to clarify the time frame early in the reference interview.

Ask the user questions such as, "What is your time frame" or "Do you need this right away?" Also, if you recognize at the onset that if the question is difficult and will take more than ten or twenty minutes to answer, it may be more efficient for all concerned to take the user's e-mail address or fax number and send the answer later.

When working with a user to answer a question that will take some time, often it's not practical to break off every thirty seconds or so to give feedback. Estimate how long it will take you to check that book in the reference stacks or to search in a periodical index and tell the user. This can be as simple as saying, "Just a moment, please" or "This will take a couple of minutes. Do you have time to wait?" A useful strategy to keep the user engaged as you look for answers is to help him get connected to one of the sources that you think may yield an answer and have him search in tandem. Even if the person doesn't find what he was looking for in the database or web site, it may help him clarify his question, thus assisting you in determining exactly what he needs. In addition, the user is an active participant in the search process and may be more willing to wait until you find the answer.

Follow-up

Although any question can be asked in chat, not every question is best answered there. Librarians have a tendency to feel pressured to answer every question online when they first start working in a chat service. As we know from experience at the reference desk, this is not practical. The *RUSA Guidelines* emphasize in this stage of a reference interaction to "ask the user if the question has been completely answered," to check up on users while they are researching, to consult with other librarians if needed, and to refer users to other information sources or libraries, making the referral as easy as possible for the user.

As you end a session, ask users if their questions have been answered and encourage them to return if they have further questions, especially with a user who seems pressured for time or is reluctant to stay online. Some users will pop on and off, asking short questions as they get stuck searching, rather than stay online while you demonstrate how to search or find an answer. One afternoon I worked with a young woman five separate times as she tried to find an article for a class assignment. The first time she logged on, she asked me to recommend a database where she could find articles on multimedia in medicine. I recommended a database, and before I could type in the words, "Shall I show you how to search," she had logged off. The second time she logged on, she asked for advice on selecting keywords, and logged off again, and so on. It was frustrating for me because I knew what the next question was going to be, but all I could do was to anticipate her next question and be ready to give a fast answer. At least she came back as she needed more assistance.

Consultations and Follow-up The physically isolating environment of real-time reference can lead librarians to forget that it is possible to consult with other staff who are not online when answering a question. It's important to remember to use the existing reference network at your institution or within your consortia. Real-time reference is not a standalone service; rather, it is just another aspect of your total suite of public services. When working with an online user, it is easy to pick up the telephone and call a colleague at the reference desk or to instant message the other librarian online at your library, or at your hosted service's backup reference center, for assistance. For example, if a user logs on for assistance because she cannot connect to the new interlibrary loan form, it is easy to call the department to consult on the answer. Someday all library public services will have a chat presence, especially those that directly service distance users such as interlibrary loan and document delivery. Some software allows more than one librarian to work with a user. The latecomer can often read the transcript of the session up to the point that he joined the session if using call center software. Libraries participating in *QuestionPoint* can transfer users along with the entire transcript of their session to a colleague or even to a librarian at another institution. Some software offers private messaging that allows staff to consult privately in the chat space without confusing the user.

Referrals As alluded to earlier, not every question that is asked in real time is best answered online—or even possible to answer online. Some questions involve consulting print sources, making them inconvenient to answer because of logistics. Some reference services' policies are to fax answers as given in printed sources, whereas others, such as *KnowItNow 24X7*, will scan the answer from the book and either e-mail it, or mount it on their web site or white-board feature for immediate viewing. For services operating on a small scale, with only one chat librarian on duty who may also be answering questions from in-house users, such service may be difficult to offer. Follow-up may be required.

Working with Multiple Users If the service is busy, it may be difficult to answer every question right as they come in. If you receive an involved question and the chat service is busy, you have a couple of options. Just as with busy times at the reference desk, you can get a user started with the basics of searching in a database, explain that you have another person to assist and will be back, then move to helping the other user. After a few minutes, return to the first user and ask if he needs assistance. If multitasking like this is too intense or the traffic is prohibitively heavy during your shift, take the second approach. Although I have worked with four users at once on a couple of occasions, it is hard to give quality service if the questions are substantive. Working with two users seems to be the limit. If working with more than one session simultaneously, greet each user, explain that you are working with more than one person right now, then move into reference interviewing the first user. Once you are confident you have the real question, arrange to deliver the answer to the first user later, verify that you have the correct contact information and the way that they prefer the answer to be delivered, and use closed questioning to end the encounter. It's helpful to take a few seconds to print the transcript of the session before moving on to the next person in line. Options for following up with the answer include e-mail, fax, telephone, or even to leave the answer at the reference desk for later pickup.

In conclusion, real-time reference offers librarians challenges because the medium currently lacks many visual and audio cues such as gestures and vocal intonations. Until online communication matures and reaches a stage where high-quality online communication channels are available in the typical home or school computer lab, librarians must learn to adapt the reference interview to communication conventions of text-based chat.

REFERENCES

Bellamy, Al, and Cheryl Hanewicz. 1999. "Social Psychological Dimensions of Electronic Communication." *Electronic Journal of Sociology* 4: 1–16. Available at http://www.sociology.org/content/vol004.001/bellamy.html (accessed 31 August 2002).

Broughton, Kelly. 2001. "Our Experiment in Online, Real-Time Reference." *Computers in Libraries* 21: 26–31.

Dietz-Uhler, Beth, and Cathy Bishop-Clark. 2001. "The Use of Computer-Mediated Communication to Enhance Subsequent Face-to-Face Discussions." *Computers in Human Behavior* 17: 269–83.

Donath, Judith, Karrie Karahalios, and Fernanda Viegas. 1999. "Visualizing Conversation." *Journal of Computer Mediated Communication* 4. Available at http://www.ascusc.org/jcmc/vol4/issue4/donath.html (accessed 29 May 2002).

Durrance, Joan C. 1995. "Factors That Influence Reference Success: What Makes Questioners Willing to Return?" *The Reference Librarian* 49/50: 243–65.

Janes, Joseph. 2002. "Digital reference: Reference librarians' experiences and attitudes." *Journal of the American Society for Information Science and Technology* 53: 549–66.

Katz, William A. 2002. *Introduction to Reference Work.* Volume II: Reference Services and Reference Processes, 8th ed. Boston: McGraw-Hill.

Murphy, Karen L., and Mauri P. Collins. 1997. "Development of Communication Conventions in Instructional Electronic Chats." *Journal of Distance Education* 12: 177–200.

O'Neill, Nancy. 2002. "Re: [DIG_REF] Skills for effective virtual reference." DIG_REF Listserv (January 25). Archived at http://www.vrd.org/Dig_Ref/dig_ref.shtml (accessed 29 May 2002).

Powers, Brett. 2002. "Re: [DIG_REF] Impact of Virtual Reference Being on Main Webpage." DIG_REF Listserv (23 August). Archived at http://www.vrd.org/Dig_Ref/dig_ref.shtml (accessed 12 February 2003).

RASD Ad Hoc Committee on Behavioral Guidelines for Reference and Information Services. 1996. "RUSA Guidelines for Behavioral Performance of Reference and Information Services Professionals." *RQ* 36: 200–03.

Reid, Elizabeth M. 1991. *Electropolis: Communication and Community on Internet Relay Chat.* University of Melbourne, Department of History, honors thesis. http://www.irchelp.org/irchelp/misc/electropolis.html (accessed 9 August 2000).

Rheingold, Howard. 1993. *The Virtual Community: Homesteading on the Virtual Frontier.* Reading, MA: Addison-Wesley.

Shalat, Harriet. 2001. "Re: [DIG_REF] What's in a name?" DIG_REF Listserv (6 December). Archived at http://www.vrd.org/Dig_Ref/dig_ref.shtml (accessed 7 December 2001).

Singer, Carol A. 2001. "Re: [DIG_REF] reference resources." DIG_REF Listserv (1 November). Archived at http://www.vrd.org/Dig_Ref/dig_ref.shtml (accessed 2 November 2001).

Suler, John. October 1997. "Psychological Dynamics of Online Synchronous Conversations in Text-Driven Environments." *Psychology of Cyberspace.*

Available at http://www.rider.edu/users/suler/psycybger/psycyber.html (accessed 10 November 2001).

Taylor, Robert S. 1968. "Question Negotiation and Information Seeking in Libraries." *College and Research Libraries* 29: 178–94.

Tennant, Roy. 2000. Digital Reference: Issues, Implications, & Impressions. Paper presented at 2000 RUSA President's Program: Reference 24/7: High Touch or High Tech? American Library Association Annual Conference, July 8–11, Chicago. Available at http://www.ala.org/rusa/acrobat/rtennant_2000.ppt (accessed 29 May 2002).

WEB SITES CITED

Ask A Librarian Live, University of Utah
http://www.lib.byu.edu/hbll/

Ask Librarians Online, New York Public Library
http://ask.nypl.org/

AskUsQuestions.com, NOLA Regional Library System
http://www.askusquestions.com/

AskUs.Now!, University of Tennessee, Knoxville
http://www.lib.utk.edu/refs/askusnow/chatref.html

Findarticles.com
http://findarticles.com

Journalsearch.com
http://www.journalsearch.com

KnowItNow24X7, CLEVNET Library Consortium
http://www.knowitnow24x7.net/

LION (LIbrarians Online), Orange County Public Library
http://www.ocpl.org/catdata/catdata.htm

Nutrisystem
http://www.nutrisystem.com

Q and A Café
http://www.qandacafe.org

Q and A NJ
http://www.qandanj.org

QIXO
http://www.qixo.com

QuestionPoint Collaborative Reference Service
http://www.questionpoint.org/

TalkNow, Temple University, PA
http://library.temple.edu/ref/talknow1.htm

10 PROMOTING ONLINE REAL-TIME REFERENCE SERVICES

Publicizing and promoting your real-time reference project is important to the success of your service. Unlike familiar and generally available services, such as librarians staffing a reference desk or e-mail reference, real-time reference is a new and unexpected application for your users. Simply adding links to your new chat reference service on your library web site is not enough. If this is all the promotion your library plans, some people will miss seeing the links, and others may pass it by because they do not understand that they can access valuable expert assistance instantly online. Librarians are often complacent about publicizing their services, and "have historically been confident that their products had such intrinsic merit that customers would automatically be attracted; they believed that people 'should' use the library" (Weingand 1999, 2). The fact is that online users relish convenience, and many potential users of real-time library service have already gone over to the competition. Library competitors such as *AskJeeves, Webhelp.com*, or *Jones e-global library* have marketing plans to reach users with ongoing advertising and promotions, and they enjoy high visibility in the online world that library chat services should try to emulate and even challenge. Unless you promote your chat service, many of your potential users may never be aware that your library offers a high-quality, objective alternative to settling for hundreds of hits with a search engine or paying for answers using a commercial Ask-A service.

PLANNING

The first step in any marketing or publicity effort is, of course, drawing up some type of plan. The planning process will include formulating objectives, identifying potential activities to reach people who would benefit from your chat service, and forecasting any expenses involved in implementing your promotional efforts. Take time to develop written objectives that clarify how you plan to reach each segment of your desired audience. This is important because certain types of publicity strategies, such as listserv announcements or printed flyers, might not reach all of your users. For example, publicity techniques that would work well with adults, such as newspaper articles or public service announcements on cable television, may not work for school children. You can use the worksheet given in Figure 10.1 to brainstorm and identify the best methods to reach the various types of people in your target audience.

The Benton Foundation's (2002) *Strategic Communications in the Digital Age: A Best Practices Toolkit for Achieving Your Organization's Mission* has more suggestions for promotional activities, as do many resources cited on the *Advocacy* section of American Library Association's (2002) web site. Expenses vary widely, depending on the size of your campaign. For example, developing handouts and brochures locally and reproducing them for distribution at the reference desk is a relatively cheap strategy, whereas hiring a graphic artist to develop a professional logo, graphics for your web site, and promotional material will prove much more expensive. Some larger libraries or library systems have a library public relations person or account with a public relations firm to draw on, whereas libraries with less resources may have no choice but to promote their service in a more modest way.

Identifying Resources

Local Expertise If your library has a person in charge or public relations or a department devoted to advertising and promoting library services, you have an important ally with the know-how to help you put an advertising campaign into motion. Investigate to see how your ideas for promotion fit within any marketing or public relations programs already in place within your library or organization, and what type of ideas your PR person may have for promoting chat. Ask to be kept abreast of any impending publicity opportunities, and don't be shy about seeking help in designing and implementing strategies. Our local public relations officer has been invaluable in writing press releases and articles, as well as in designing artwork, brochures, posters, and bookmarks. An experienced PR person also has an established set of media contacts to whom promotional materials can be targeted effectively.

How To Do It Yourself For readers that lack the resources of a public relations librarian or a background in this area, there are many excellent books that can lend ideas and guidelines for mounting simple promotions. Two that address nonprofit organizations specifically are Darlene Weingand's (1999), *Marketing/Planning Library and Information Services*, and Gary Stern's (2001) *Marketing Workbook for Nonprofit Organizations*. Marc Meola and Sam Stormont's (2002) manual, *Starting and Operating Live Virtual Reference Services*, has a chapter devoted to marketing. In addition, many good web sites offer step-by-step guidelines. One particularly comprehensive online guide is *How to Develop Your Marketing Plan: A Forty*

Figure 10.1. Checklist of strategies for promoting chat reference to users.

Media/Channels	How My Library Could Use Them
Press releases	
Photographs	
Press kit	
Newspaper articles	
Bibliographic instruction	
Feature story	
News conference	
Special event	
Give-aways: buttons, bookmarks, bumper stickers, notepads, self-sticking notes, pencils, etc.	
Annual report	
Posters	
Brochures	
Direct mail	
Public service announcements (PSAs)	
Newsletters	
Speeches/public appearances	
Media presentations	
E-mail	
Listserv announcements	
Web site	

Part Workshop by Joscon Networks. Regardless of whether your public relations office or your chat planning team gets involved in promoting chat reference service to users, you'll find many distinct avenues for accomplishing outreach. These different promotional activities fall into three basic areas: publicity, direct contact, and advertising. All three should be creatively examined for deployment, if your new service is to reach all potential users.

PUBLICITY STRATEGIES

Marketing professionals define publicity as promotional strategies or activities that have little or no cost. In a library setting, this would include familiar methods such as bookmarks, posters, library newsletter articles, and brochures. But other avenues that librarians might not think of can be used to generate interest in real-time reference. Several possibilities exist for publicity:

- Press releases for submission to local newspapers, television, and radio stations
- Public service announcements produced for broadcast outlets
- Articles in library-based newsletters for users
- Articles in professional or organizational journals
- Announcements on listservs
- Marketing letters
- Brochures, fliers, slip sheets (small 4 x 5 inch fliers)
- Posters, handouts, bookmarks
- Business cards for librarians
- Press kits
- Sponsorships of special events
- Open houses, receptions, get-togethers, dedications
- Product placement on library web site and related web sites

Using the Media

Newspapers, television, and radio have the potential to reach a wide range of people outside the confines of your library for little to no cost. The Ohio consortium of public and academic libraries, *KnowItNow 24X7* experienced a dramatic surge in use after the local National Public Radio station featured a segment on the new chat reference service. Unfortunately, most libraries have to work at getting that type of free coverage in the local media. One way to solicit media coverage is by issuing press releases. If you don't have a contact of your local newspapers, magazines, and radio or television stations, create one. The *Gale Directory of Publications and Broadcast Media* (2003) is one popular reference work that offers geographic listings of radio and television stations, as well as listings of weekly and daily newspapers. Don't forget about Internet streaming radio stations. *The Radio-Locator, RadioTower.com,* and *Web-Radio* are helpful in finding locally based Internet radio stations.

Tips for Writing an Effective Press Release

When writing a press release, keep it brief—no longer than two pages. Write in short, clear sentences minus any library jargon and place the most important information (the lead) at the beginning. Keep in mind that the point is not to write a lengthy detailed article but to convey basic information to reporters and journalists, interesting them enough to cover the story or to give the newspaper editor enough concrete information to run a brief public interest piece. The parts of a typical press release include the date, a contact name and phone number, and the release date. Include a bold-faced statement at the top of the page that says, "FOR IMMEDIATE RELEASE," if the news is time sensitive. The first couple of sentences in the narrative should distill the most important facts for readers, attempting to grab their interest. When writing this portion of the press release, try to answer the questions, who, what, when, where, why, and how, in the order of importance. Placing the most important information at the top of the release helps to ensure that critical information is not cut by editors or reporters. Keep information factual, and remember to attribute any opinions or positions to an identifiable source. If possible, work in a catchy quote from a local dignitary or personality who has used the service. Some authorities recommend keeping a press release to a single page, whereas others say keep it under two. Remember that you can get more information to a reporter by including supplementary material in the form of a fact sheet, handouts, or brochures and a list of "FAQs"(frequently asked questions). A fact sheet should contain basic information such as the beginning date of the service, the software used, number of librarians, hours of service, and statistics. The FAQ would succinctly answer questions new users might ask. "What is chat?" "What is chat reference?" "Why did you start this service?" "Are other libraries doing this?" "Who can use the service?" "Will chat replace the reference desk and librarians?" and "Why would I want to use chat reference?" are all questions that a FAQ can quickly and cost effectively cover.

The Press Kit

Libraries with a healthy budget for promotion may wish to take the press release a step further and develop something called a press kit. A press kit includes the press release but also includes brochures, photos, and a wealth of background information about the service. It is not something that would be sent out regularly to reporters or other media contacts but is a relatively expensive package of photos, news clippings, articles, and other materials that provide extensive background on the project. In a library setting, uses might be to give nationally known journalists easy-to-digest background information on your service for the purpose of enticing them to cover it, to encourage potential donors to lend financial support to the project, or for the library director to distribute to the local library board.

One other type of media that reaches a smaller but more targeted audience is your local public access television channel's community bulletin board channel, or the internal cable network for students or school children on your campus. Public access television and internal cable networks usually accept ads or announcements in PowerPoint format, making them easy to create and free of cost.

This is a unique and visually appealing way to publicize a new library service, even though the audience may be relatively narrow.

Publicity Strategies for an Educational Setting

In the academic setting, it is helpful to enlist the aid of faculty and advisors to publicize chat reference. Send a letter to department chairs and deans, asking them to try the service. One method I have found to be productive is to identify faculty with online syllabi. I then send each instructor a letter on official library letterhead introducing our chat reference service, complete with scenarios in which the real-time reference could assist students in the course. The letter also asks them to announce the service in their classes and easy-to-follow instructions for programming a hyperlink to chat reference from their syllabus. You can also reach users by encouraging agencies and organizations that also serve your targeted audience to link to your chat reference on their own web sites. This might be local social service agencies or city government web pages for a public library, whereas in an academic setting, it might be student services offices or campus organizations. Of course, web sites aren't the only way to reach clientele electronically. Electronic mail discussion groups are good places to reach target audiences. Use relevant listservs and other online e-mail lists to make periodic announcements about your service and to keep users updated on software, new hours, or even that a new librarian or library is joining your chat service, thereby broadening subject expertise, for example. Highlighting new developments in the program allows you to repeat your basic publicity information to your media contacts and other targeted groups.

Events

Finally, another fun way to publicize your real-time reference service is to hold a special reception or open house at the library, or to participate in or help sponsor a community event. Good times to hold receptions are for your service's grand opening and for important milestones that you reach along the way, such as your 100th or 1,000th question. Community events are also effective ways to encourage awareness. Maybe you have a limited budget, but you could afford to have T-shirts emblazoned with your chat service's logo for librarians to wear as they run in the local marathon. Setting up a special booth at the student activity fair or even as part of a special event at the local shopping mall allows you to promote services face-to-face with users who may not receive traditional media channels. Opportunities for publicity are enormous, as are opportunities to network with users.

Promotion through Direct Contact

The informal network that your librarians and staff have established with clients and daily contacts with users at public service points can be used to help promote a chat service. Suggestions for initiating direct contact with your targeted audience include the following:

- Referrals from public service points (reference desk, circulation)
- Demonstrations in classes, tours, workshops, public events
- Speeches
- Signature files in e-mail reference responses or other staff e-mails
- Message on reference desk answering machine

If you train your staff to promote the chat service in-house at the reference, circulation, and interlibrary loan desks, you will reach many users. In the process of the reference interview, it often becomes obvious that a person could have benefited from help while online, if they had been aware of the library's chat service. For example, many times a user will say in passing, "I was trying to search for this yesterday at home, but gave up until I could come in to the library." Encourage staff to promote your chat service to anyone who reveals they research at home, as well as to point out connection points on your home page to the person. If you have chat service hours beyond those of your reference desk, put a recording on an answering machine and a sign at the reference desk directing users to the service for immediate assistance. Encourage student staff members working late hours to direct questions to the library's real-time reference service.

One night at 10:30 P.M. after our in-house reference desk was closed, I had a chat with a student looking for an accounting standard for a paper that was due the next morning. I knew we had this standard in an accounting work in our reference collection, but couldn't find it anywhere online. In desperation, I asked the student if she happened to be working in the library. To my great surprise the student was working at a library computer across from the reference desk. The main point of this story is how the accounting student discovered she could reach a librarian using chat. As is the case often when the reference desk is closed, the frustrated accounting student turned for assistance to the student assistant working at the circulation desk. Although the student assistant was unable to answer the question, he had the presence of mind to encourage the accounting student to try reference chat.

Contacts your library director or other librarians have can be used to help promote the new service. A good argument for developing and maintaining a press kit is that you can provide librarians, administrators, and staff with easy-to-digest facts that they can work into their own presentations and meetings with users, the library board, deans and faculty, and so on, thus widening your outreach. In a college or university environment, ask your director to draft a letter or e-mail to deans, department chairs, or faculty asking them to try the service. Encourage librarians who are subject liaisons to faculty to distribute literature and demonstrate the service in meetings. Public librarians may wish to target local dignitaries, such as civic or business leaders and city officials, the teacher's union, or community groups such as the Sierra Club or a local Girl Scouts troop. Oftentimes service clubs such as the Kiwanis or Rotary seek out speakers for their gatherings. Network with local librarians to see if you have a member of one of these organizations on staff that can help you arrange a speaking engagement. Corporate librarians may want to make appointments with executives, project teams, or departments that use the library resources heavily, to demonstrate the benefits. Another way to promote chat reference through existing contacts with users is to add a signature line that advertises chat reference and gives the URL to connect to the service in responses to e-mail reference questions.

If your library has an active instruction program offering tours, hands-on workshops, or other programs for users, encourage librarians to work a mention of the chat service into the content. Demonstrate the chat service whenever you can to groups of students or patrons. At my library, we have worked out a consistent question for these demonstrations so that the librarian on duty will be able to show features such as push page quickly, keeping the demonstration to a couple of minutes. The question that we use is simple: "Is the Alligator online?" It is a good demonstration example for four reasons. The question is short and easy to key in, it is slightly ambiguous; even at the University of Florida, it requires a short dialogue to get at the real question, and students are interested in the answer, because they like to read *The Independent Florida Alligator*, the university's student newspaper. The most important reason the example works, however, is because when the chat librarian pushes *The Independent Florida Alligator* web page, a colorful banner fills the top part of the web browser window, underscoring the fact that the chat librarian can send information, not just talk with users. When demonstrating a chat service featuring push page to an audience, be sure to choose a colorful but fast-loading web page with a strong graphic.

Promoting your chat service to faculty may result in an added avenue for outreach—the professor or schoolteacher using your service in a library assignment. We recently had an instructor feature *RefeXpress* as part of a library research assignment in her university writing class. Students were asked to log on to the chat service and work with the librarian to locate three journal articles in the area of their research interest. Students were also required to forward copies of their session transcript that is e-mailed at the close of chat session to their instructor, and provide a critique of their experience. Figure 10.2 is a copy of the assignment as posted on the instructor's web site.

ADVERTISING

Another option for promoting chat reference to users is advertising using purchased time or space in the local media to deliver your message. Launching a professional advertising campaign can be expensive, and the size of your budget will determine the available venues. Many libraries or consortia include a separate budget line for advertising in their grant proposals when seeking funding for a new chat reference service. The major options in the area of advertising are as follows:

- Newspaper, magazine ads
- Direct mail
- Ads on billboards, electronic message boards, bus boards
- Giveaways

Figure 10.2. Example of library research assignment using RefeXpress.

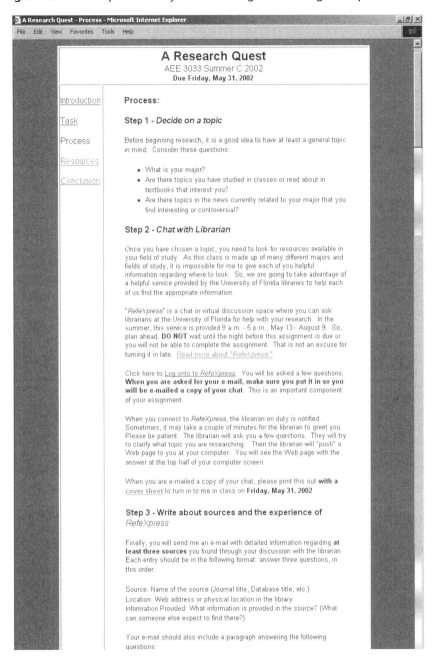

If you have set aside funding to cover advertising, consider using an advertising agency to create professional looking copy for newspapers, billboards, or radio spots. Academic and larger libraries may be able to work with their institution's public relations office to work real-time reference into the institution's overall advertising campaign. If using an advertising agency is cost prohibitive, as it was for my chat reference project, many relatively inexpensive ways to use advertising can still be found. In exchange for a public endorsement of their donation to the library, local newspapers or radio stations may be willing to help develop a print advertisement or script and record a brief radio spot. Such donations in kind might also include a local business including a "bug" or brief reference to your service in one of their advertisements. For example, a local bookstore or computer store may be willing to include a sentence or two about your library's chat service in one of their ongoing ads on television, the radio, or the newspaper.

Many libraries focus their advertising efforts in the area of giveaways, or items emblazoned with the logos of their library and real-time reference service. These might include mugs or mouse pads, self-adhesive message pads, highlighters, tote bags, pencils, pens, or magnets. Giving away trinkets with your service's logo and URL helps keep the service present in the customer's mind. When selecting giveaways, keep in mind the following tips.

Choose items that are useful to your users and that have a natural link with chat reference, such as a pencil to jot down notes or a mouse pad to sit next to the user's computer. You might be able to get a good deal on key chains, but will it remind a person to ask a reference question via chat? In addition, a key chain doesn't advertise your service to other people who see the person with the giveaway using it, like a bumper sticker or clear sticker for a car window would. If you are serving a wide audience of users, keep in mind that the type of giveaway that might appeal to a working mother might not work for a child. A coffee mug probably wouldn't appeal to a twelve-year-old, but a sport bottle might. Personalize the item with the logo of your chat service and library name, the URL, and even an e-mail address. Add a catchy slogan. Avoid consumables. Candy and gum are popular giveaways, but your advertising disappears when the user tosses the wrapper in the trash. Unfortunately, the most carefully crafted library handouts also frequently suffer this fate. It's better to choose something that a person will use at their computer such as a notepad or a bright sticker to put on their monitor.

It takes time and promotion to build up a user-base for a new service such as real-time reference, and in some environments publicity is a continuing need because of user migration. This is especially the case for school and colleges. Happily, there are any number of creative ways to spread the news among potential users, ranging from formal advertising and press releases for the media to more intimate methods such as networking with people. Promotion is necessary for the success of a real-time reference service but need not drain your budget.

REFERENCES

American Library Association. 2002. *Advocacy* (24 April). Available at http://www.ala.org/pio/advocacy/ (accessed 28 May 2002).

American Marketing Association. 2000. "Marketing Definitions." *Marketing Power.com*. Available at http://www.marketingpower.com (accessed 23 May 2002).

Benton Foundation. 2002. *Strategic Communications in the Digital Age: A Best Practices Toolkit for Achieving Your Organization's Mission* (17 May). Available at http://www.benton.org/Practice/Toolkit/home.html (accessed 28 May 2002).

The Gale Directory of Publications and Broadcast Media. 2003. Detroit, MI: Gale Research.

Joscon Networks. n.d. *How to Develop Your Marketing Plan: A Forty Part Workshop*. Available at http://linz1.net/biz/mkadmedium.html (accessed 25 May 2002).

Stern, Gary. 2001. *Marketing Workbook for Nonprofit Organizations*, 2nd edition. St. Paul, MN: Amherst H. Wilder Foundation.

Weingand, Darlene E. 1999. *Marketing/Planning Library and Information Services*, 2nd edition. Englewood, CO: Libraries Unlimited.

WEB SITES CITED

AskJeeves
   http://www.askjeeves.com/

The Independent Florida Alligator
   http://www.alligator.org/

Jones e-global library (JonesKnowledge)
   http://www.jonesknowledge.com/eglobal/

KnowItNow 24X7, CLEVNET Library Consortium
   http://www.knowitnow24x7.net/

The Radio-Locator
   http://www.radio-locator.com/

RadioTower.com
   http://www.radiotower.com

RefeXpress
   http://refexpress.uflib.ufl.edu/

WebHelp.com
   http://www.webhelp.com/

Web-Radio
   http://www.radio-directory.fm/

11 GIVE THEM WHAT THEY ALREADY USE— AOL INSTANT MESSENGER: A CASE STUDY

Wilfred (Bill) Drew
Associate Librarian, Systems and Reference
SUNY Morrisville College Library
drewwe@morrisville.edu

Talk to a Librarian LIVE

Software: *AOL Instant Messenger* (http://www.aol.com)
Started: August 1998
Staff: Five full-time librarians and two part-time librarians
Hours: Regular library hours

Imagine the following scenario. You are working from home on your term paper due Friday morning. It is Thursday night at 8 P.M. You are working on your bibliography and only have part of a citation for a magazine article. You panic. What do you do now? You go to the library web site, but in your panic you forget how to use the databases. You need help and click on *Talk to a Librarian LIVE* and up pops *AOL Instant Messenger*. Now here is something you know how to use. You type in your message asking for help and the librarian on duty makes some suggestions. You find what you need and finish the paper in time to get some sleep. This is how many students get help from home or their dorm rooms at SUNY Morrisville College.

THE COLLEGE

Morrisville College of Agriculture and Technology is part of the State University of New York (SUNY) and is located five miles from the geographic center of New York State. Founded in 1908, it is a residential college of agriculture and technology offering two- and four-year degrees in more than seventy academic programs and options. The college community is made up of approximately 2,900 full-time students with more than 102 full-time faculty. The college has an extension campus in Norwich, New York. The college has been named Yahoo! Internet Life's "Most Wired Two Year College" for both 2000 and 2001. The mission of the college is to "provide access to quality post-secondary education to all who can benefit." The vision of the college, as stated by our president, Dr. Ray Cross, is to aspire "to be an academically challenging, business-oriented, technology-focused entrepreneurial learning community."

THE COMPUTING ENVIRONMENT

The college is an IBM Laptop University institution. Approximately two-thirds of all students participate in the laptop program. All students in a laptop program get an IBM laptop and Raytheon wireless card. Currently, more than twenty-seven curriculums require students to have a laptop. Laptops can be covered by financial aid.

The college computing infrastructure consists of a fiber-optic gigabit Ethernet to all college buildings. All desktop computers have a link to the backbone via 10Base-T cabling with a bandwidth of up to one hundred megabits. The college links to the Internet via eight T-1 lines. All classrooms are wired with at least one port. All faculty and staff offices are wired. A student or faculty member with a laptop using his or her wireless card can walk from one end of campus to the other and stay connected the entire time. Wireless connectivity is available in all academic buildings, including the library and dorms plus all dining areas.

THE LIBRARY

The library has an extensive collection of more than 90,000 books, 12,000 microfilms, 400 serial titles, 12,000 full text e-journals, and 1,500 audio and videocassettes. It is open eighty-two hours per week during the semester and forty hours a week during the summer. In March 2002, the library migrated from DRA MultiLis integrated library management system to Ex Libris ALEPH 500. It was fully operational by the end of May 2002. Other resources include many online databases and full text resources. All are accessible off campus to anyone in the college community. Wireless and network connections are available throughout the library. The professional staff consists of five full-time and two part-time librarians. All are experienced computer and internet users.

Figure 11.1. Link to *Talk to a Librarian LIVE.*

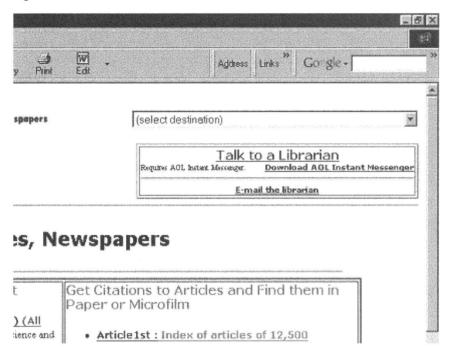

TALK TO A LIBRARIAN LIVE

Started in its present form in August 1998, the purpose of *Talk to a Librarian LIVE* (Figure 11.1) is to provide live synchronous reference service via the Internet. The service is aimed at several clienteles that all need help from the library. It allows Norwich campus students and faculty to reach a reference librarian when one isn't available at Norwich. It allows distance-learning students to get help without visiting the library and without making a long-distance phone call. For the Morrisville campus, the service allows the student and faculty member to get assistance without going to the library. For users with a dial-up connection, it allows them to contact the library when they would otherwise be unable to use the phone to call the reference desk without disconnecting from the Internet.

Requirements for the service are minimal. All that is required for the user is having *AOL Instant Messenger (AIM)* on his or her computer and a connection to the Internet. America Online provides its instant messaging (IM) software at no charge and does not require the user to be an AOL subscriber. Instant messaging allows two or more people to exchange messages in real time almost instantaneously. AIM can also be used to access chat rooms. It works through servers maintained by America Online. No local server is required. Figure 11.2 shows a *Talk to a Librarian* session in action.

Figure 11.2. *Talk to a Librarian LIVE.*

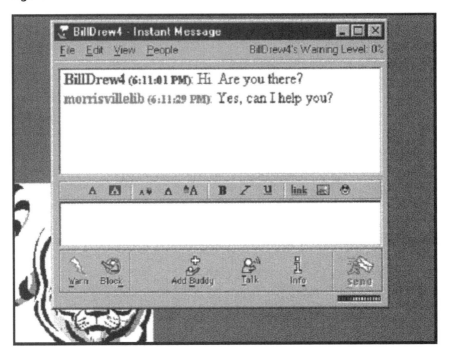

WHY AIM?

To decide what IM program to use, I conducted a survey of thirty-five laptop students in journalism. The survey showed 95 percent of the students used AIM already. I also did more subjective surveys of students and staff and most were familiar with AIM. AIM is easy to download and install and is available at no cost to the library or the patron. Any staff member can cover the service by logging in under the "morrisvillelib" screen name. It is also easy to implement by inserting a link into each webpage. The code to do this is

<a href = "aim:goim?screenname = morrisvillelib&message = Hi.+Can+you+ help+me+?"> <img src = "http://www.morrisville.edu/library/images/talk.gif " alt = "Talk to a Librarian LIVE" border = "4"></a>
<font size = "2">Requires AOL Instant Messenger.
<a href = "http://dynamic.aol.com/cgi/redir?http:// www.aol.com/aim/imreg_download_template?pageset = aol&promo = 106695"> Download AOL Instant Messenger</a>

AIM offers many useful features for the user and for the librarian on duty. Users can log on without giving the library any personal identifying information. AIM requires a screen name registered with America Online but not with the library. The librarian can easily insert links to web pages (Figure 11.3). This allows the user to go directly to the appropriate page without having to go through intermedi-

Figure 11.3. Example of a "clickable" URL in text of *Talk to a Librarian* (AIM).

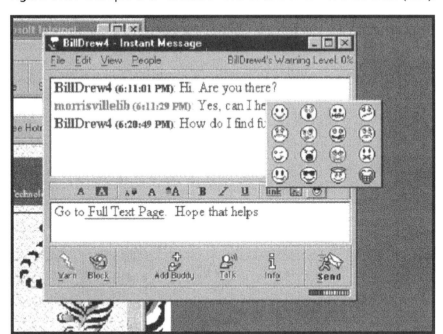

ate pages or menus. The librarian or the patron can print transcripts of the session for later reference. Occasionally useful is a feature allowing the librarian to block abusive users. Some users may find AIM's emoting feature useful (Figure 11.4).

As with any service, there are some disadvantages. For one thing, AIM does not record statistics, so staff members must make an effort to keep a count. AIM has many features that the library staff does not use, which can make it difficult for the occasional user such as our part-time librarians. Another potential problem is that anyone using AIM can contact the service even if he or she is not part of the Morrisville College community. AIM also does not allow you to push the user's browser to particular pages.

STAFFING

Talk to a Librarian LIVE is available any time the library is open. The librarian at the reference desk monitors it. It is treated no different in priority than a phone call or face-to-face reference interview. All five full-time librarians and the two part-time librarians cover the service when they are on the reference desk. Staffing can be a problem when people are sick or away at meetings. This is handled either by using the "Away" message feature or by having someone monitor *Talk to a Librarian LIVE* from their desk.

Figure 11.4. AIM emoting feature.

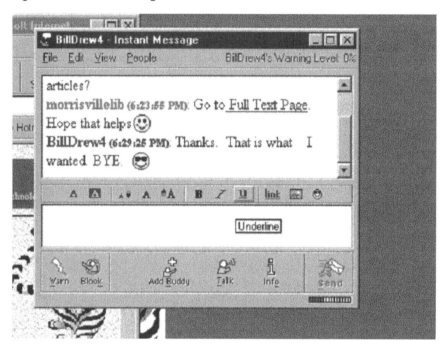

OBSERVATIONS

The volume of questions seems to vary a great deal. The library receives anywhere from one to twenty real-time questions on a typical day. I have had as many as fifteen in one hour. The other librarians report about five per hour as maximum.

Questions asked are similar to questions we get at the reference desk or over the telephone. One librarian reported that most questions are "Which database do I use for...?" and "Where would I find...?" Another felt she received primarily questions that the patron could have answered by looking over our web page more carefully. One of our part-time librarians reports that the most common questions for her are "When does the library close?" and questions about finding books.

The librarians have accepted the use of AIM quite well. Two have started using it to chat with their children who are away at college. Another dislikes "the cryptic code, lowercase letters, that people write in!" One librarian complained about conversing with anonymous patrons and told me this tale of woe: "One night I had a patron asking about books on the Taliban—then he (or she) asked if I thought Bin Laden was dead. No, I replied, he's probably hiding in Pakistan. The patron then opined that Bin Laden was actually hiding in Seneca Dining Hall."

One problem we have yet to solve is the one of missed messages. This happens when the librarian at the reference desk leaves to help another patron. The librarian will often come back and find one or more messages waiting. When he or she tries to respond, the patron is no longer online. We are investigating possible solutions to this problem. One obvious solution is to have this service covered by someone not at the reference desk. The problem with that is that we are busy and cannot guarantee someone else would be at his or her computer when needed. Another alternative is to use the "Away" message function within AIM. This may be the most desirable method.

MARKETING *TALK TO A LIBRARIAN LIVE*

Marketing of the service was done via e-mail and handouts. The following message went out to the entire college community:

SUNY Morrisville Library now has two new services for use of the students, faculty, and staff when they are not in the library. These services allow the library patron to have access to the reference desk and to all of the library databases and full text resources without having to be in the library.

Talk to a Librarian LIVE lets the remote library user reach a live reference librarian in real-time without having to disconnect from the internet. This service is available any time the library is open.

Off campus library users can now use any of the resources available via the library web pages from home or any other location where they can get access to the Internet. This service is available 24 hours a day, 7 days a week. All the user needs is a username and password provided by the computer center to every student, staff, or faculty member of the SUNY Morrisville community.

Marketing also involves placement of the product. *Talk to a Librarian LIVE* is placed on most of the library web pages. There is a live link at the top and bottom of each page.

THE FUTURE?

It is likely that SUNY Morrisville will stay with AIM for our *Talk to a Librarian LIVE* service. As one patron stated after a chat session, "Librarians Rule!" and because the students like this service, we will continue it. With AIM clients now available for personal digital assistants (PDAs) and other handheld devices, the future looks bright for our use of AIM. There has been some interest expressed across libraries in our system for a SUNY-wide virtual reference service. The discussion of such a service is just beginning, and its future remains unknown. What is known is that we will continue our *Talk to a Librarian LIVE* service because, as one of our librarians said, "The best times are when a patron says 'thanks' for the help they've received."

12 AUSTIN PEAY STATE UNIVERSITY— *ASK A LIBRARIAN:* A CASE STUDY

DeAnne Luck
Electronic Resources Librarian
Austin Peay State University
LuckDL@apsu.edu

Ask A Librarian (http://library.apsu.edu/5_0.htm)

Software: *LiveAssistance* (http://www.liveassistance.com/)
Started: May 2001
Staff: Eleven (reference desk staff)
Hours: 8:00 A.M.–9:00 P.M. Monday–Thursday; 8:00 A.M.–4:30 P.M. Friday; 10:00 A.M.–5:00 P.M. Saturday; 3:00 P.M.–9:00 P.M. Sunday

---

The Austin Peay State University (APSU) library began offering online reference services in May 2001 (Figures 12.1 and 12.2). APSU is a public university of 5,700 full-time-equivalent students located in Clarksville, Tennessee. The library faculty consists of eleven librarians, all of whom work at the Reference Desk in addition to their other duties. The library began investigating chat reference in spring 2001. Several factors influenced our decision to pursue this new service. First, online classes, which did not require students to come to campus at all, were becoming popular (Spring 2002 online class enrollment topped 1,500). Second, our reference desk statistics had been declining for several years, demonstrating our need to reach out to the students. Third, we have a large proportion of nontraditional

Figure 12.1. Log-on screen for *Ask A Librarian*.

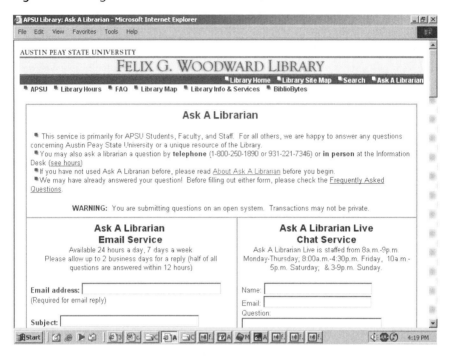

students, whose work and family responsibilities often prevent them from coming to the library. The fourth and prompting factor was a mandate from the university to improve library services to an off-campus center, in preparation for the Southern Association of Colleges and Universities reaccreditation. Chat reference appeared to be a way to address all these issues, and thus a pilot project was planned for summer 2001.

SOFTWARE

Some funding accompanied our mandate to improve off-campus services, so we were not limited to free services. We investigated free services but determined that reliability, performance, and privacy concerns made them undesirable. The full-featured and high-cost packages aimed at libraries were also evaluated, but annual fees in the thousands of dollars were too much to invest in a new service of undetermined popularity. Our choices narrowed to the midrange packages that provided the basic functionalities we considered crucial. The best value for us was *LiveAssistance*.

LiveAssistance does not require any hosting or setup on the library's part, other than adding code to the library's web site. The code is provided by *LiveAssistance*, but the library can easily customize it. More important, it does not require any

Figure 12.2. *Ask A Librarian* session in action.

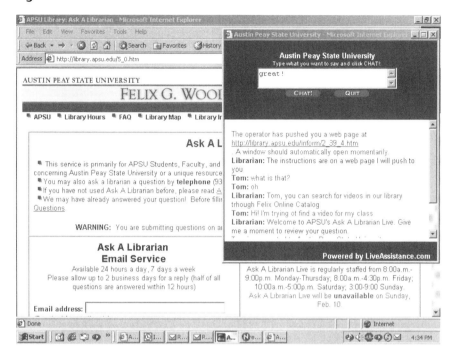

software installation on the patron's part. We considered any type of software or plug-in requirements as an unacceptable barrier to our not-always-tech-savvy student population. *LiveAssistance* also includes the basic features we considered most important: predefined quotes (also called canned responses), transcript e-mailing, statistic gathering, and the ability to push pages.

After using the software, we have found the first two features to be particularly useful. The statistics function, however, suffers from its not being designed specifically for libraries. The inability to categorize the transactions into usual reference categories causes us to simply collect the statistics by reviewing the transcripts and entering the information into a spreadsheet for processing. Other methods of categorization, combined with the built-in statistics (chats by day, by hour; average length of chats; average wait length) can be used to produce complete reports.

The ability to push pages seemed, at first, like a desirable feature (Figure 12.3). After a few months, we found it to be of limited utility in our chats. Many of our library databases do not have static URLs for pages of search results or specific items. Others that do use static URLs require patron authentication of off-campus users. In either instance, pushing a page of search results or even the search screen is not practical. Even when we want to show the patron a page on the library's or a public web site, it seems to be less confusing for patrons to send the URL in the chat and let them open it when they are ready.

Figure 12.3. Librarian pushes a page in *Ask A Librarian* (displayed at top right).

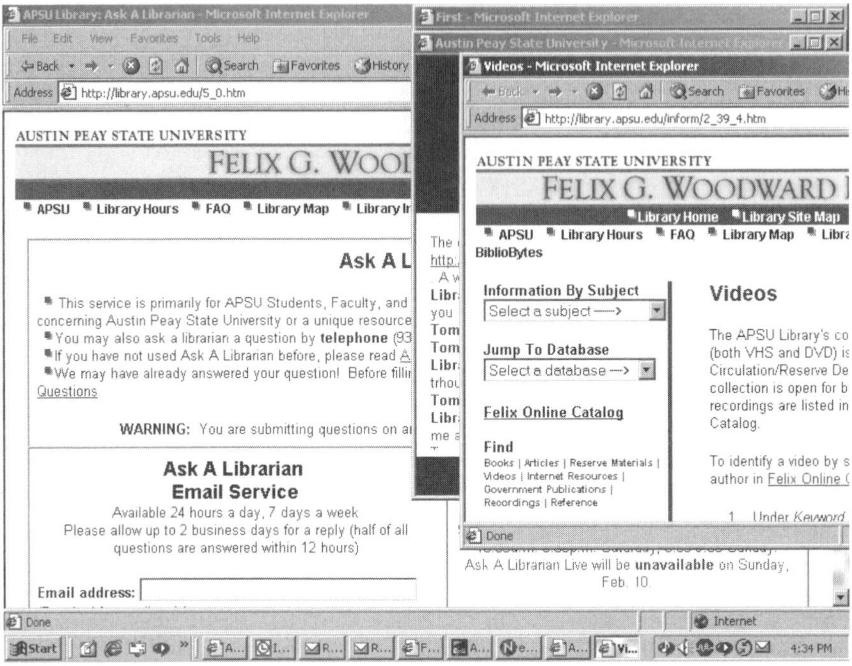

LiveAssistance works well for us, with the exception that it occasionally crashes for no diagnosable reason. The librarian screen is a little busy, which can be intimidating to staff at first, but it is not difficult to use. On the whole, the technical support staff are helpful and quick to respond to questions. *LiveAssistance* also includes an after-chat patron survey that the librarians can customize to their liking.

STAFFING

Our *Ask A Librarian* service was unveiled officially with minimal publicity in May 2001. We determined that offering just a few hours of coverage a day would not provide our students with real service, so we decided to provide chat reference during the same hours that we provide face-to-face reference. Of course, not having any additional staff, we needed to staff chat reference while on the reference desk. We experimented briefly with staffing afternoon hours from offices, but our question volume was not high enough to justify the separate coverage. Our reference desk is staffed by only one person, so occasionally questions arrive simultaneously from in-person, chat, and telephone patrons. Our policy is to give in-person patrons priority, but in practice this varies according to the situation. As our volume increases, we expect to use our reference desk and chat reference statistics to identify hours when both are busy and cover those hours (2–4 per day, Mon–Thurs) from librarians' offices.

TRAINING

The electronic resources librarian led the chat reference project. She learned the basics of the software from *LiveAssistance* telephone training and the basics of chat reference service from reading the fledgling literature and listservs. She trained two other librarians, who formed a core group to train the rest of the staff. The reference desk staff (ten librarians plus one professional staff member) were introduced to the project by reading a few selected articles about chat reference services in other libraries, chat communication tips, and step-by-step instructions on using the *LiveAssistance* software. Next, a workshop was held in which the three core librarians demonstrated the software from the patron's and librarian's points of view. Following the demonstration, staff members made appointments with one or more of the core librarians for individual practice sessions. These sessions were repeated until the librarian was at least somewhat comfortable with providing chat reference service. Problems and newly discovered tips were shared during faculty meetings and through e-mail. A refresher workshop was held in January 2002.

ASK A LIBRARIAN

Use of the service started out slowly, and our question volume is still low, having hit a high of twenty-six questions in October 2001 (excluding those from other librarians). We hope to raise patron awareness and use of the service by increased nonelectronic publicity. Figure 12.4 charts questions per day for Fall 2001, and Figure 12.5 charts questions per hour for the same period.

The questions we receive (excluding the many from other librarians asking about the service) fall into two basic categories: reference questions such as "How do I find scholarly journals in sociology" (93 percent) and technical questions about accessing databases, electronic reserves, and so on (7 percent). Technical questions are defined as those that require troubleshooting beyond simply instructing the patron how to access a resource. Ready reference questions and questions concerning our special collections (popular in our e-mail service) are virtually nonexistent.

We also attempted to categorize our questions as successfully answered or not. Although this determination is subjective, 80 percent of the questions were categorized as successful and 20 percent were unsuccessful. The unsuccessful questions are generally those that include some interaction between the librarian and the patron, but the patron hung up, was disconnected, or simply indicated dissatisfaction with the answer. We hope to improve this percentage as we become more comfortable with chat and improve our technical capabilities. Figure 12.6 shows the *LiveAssistance* exit survey we used to determine whether our service was successful.

Figure 12.4. Austin Peay State University Questions by day (Fall 2001).

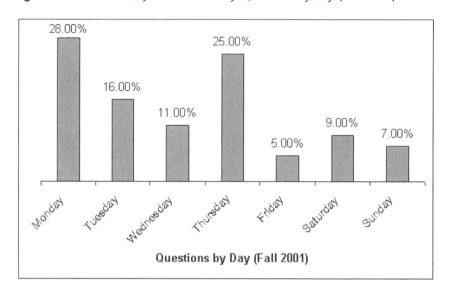

Figure 12.5. Austin Peay State University Questions by hour (Fall 2001).

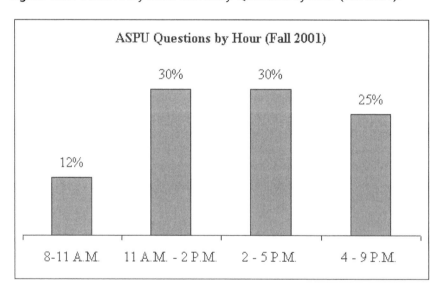

Figure 12.6. *Ask A Librarian* exit survey.

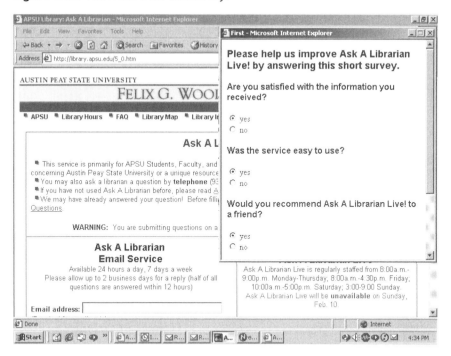

LOOKING BACK AND AHEAD

In hindsight, we would create more publicity earlier in the project. We were concerned about being overwhelmed, but so far our question volume has been decidedly underwhelming. Publicity so far has been largely electronic (notices on our web site, e-mail). We hope that by expanding publicity to flyers, bookmarks, and so on, we will reach a larger proportion of the university.

We would also devote more time to training. Although we tried to make individual training sessions available to all the staff members, some remain uncomfortable with chat reference. These staff members should have follow-up sessions, but time constraints and busy schedules have prevented this from happening. One aspect that should have been stressed more in the training was that we are all new at this, and some trial and error is to be expected. Librarians who are good at face-to-face and even e-mail reference were often frustrated by this new medium. The detailed answers we were used to providing in e-mail reference did not work in chat, and yet we didn't have the body language and voice cues we were used to in face-to-face and telephone reference. Teaching ourselves to be brief and to keep the patron's attention was a challenge, and no quick-fix answers were available. Librarians everywhere are still struggling with these issues.

Librarians were also frustrated by the limitations of page pushing and straight chat when providing answers to complex questions and especially when trying to fulfill our instructional mission. Because of these problems, which were the cause of some of the unsuccessful chats noted here, APSU is planning to "upgrade" to one of the more expensive packages that support cobrowsing. We feel this is a crucial component of a service that is truly comparable to other modes of reference and of our instructional mission.

CONCLUSION

Although use of the APSU *Ask A Librarian* service has been relatively low to date, we believe it will play a major role in our future reference services. After all, use of library web sites was low at first, but as public awareness of the web increased, the web became one of our most important tools. We hope that given evolution of the technology, increased patron awareness, and increased librarian confidence, *Ask A Librarian* will provide much-needed reference service to those who are unable or unwilling to ask in any other way.

13 LIBRARIANS ONLINE— VIRTUAL REFERENCE AT A MULTI-CAMPUS INSTITUTION: A CASE STUDY

Shelle Witten
Library Faculty
Paradise Valley Community College
shelle.witten@pvmail.maricopa.edu

Librarians Online

Software: LSSI *Virtual Reference Toolkit*, two seats
Piloted: Spring 2001, evening service, using *AOL Instant Messenger* and Hipbone
Continued: Fall 2001 as a weekday service using LSSI's *Virtual Reference Toolkit*
Staff: Nineteen librarians from nine of ten Maricopa college libraries
Hours: Pilot: Sundays 7 P.M.–11 P.M., Monday–Wednesday 8 P.M.–11 P.M.
Current hours: Monday–Friday 10 A.M.–4 P.M., closed evenings and summers

---

THE MARICOPA COMMUNITY COLLEGE DISTRICT AND ITS LIBRARIES

The Maricopa Community College District spans the greater Phoenix, Arizona, metropolitan area. Ten colleges, plus satellite centers, serve more than 277,000 credit and noncredit students year round. Although the colleges share a governing board along with a chancellor-led administration, the colleges operate autonomously. This autonomy carries over to the college libraries. Even with a shared library automation system, as well as centralized technical services, policies and procedures vary among the libraries, often significantly. Thus, implementing a virtual reference service presented a challenge.

THE GENESIS OF LIBRARIANS ONLINE

In the fall of 1999, I undertook an exploratory sabbatical to see how premiere services such as Central Michigan's Off Campus Library Services, the Internet Public Library, Nova and Walden Universities provided reference assistance to their "distant" patrons. As a result, the districtwide Library Technology Group formed an ad hoc committee dubbed RAD, Reference at a Distance, to further explore the possibility of a virtual reference service.

RAD began with philosophical discussions touching on issues such as: Should this be a centralized or distributed service? How will we staff the service? Where will the service be housed? How will we pay for it? Is a virtual reference service even necessary?

Given the steady growth in off campus course enrollment, as well as the increase in remote access to proprietary databases offered by our libraries, the RAD members felt it a worthwhile endeavor to pilot a virtual reference service.

The spring 2001 pilot operated as an evening service, thus extending our traditional library hours. In fall 2001 and spring 2002, *Librarians Online* became a daytime service. Figure 13.1 shows the log-on page for the service.

Software

AOL Instant Messenger (AIM) was our chat medium of choice for the spring 2001 pilot. We also brokered a free trial of Hipbone, collaborative browsing software.

Although we had a small grant for staffing, we had no leftover funds for software. *AIM* was the most widely used chat ware at the time. Even though *AIM* requires a download on the customer's part, we banked on the fact that most people either already had *AIM* installed on their computers or they could do so fairly easily. We provided a link on our web page with instructions on how to install *AIM*. Hipbone only required installation on the librarians' computers.

We had cobbled together a multifeatured virtual reference service. *AIM* worked well. It includes features such as emoticons, knowing when the other person is typing, image sharing, and temporary "Away" message capability that are not yet available on the more robust virtual reference services. Hipbone was problematic. Not only did it cause computer crashes, but also it wasn't compatible with Macintosh computers. When it did work successfully, it gave us a taste of the usefulness of being able to share web pages with our students.

We had planned to switch to the free version of *Livehelper* for fall 2001, as it included web pushing capability. To our surprise, our vice chancellor of information technologies agreed to provide funding for a full-featured virtual reference software. We selected LSSI's *Virtual Reference Desk* software, now known as the *Virtual Reference Toolkit, VRT.*

Figure 13.1. Logging on to *Librarians Online.*

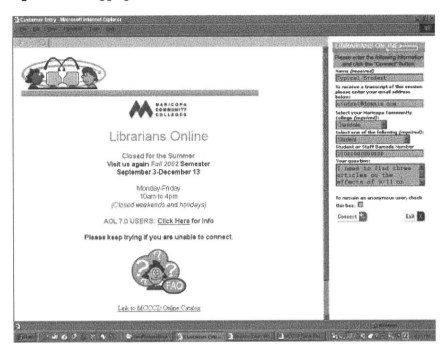

VRT's benefits today include the following:

- truly interactive collaborative web browsing that allows sharing of most proprietary databases

- no need for a patron download

- transfer and conference messaging

- ability to share documents created in application software such as Microsoft Word

- pushing of slide shows created in PowerPoint

- transcript e-mailing; meeting and waiting room features

- a patron anonymous checkbox that removes all identifying information

- exit patron survey

- scripted messages and bookmarked web pages which can be shared amongst all librarians

- comprehensive statistical reporting capability

In addition to the software features, LSSI's customer service has been responsive, as have the developers and programmers to suggestions for software enhancements.

During the last three weeks of our spring 2002 service *Librarians Online* went live with the newest version of *VRT*. Although we experienced technical difficulties, several of us managed to have successful sessions that included collaboratively browsing in several of our proprietary databases. With true interactive collaborative browsing, the potential to teach students lifelong research skills becomes possible.

Notwithstanding these benefits, *VRT* is not without its problems. We have lost patrons because of computer crashes on both sides. Obviously, this is not good PR for a new service. When an e-mail address has been provided, we try to contact the students who were disconnected. Some of the features of *AIM* described, such as "Be Right Back" messaging are yet to be incorporated in *VRT*. We would also like to see a "back chat" feature incorporated so that librarians may communicate with one another. Ultimately, voice and video capability would provide the opportunity to truly simulate a reference interaction very similar to a face-to-face reference interview.

Staffing

During the spring 2001 pilot, the grant money covered the wages of the librarians who were working evening and Sunday hours. In fall 2001, it was reversed. We had funding for software, but not for personnel. Therefore, we switched to a daytime service, staffing creatively with "volunteers."

Most of us have some scheduled office hours. We put out a call to our more than sixty librarians across the district asking for those interested to volunteer one to three hours per week of their office time to staffing *Librarians Online*. From fall 2001 to spring 2002, we've had up to nineteen librarians involved in a semester. Although the original call was for individual librarians to make a commitment, a hybrid has evolved. Two of our college libraries are committing two to four hours of the library's time, and they work out the scheduling among their librarians. Piecing together a solid thirty-hour-per-week schedule with one librarian staffing at a time is challenging, but with everybody's cooperation it ultimately falls into place. Once in place, it is up to the librarians to work out any trades that may come up. At this juncture, we have limited participation to librarians. Potentially, we may be comfortable opening it up to our paraprofessionals in the future. Another piece of the staffing puzzle is the coordinator of the service. Currently this is simply an "add-on" responsibility for me. I estimate that I spend fifteen hours a week performing tasks related to *Librarians Online*.

RAD members realize that relying on volunteers will not withstand the test of time. We predict a few things will change in the next two years. If the library directors determine that *Librarians Online* is an essential service, they will make a commitment that would include participation in *Librarians Online* as part of our job descriptions. Another approach that might be taken is that the library directors appeal to the district administration for funding to cover coordination and staffing of the service, as a centralized service much like our technical services department. We also realize that as the service's popularity grows, one librarian will not be able to handle the volume of sessions. Though it is possible to juggle several at once, three is the outside comfortable limit.

EVALUATION AND STATISTICS

In our pilot, evening service semester, we had thirty chat sessions. Even with so few questions, we gained a sense of the types of questions we would be asked, the inevitable technological problems we would have, as well as some confirmation that the wee hours of the night wouldn't be popular. We were gratified to find that we were not being asked exclusively procedural questions, but genuine reference questions, no different from those fielded at the physical reference desk. And we found that although we offered services until 11 P.M., as well as on Sunday evening, the majority of our questions were fielded earlier in the evening, and seldom on Sundays. This experience bolstered our decision to try a weekday service.

We had an online evaluation for which we sent students the link. Several filled it out, and others gave us feedback in the context of the chat. Overall, the students who tried out our neophyte service were grateful for it and encouraged us to continue offering it.

Fall 2001 we had 177 chat sessions. In the spring, our service was open three additional weeks; nevertheless, when comparing each week of the service, spring 2002 exceeded the number of questions.

Questions by Day*	Fall 2001	Spring 2002	AVERAGE
Monday	18 percent	19 percent	19 percent
Tuesday	22 percent	24 percent	23 percent
Wednesday	23 percent	22 percent	22.5 percent
Thursday	19 percent	22 percent	20.5 percent
Friday	18 percent	13 percent	15 percent
Questions by Hour			
10 A.M.–11 A.M.	17 percent	23 percent	20 percent
11 A.M.–12 P.M.	17 percent	18.5 percent	18 percent
12 P.M.–1 P.M.	16 percent	14.5 percent	15 percent
1 P.M.–2 P.M.	19 percent	15.5 percent	17 percent
2 P.M.–3 P.M.	14 percent	12 percent	13 percent
3 P.M.–4 P.M.	16 percent	15.5 percent	16 percent
After 4 P.M.	1 percent	1 percent	1 percent

*Percentages calculated minus holiday weeks to provide truer picture of which days of week were used most.

The questions continue to range from ready reference and procedural to genuinely complex reference questions. And, as is true at the physical reference desk, we've had some rather unique questions such as the guy on his wireless laptop driving on I-10 who needed to know which exit to get to Bank One Ballpark. Another was the student who was looking for biographies of mail-order brides.

From our exit survey, as well as comments within our chat sessions, the students who are using our service are overwhelmingly positive. They have asked for expanded coverage in the early evening hours as well as some weekend hours.

MARKETING

Marketing is the key to making a virtual reference service successful. Because we are ten distinct colleges, our marketing has not necessarily been consistent. We have a friendly logo that has remained constant from the beginning and is used to brand our publicity. The logo can also serve as the actual hyperlink into *Librarians Online*.

We have developed half-page flyers and bookmarks. Several colleges have had articles in their student newspapers and employee newsletters. Many librarians mention our service during their face-to-face instruction sessions. An e-mail is sent to all district employees at the beginning of each semester with a reminder about the service, as well as a little bit of statistics and examples of questions the librarians have fielded. An invitation to faculty and department heads to include a link to our service on their department web site and their web-based or web-enhanced courses is also included. All the college library web sites include at least one link. Those that include the link on their top web page tend to get the most hits.

CHANGES AND THE FUTURE

Although we got a relatively early start in the realm of virtual reference, it was not without its problems. We probably would have all been more comfortable if we had spent more time in real-time practice, which may have helped us identify the technical problems ahead of time. Because we have a variety of hardware configurations districtwide, including network and firewall-related differences, some of our librarians had glitches that were addressed by LSSI and the local computer services department.

We also weren't prepared for the procedural and policy-related questions that were unique to each college library. Questions about checkout and renewal policies, or unique e-mail services offered at one college were unexpected.

As a result, two librarians are working on two intranet web documents for the fall 2002 start-up. One will be a compilation of each library's policies and procedures. The second will be a procedures manual for the online librarians. The procedures manual will cover such things as how to end of chat sessions gracefully, which begins two minutes before closing.

We have been fortunate that LSSI has provided the training in the use of the software, with the coordinator acting as backup trainer. The online librarians are also expressing a need for training in how to be an online librarian. How does one conduct an effective reference interview in a chat modality? What are some shortcuts to make chat less tedious? How can we best "teach" research methods rather than spoon-feed answers? Do I really need to pick up a patron the minute she or he "rings my bell," or can I keep him or her waiting as I would at the reference desk? We will tackle these more subtle training issues in several informal discussion sessions each semester.

Finally, funding issues will continue to inform our decisions. Until we legitimize the service with line-item funding, our service will rely on the good will of our librarians to volunteer their time. Potentially the use of *Librarians Online* will flourish. With statistics as well as testimonies from students and faculty will make a case for creating a fully funded, weekday, evening, and weekend virtual reference service for the Maricopa community.

reserve material. Students often find this confusing or have trouble with the library card number needed for this verification. The Virtual Library Reference Chat service is intended to help field some of these types of questions, as well as other general research questions students may have while online.

HISTORY

The *Virtual Library Reference Chat* service became available to the USF community in the fall of 2000. The reference chat service started out being available fifteen hours per week, from 9:00 A.M. to noon, Monday through Friday. In the fall of 2001, the library expanded the hours to include 2:00–4:00 P.M., providing twenty-five hours per week of coverage. This semester, spring 2002, there are now eight additional hours, from 7:00–11:00 P.M. on Wednesday and Sunday nights (see Figure 14.1). There are fifteen librarians plus one graduate assistant from the USF School of Library and Information Science (SLIS) staffing the chat service during these hours. The librarians are from the Tampa Campus Library and the Jane Bancroft Cook Library at USF–Sarasota. Librarians volunteer to staff the desk during certain hours. When librarians are unable to be there during their scheduled hour (due to vacation, illness, or another conflict), they e-mail the other librarians to ask for a volunteer replacement.

The graduate assistant is a student from the SLIS program who was originally hired with money earmarked for distance learner services. The Florida Distance Learning Reference and Referral Center (RRC), which was housed in the USF Tampa Campus Library, closed in December 2001. The RRC assisted distance learners throughout the state of Florida via chat, e-mail, and telephone service, so the reference librarians are now performing more of these same services for distance learners. This graduate assistant helps patrons in remote locations needing reference assistance by staffing the *Virtual Library Reference Chat Service* during the eight evening hours, answering e-mails and returning calls from our new toll-free number. Because of recent budget cuts, the reference department currently has eight graduate assistants working at the reference desk, each of whom work approximately twenty hours per week and are currently enrolled in the SLIS program. Only the graduate assistant hired with the money earmarked for assisting distance learners is staffing the chat room.

In Tampa, the librarians stay in their offices or near a computer for the hour that they cover. Usually librarians do one to three hours per week in the chat room, in addition to their regular desk time, and only one librarian staffs the chat room at a time. Because the desk is so busy during the day in Tampa, the reference librarians were afraid of losing business trying to help a live patron and a virtual one simultaneously. Also, at the Tampa reference desk, the computers are not sound enabled, so if someone were to come into the chat room, the librarian would not hear him or her. (Normally there is a doorbell sound when a patron enters the chat room.) The graduate assistant, on the other hand, handles the chat room while at the desk during her evening hours on Wednesday and Sunday nights. This has been an experiment for this semester, and because the chat room is

Figure 14.1. Log-on screen for *Virtual Library Reference Chat.*

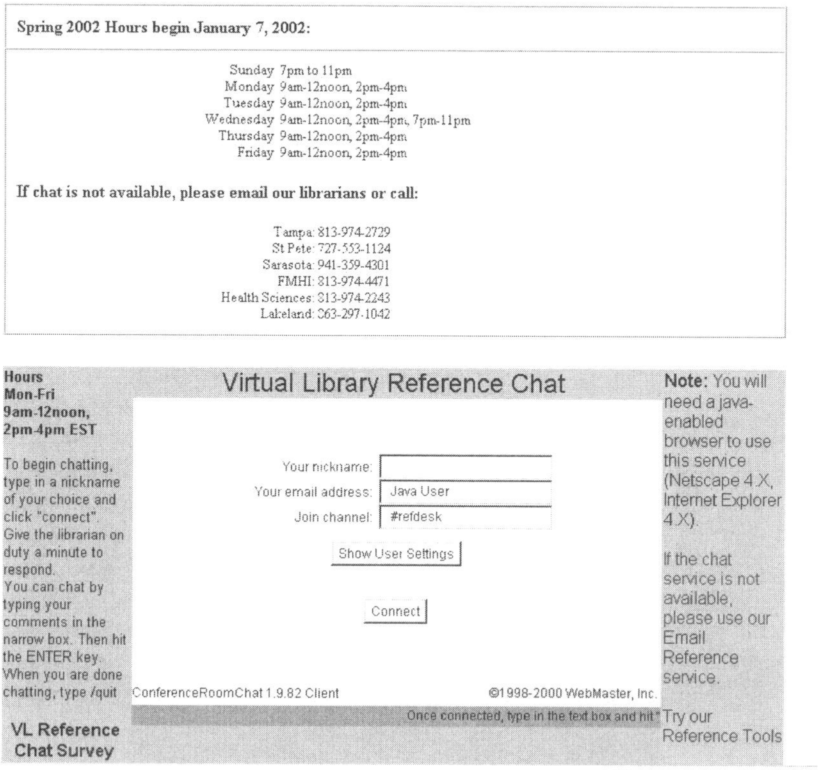

generally not very busy during those times, juggling the traffic from the chat room and the desk has not yet been a problem. The librarians at USF–Sarasota also keep the chat service open while they are on the reference desk. The USF–Sarasota library's involvement has enabled us to expand the chat service hours, and we hope to be able to create consortial agreements with other state university system institutions to continue to expand the current service. This will be particularly important because the RRC recently closed. Distance learners who relied on its services now need to find some other means of assistance, and the chat service can help to fill that hole.

ADMINISTRATIVE FEATURES

The USF Library System has been using the Professional edition of the *ConferenceRoom* software, available from WebMaster. This software allows 1,000 simultaneous users in the chat room, and the librarian can sign in as a channel operator or an Internet Relay Chat (IRC) operator. The channel operator panel is available to either type of operator and has the option to kick and ban users (see

Figure 14.2. Channel operator panel (*ConferenceRoom*).

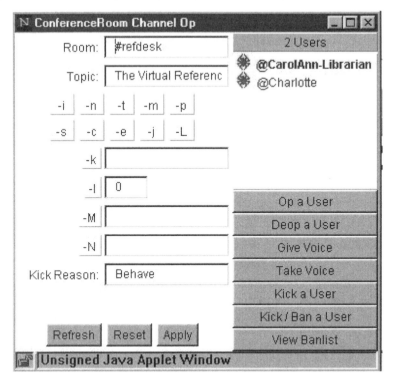

Figure 14.2). An IRC operator can also create additional chat rooms in which they are automatically the room operator and can move patrons into them. This allows the librarian control in the event that too many users are in the system at once, that they become unruly, or that a user has a question to ask of a more personal nature. To create new rooms and move people into them, a librarian signs on as an IRC operator. If one librarian is staffing several rooms at once as an IRC operator, there will be gray bars with the room names at the bottom of the chat area (see Figure 14.3). The gray area turns white when someone has typed something new, so the room operator can see which rooms are active and ready for a response. For example, in Figure 14.3, there are two rooms, #test and #test2. CarolAnn-Librarian has pulled Ilene_Librarian into the room #test with her, but chose in this case not to move her completely out of the original default room, #refdesk. The bar for the room #test2 at the bottom of the screen is white to indicate that another patron has typed a statement in that room. Now CarolAnn-Librarian knows to click on that bar to see what that person has written. The librarian can also type in a command to see a user's IP address and email address, if they have entered one, and their idle time. Therefore, if a patron leaves the chat area without signing out, the librarian can remove that person.

Figure 14.3. Librarian chatting in the main reference room, *Virtual Library Reference Chat.*

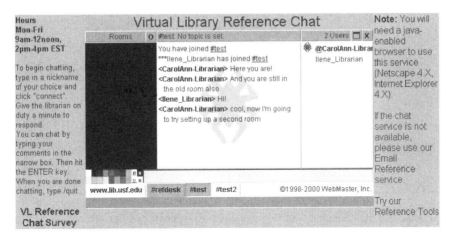

Usually, there are only one or two patrons at a time visiting the chat room, unless one of the librarians has taken an entire class in simultaneously to demonstrate the software. Although the morning hours tend to be the busiest, the chat room has been frustratingly slow during the hours it has been open. Sometimes there will be a patron who just wants to chat with someone, such as the person who was "trying to meet some American girls" online. In one case, a number of users were acting childish in the chat room, and the librarian e-mailed the reference department to request assistance in handling the situation. One or two other librarians signed in as IRC operators and pulled the patrons into individual chat rooms. Occasionally, visitors or other librarians use the chat service to see what it is like. Actually, when USF was deciding to start this service, this is how the librarians investigated different software. Reference librarians from USF contacted librarians at other institutions either by e-mail or in a live chat room to see how the software worked and to inquire about its advantages and disadvantages.

During the time that the service is not open, the server, "Charlotte," acts as the channel agent to inform people that a librarian will be right with them but that if it is during our off hours to please use the "e-mail reference" link to contact someone (see Figure 14.4). Charlotte acts as an automated channel operator to preserve the room settings and provide a message to anyone signing on at any hour of the day.

STATISTICS

Questions in the chat room have varied. Usually they are simple, such as how to find a video, how to locate electronic reserves, or finding some other resource on the Virtual Library interface. Occasionally questions are more in-depth or

Figure 14.4. Charlotte, a "bot," manages the reference room in librarians' absence, *Virtual Library Reference Chat.*

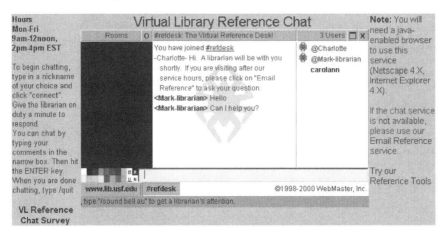

obscure, asking for a specific piece of information or how to get started on their research. Less than 1 percent of the total reference questions are coming from the chat service, with another 1 percent coming from e-mail reference. The remaining questions are still coming through the more traditional channels of telephone (18 percent) and in person (80 percent). We would estimate that 15 percent of our chat service questions are ready reference, with another 10 percent being research questions, and the bulk of the questions (75 percent) being questions specific to the library's collection, facility, or campus. Again, these are estimates, because the library does not have the capacity with the *ConferenceRoom* software to break statistics down by type of question.

Using the *ConferenceRoom* software, the library has not been keeping statistics or transcript logs of online sessions. The statistics available with *ConferenceRoom* are limited, so we only have a total number of questions, not types of questions, busiest times, or types of patrons (faculty, undergraduate and graduate students, general public, etc.). The library will be switching to *RightNow* software in the near future, which will facilitate collection of statistical information and other record-keeping. Currently, the Academic Computing department here at the University of South Florida is using *RightNow* software for their online chat help service. *RightNow* will also keep patrons in separate areas automatically, which will serve to preserve their privacy and allow the librarian to handle one patron at a time. Unfortunately, with the new software, librarians will not be able to have an entire class in one chat room simultaneously to demonstrate the software. One person will be in each chat room with a librarian with the others waiting in a queue.

The purchase of the *ConferenceRoom* software was a one-time expense, and we have been able to run it from within the library. The software is easy to use and requires minimal training. A two-page help sheet is given to all librarians when they offer to staff the service (and to the graduate assistant), which provides basic commands for signing on, acting as a channel operator or IRC operator, moving users into rooms, and checking to see from which computer or location a user is typing. Another advantage of the software is that patrons using it do not need to download any software or plug-ins to access the service. They can access it through a java-enabled browser, and the instructions and hours are on the screen. Users and librarians log in with a nickname or alias. Librarians usually attach the word "librarian" to the end of their first name, such as "CarolAnn-Librarian." Patrons using the service do not have to be from the university's community; access is open to anyone who chooses to use the service. Access to the library's database and electronic reserves services through the Virtual Library is restricted to USF staff and students, however.

The library has been advertising the online chat service in its bibliographic instruction classes, on the main Web page for the Virtual Library, and in library newsletters, such as the spring 2002 Reference Department newsletter. Currently there is no official name for the chat service at the USF libraries, just "Virtual Library Reference Chat." The chat service is supplemented by the USF Virtual Library email reference service, in which the Reference Department promises a twenty-four-hour turnaround on questions but is usually able to answer most questions in twelve hours. The *ConferenceRoom* software offers a number of advantages to the library including its low cost, ease of installation and use, and ability to create rooms and handle difficult users. The system is easy to learn and requires no plug-in from the patron's end. The biggest drawback of this software for USF has been the difficulty in collecting useful statistical information and keeping a transcript log of online transactions. These problems should be solved with the new *RightNow* software.

For further information about the *ConferenceRoom* and *RightNow* softwares, or to see the Virtual Library Reference Chat or the USF Academic Computing Help Desk Online, please go to the following pages:

- USF Virtual Library: http://www.lib.usf.edu/virtual/
- USF *Virtual Library Reference Chat:* http://www.lib.usf.edu/virtual/chat/
- *ConferenceRoom* Products: http://www.conferenceroom.com/products/products home.shtml
- *RightNow* Products–Live Collaboration: http://www.rightnow.com/products/ live.html
- USF Academic Computing Help Desk Online: http://www.acomp.usf.edu/ help.html

15 *REFEXPRESS* AT THE UNIVERSITY OF FLORIDA: A CASE STUDY

Mimi Pappas and Colleen Seale
Humanities and Social Sciences Services
George A. Smathers Libraries, University of Florida
mimipappas@mac.com
cwseale@mail.uflib.ufl.edu

RefeXpress

Software: *Virtual Reference Desk (VRD),* based on divine *NetAgent,* divine Inc.
http://www.divine.com
Started: March 13, 2000
Staff: Thirty-one librarians and professional staff
Hours: Fifty-six hours per week (Monday–Thursday 9 A.M.–9 P.M., Friday
9 A.M.–5 P.M.)
RefeXpress URL: http://RefeXpress.uflib.ufl.edu/

The University of Florida (UF) is a large, land-grant institution serving more than 46,000 students with researchers and students all over the state of Florida and the world. Seven of the nine UF Libraries are under the George A. Smathers Libraries umbrella and are currently participating in our chat reference service.

Our foray into interactive reference service first began in the fall of 1999 when an Interactive Reference Planning Committee was charged with exploring the feasibility of providing a chat reference service; looking at technical, staffing, and policy issues; initiating a pilot project; and making final recommendations.

Initially, *RefeXpress* began with the pilot project that ran from March 13–May 4, 2000. The hours of service were limited to twenty hours per week, Monday–Thursday 9 A.M.–11 P.M., Friday 9 A.M.–11 A.M., Sunday 9 P.M.–11 P.M. The software chosen for the *RefeXpress* pilot was *JHCore MOO*. MOO (MUD Object Oriented or, less commonly, Multi-User Object Oriented systems) is a type of virtual reality software used to create virtual rooms in which people can congregate and communicate. We decided to begin with MOO software primarily because it was free and because many of the freshman composition classes on campus use a MOO as a pedagogical tool.

User response was positive, and after several meetings with library staff the committee recommended continuing the service with a more sophisticated software package. Throughout the summer of 2000 the committee investigated chat software packages. We recommended *NetAgent* from eShare, which was purchased in late fall 2000. Using *NetAgent*, in January 2001 we opened *RefeXpress* for twenty hours a week. The full implementation of *RefeXpress* began in February 2001. In 2002, divine purchased eShare Communications and rebranded *NetAgent* as *Virtual Reference Desk (VRD)*. Figure 15.1 shows the user's view of the system.

SOFTWARE

We began our project by purchasing three seats and an e-mail management package. A year later, the Documents Department added two additional seats, in preparation for the start-up of their new grant funded service *GovXpress*, which provides online government documents assistance to public libraries and users in the state of Florida, operating independently with *RefeXpress* using the same server. *VRD* software permits up to six simultaneous users per seat. The software is flexible, however, and we set our staff, depending on comfort level, to have up to two users at one time.

Our Libraries' Systems department strongly supported the purchase of *Net Agent* software because we could host it in house. This leads to greater security and speedy response, and we have had virtually no downtime since *RefeXpress* has been in operation.

The *VRD* client software has to be downloaded for each library staff member providing *RefeXpress* service, although there is a web-based Java client available for emergencies. Users just need an Internet connection with MAC or Windows OS and a web browser.

The features of the *VRD* software met almost all of our needs. Staff features include built-in e-mail management for e-mail reference; push page technology; escorting or cobrowsing; private messaging between librarians; the ability to transfer questions; AutoPilot (a feature that can send question-answer scripts to the user); the ability to create and customize databases of frequently used sayings, web pages, and files; the ability to retrieve historical statistics; and the ability to customize the interface with graphics, messages, hours of service, and so forth. Another important feature is that the librarian interface combines the chat win-

Figure 15.1. Chat session from the user's view, University of Florida (divine *Virtual Reference Desk*).

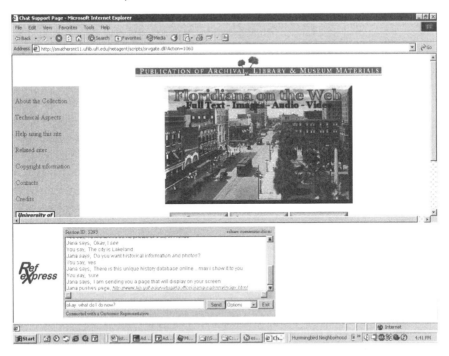

dow, web browser, and librarian's tools on one screen (Figure 15.2). Auditory and visual cues let us know when a user has typed a message and when a user is calling in. The administrator side of the software is accessible via a web browser and is easy to program.

User assets include transcripts, one-on-one private conversations, the fact that no special software is necessary, cobrowsing, cross-platform capabilities, and the chat interface and web browser are contained on one screen.

Despite having all these features we wish that we still had the ability to chat in a multiple-user forum for classroom projects, training, and so on. For example, during our pilot project, we hosted two online meetings, on the *RefeXpress* MOO (May 4 and May 16, 2000) at which librarians from around the world discussed chat reference issues.

STAFFING

During the pilot of *RefeXpress*, eight librarians covered the twenty service hours during the week on a volunteer basis. Based on this pilot, we initially recommended that only librarians staff the service. With the development of extensive training, and the reality of staffing the service for more than forty hours a

Figure 15.2. Chat session from the librarian's view, picturing an active session with a user and a private one-on-one session between two online librarians.

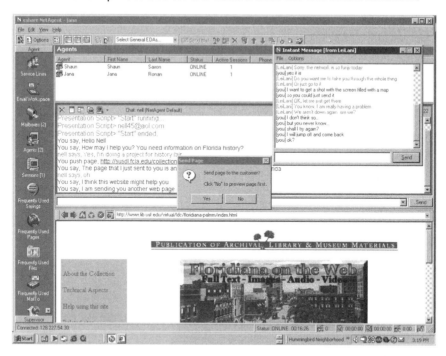

week, we invited other staff to participate. With the full implementation of the service, this group has expanded to thirty-one librarians and professional staff. Interest, training, and familiarity with online sources have helped to determine who is staffing the service.

The librarians and professionals who currently staff *RefeXpress* work in many areas of the library including science, art, technical services, documents, humanities and social sciences, medicine, business, music, and education. *RefeXpress* is treated as a separate service activity conducted during off desk hours usually in staff offices or at home. Some additional laptop computers were purchased to facilitate staffing the evening hours from home.

Before the beginning of each semester a new master schedule is created with staff members choosing their own hours. Gaps are negotiated, and most people staff the service for two or three hours per week. Compensatory time is allowed for staff working *RefeXpress* shifts during evening hours.

TRAINING

Training for our chat reference service has been offered in multiple phases and began with the vendor once we purchased our software.

eShare Communications provided three days of administrator training at its training center in Atlanta. In addition, eShare provided onsite staff training (two half-day sessions), onsite supervisor training (half-day session), and onsite administrator training (one full-day session). Since acquiring *NetAgent*, divine continues the training program and ongoing technical support via e-mail, chat, and a toll-free number.

In-house staff training has continued with several introductory, refresher, and practice sessions offered in groups, one-on-one, and at point of need as library staff members work their shifts. Another training option we have explored is using an online buddy system for help and practice. Our ongoing training has included large group workshops on chat etiquette, adapting RUSA behavioral guidelines to online reference, role-playing, back channel communication, and troubleshooting connection problems.

An e-mail list of *RefeXpress* staff was initially put together to find substitutes to cover assigned service hours. It has also been used to communicate problems and issues, for example, the best way to end a reference interview, the best way to handle two simultaneous users, and so on.

POLICIES: WHO, WHAT, WHEN

In planning *RefeXpress* policies, we decided to expand on our already successful existing e-mail reference policies. The service is open to anyone who logs on, and our overall service policy is that we help users as much as we can online without doing their research for them.

We answer ready reference questions, basic questions about connecting to databases and database navigation, provide guidance to appropriate information sources for research, interpret citations, and make referrals to subject specialists when appropriate. We also provide follow-up to *RefeXpress* questions by e-mail, phone, or appointment.

The Interactive Reference Planning Committee made the decision not to limit the use of *RefeXpress* to UF affiliates and we have not limited the amount of time spent on each chat transaction. Sessions with users last an average of eight to nine minutes, but twenty to thirty minutes is not uncommon.

SERVICE HOURS

RefeXpress is currently staffed fifty-six hours a week (Monday through Thursday 9 A.M.–9 P.M., Friday 9 A.M.–5 P.M.) covering most of the hours that the reference desk is staffed. During pilot phases and the initial implementation of our service, fewer hours were staffed.

Usage and User Statistics

We receive a range between four and fourteen questions a day. The volume from the first thirteen months *RefeXpress* was offered totaled approximately 1,400 questions. A feature of the *VRD* software allows us to categorize our chat sessions for keeping relevant statistics. A window pops up as soon as an individual chat session is completed, allowing us to categorize the type of question we were asked. The administrator can program in our own categories, which we have expanded over time to cover the most common kinds of questions we receive. The number of questions in the different categories for the time period January 8, 2001, through February 22, 2002, is as follows:

Usage patterns and types of questions:

What index to use?	6
ILL	7
Lost the Patron!	8
Referral	13
Full-Text Articles	43
Circulation	50
Other	69
Directional	94
Connection Problems	373
Reference	727

We have discovered that because questions are nearly always multifaceted, it is often difficult to put one session into a single category. For example, our own experiences reflect that many users are having problems connecting to our databases. Many are not using the campus Internet service provider and do not understand how to connect to the libraries' proxy server. In addition to users logging on with specific questions about how to connect, many begin by wanting to find articles, which then leads to connectivity issues.

Despite the low number of reported referrals, we know that our staff is making referrals to subject specialists. We have noticed that *RefeXpress* staff have used the instant messaging feature or the telephone while online with a user either to discuss a question or to transfer a chat call.

One aspect of *RefeXpress* that does not show up in the statistics is that questions cannot always be answered during the initial chat transaction. Many staff members are taking the information from difficult questions or ones that cannot be answered immediately and following up with an answer via e-mail, telephone, or in-person consultation.

Chat Evaluation and User Statistics

In addition to usage statistics provided by the *VRD* software, we decided to send an evaluation survey to each user's web browser as they disconnect from a chat session. Responses are completely voluntary and have been overwhelmingly positive. Not all users answer the survey or all parts of the survey, and some questions allow users to choose more than one answer. Following are findings from some of the questions.

Figure 15.3. Hours of user online activity.

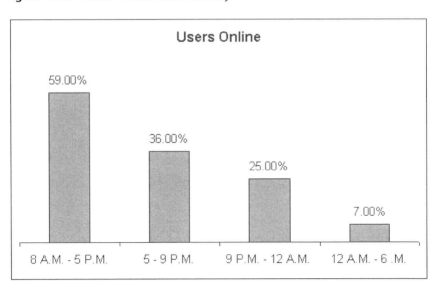

Users were asked when they were online (they were able to choose more than one response; Figure 15.3) During the pilot phase, we suspected that use would be heavy after the reference desk closed, but that was not the case. Our current service hours run from 9 A.M.–9 P.M.; however, most of the usage of *RefeXpress* has occurred during "business hours" between 9 A.M. and 6 P.M.

Survey results show that 65 percent of those who complete the *RefeXpress* survey have heard about our chat service from the UF Libraries' Web site. We worked to have our logo placed prominently on the UF Libraries' home page, within the libraries' catalog, and in locally loaded databases. Most of our users are UF affiliates, even though we have not restricted access to *RefeXpress* in any way (Figure 15.4).

ADVERTISING AND MARKETING

Selection of a name and a logo were the first major decisions made to advertise and promote our new service. Librarians developed the trademark and logo in house. Bookmarks, posters, news articles, and news releases have been facilitated by Barbara Hood, the Smathers Libraries' chief information officer. Figure 15.5 breaks down how users discovered the chat reference service.

We are still inventing new ways to advertise *RefeXpress*. We have recently added links to the service in the Libraries' Catalog and locally loaded databases. *RefeXpress* is mentioned in library instruction classes and at various public service points such as the reference and circulation desks; flyers and door hangers are

Figure 15.4. Chat reference usage at the University of Florida.

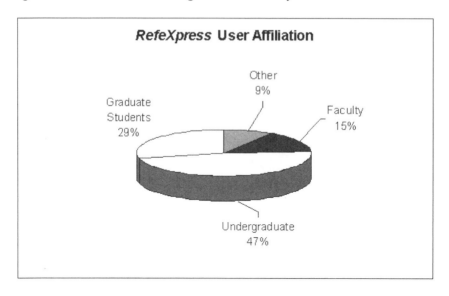

Figure 15.5. How users discovered chat reference at the University of Florida.

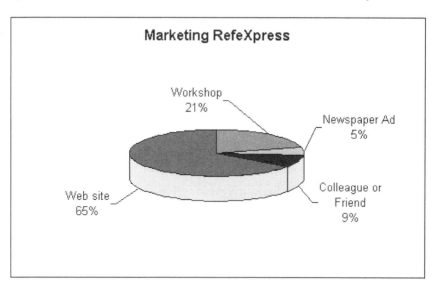

posted in dorms and other locations on campus, and we advertise in e-mail reference responses with a signature file.

CONCLUSIONS

Some of the key decisions that have helped to make our service a success include the following:

- Assigning roles for coordination of the service including a technical coordinator (to manage the server and software) and two key people to maintain the day-to-day operations (one person serving as the main service coordinator and one as a backup)
- Getting system support
- Soliciting feedback from users and staff
- Providing for the early involvement of all participating staff
- Providing extensive training
- Keeping morale in mind during start-up and slow periods
- Setting realistic hours
- Starting with a free or low-cost software
- Anticipating resistance to change, additional service hours, learning new software

What makes it work:

- Receiving support from library administration and our Systems Department
- Developing a core team of librarians to manage and make recommendations
- Housing the chat software on our own server provides quick and dependable service
- Forwarding positive survey responses on to the whole group of librarians staffing the service, or if an individual is mentioned, then to that person
- Placing prominent hotlinks to *RefeXpress* on as many library web pages as possible
- Remaining flexible
- Purchasing flexible software that can grow with our needs

INDEX

About the Author

JANA SMITH RONAN is Interactive Reference Coordinator for the George A. Smathers Libraries of the University of Florida, Gainesville.